THE SOCIAL WORK AND
SEXUAL TRAUMA CASEBOOK

This volume offers a collection of 10 case studies from clinical social workers who work in the field of sexual trauma, with the objective of challenging and informing social work practice with survivors and perpetrators of sexual trauma. These steps are meant to help the process of treatment by breaking down the experience of trauma to a set of steps and interventions aimed at resolving traumatic symptoms within a given time frame. Our text seeks to challenge the tendency toward reductionism inherent in the dominant social paradigm by encouraging the development of a phenomenological and interdisciplinary approach to understanding sexual trauma. In doing so, the examples of interventions presented in each case study reflect practice methods that honor the complexity of the human experience of sexual trauma, suffering, and recovery.

Miriam Jaffe, MSW, PhD, is the director of the Rutgers University Doctorate in Social Work Writing Program. She specializes in issues of autobiography, life writing, and the case study method. Her publications, including the textbook *Social Work and K–12 Schools*, focus on pedagogies that de-silo academic disciplines. She practices with clients ages 7–80.

Jerry Floersch, LCSW, PhD, is an associate professor at the Rutgers University School of Social Work. He is the author of *Meds, Money, and Manners: The Case Management of Severe Mental Illness* and coauthor of *Qualitative Methods for Practice Research*. His clinical practice focuses on adolescents and adults.

Jeffrey Longhofer, LCSW, PhD, is associate professor of social work at Rutgers University. He is the author of *A-Z of Psychodynamic Practice* and coauthor of *On Being and Having a Case Manager*. His clinical practice focuses on children, adolescents, and adults.

Megan Conti, LCSW, DSW, is a specialist in sexual trauma. She practices through a psychodynamic, feminist lens with clients ages 3–75 in both community-based mental health agencies and in private practice. Her publications include *The Case Study of Jacob: Childhood Sexual Abuse and the Limitations of the Holding Environment*.

THE SOCIAL WORK AND SEXUAL TRAUMA CASEBOOK

Phenomenological Perspectives

Edited by Miriam Jaffe, Jerry Floersch,
Jeffrey Longhofer, and Megan Conti

Routledge
Taylor & Francis Group

NEW YORK AND LONDON

First published 2018
by Routledge
711 Third Avenue, New York, NY 10017

and by Routledge
2 Park Square, Milton Park, Abingdon, Oxon, OX14 4RN

Routledge is an imprint of the Taylor & Francis Group, an informa business

Library of Congress Cataloging-in-Publication Data
Names: Jaffe, Miriam, author.
Title: The social work and sexual trauma casebook : phenomenological
    perspectives / edited by Miriam Jaffe [and three others].
Description: New York, NY : Routledge, 2018.
Identifiers: LCCN 2017052830 | ISBN 9781138727007 (hardcover :
    alk. paper) | ISBN 9781138727014 (pbk. : alk. paper) |
    ISBN 9781315191072 (e-book)
Subjects: LCSH: Sexual abuse victims—Services for. | Sexual abuse
    victims—Rehabilitation. | Sex offenders—Services for. | Social work
    with sex offenders. | Social services.
Classification: LCC HV6556 .S545 2018 | DDC 362.883/53—dc23
LC record available at https://lccn.loc.gov/2017052830

ISBN: 978-1-138-72700-7 (hbk)
ISBN: 978-1-138-72701-4 (pbk)
ISBN: 978-1-315-19107-2 (ebk)

Typeset in Bembo
by Apex CoVantage, LLC

CONTENTS

CONTRIBUTORS

Kara Beckett, BS in Family Studies (University of Maryland at College Park), MSW (Howard University), and DSW (Rutgers University), is a licensed clinical social worker in Georgia. As the Child & Youth Services director for the Georgia National Guard, she develops and implements programming for military youth. In addition, she maintains a part-time private practice where her areas of specialization include treatment for children and adolescent victims of commercial sexual exploitation, trauma, mood disorders, crisis counseling, stress management, parent training, and veteran services. Her previous experiences range from working with severely emotionally disturbed children and adults in a community-based setting to working with individuals and families in a therapeutic setting. She has conducted biopsychosocial assessments on children that were placed in the care of the Department of Family and Children Services (DFACS); served as an advocate for victims; and worked in a consultative capacity with local and state law enforcement agencies. Her therapeutic approach is eclectic and includes utilizing treatment modalities such as cognitive behavioral therapy, solution-focused therapy, and dialectical behavior therapy.

Lauren Busfield, BA in Women's Studies (West Chester University), MSW (West Chester University), and DSW (Rutgers University), is a licensed clinical social worker in Pennsylvania. While earning her bachelor's degree, she worked at a center for domestic violence managing crisis calls, which prompted an interest in counseling and social welfare, as well as a return to school for a graduate degree. She began her social work career as a medical social worker and expanded to experience in inpatient and partial hospitalization settings, as well as hospice work. She currently works in a group practice serving Bucks and Philadelphia counties in Pennsylvania, providing outpatient therapy to children, adolescents, adults, couples, and families. While she provides services to a variety of clients with a plethora of mental health challenges, she is particularly interested in adolescents and trauma. She has completed many professional trainings, including mindfulness-based stress management courses through the Penn Program for Mindfulness and those focusing on complex trauma. Her clinical interests include mindfulness-based therapy, technology and interpersonal trauma, and the impact of companion animals on mental health.

Megan Conti, LCSW, DSW, is a specialist in sexual trauma. She practices through a psychodynamic, feminist lens with clients ages 3–75 in both community-based mental health agencies and in private practice. Her publications include *The Case Study of Jacob: Childhood Sexual Abuse and the Limitations of the Holding Environment*.

Jesselly De La Cruz, BA in Political Science (Rider University), MSW (Rutgers University), and DSW (Rutgers University), is a licensed clinical social worker in New Jersey. She completed a post-graduate certificate in family therapy at The Multicultural Family Institute, Inc. in Highland Park, New Jersey. Having originated from an underprivileged background and being a child of an immigrant family herself, her education and work has been motivated by her desire to support traditionally underserved populations. Toward that overarching goal, she has worked with Latino advocacy nonprofit agencies in positions such as project manager and program coordinator. She has also worked in providing emergency screening of persons in mental health crisis at an inner-city hospital, outpatient and in-home child and family therapy, and clinical consultation for nursing homes with primarily Spanish-speaking residents. She has extensive experience working in the prevention of child sexual abuse by conducting forensic evaluations, individual, group, and family therapy at an intensive outpatient program for court-mandated youth who have sexually abused and/or have fire-setting behaviors. Currently, she coordinates the psychological treatment of child sexual abuse survivors and their non-offending families in Hudson County, New Jersey. Her research interests focus on systemic approaches to the prevention and treatment of sexual abuse, and the healing of intergenerational trauma in families through the use of mindfulness based psychotherapies, play therapy, and multi-systemic family therapy.

Jerry Floersch, LCSW, PhD, is an associate professor at the Rutgers University School of Social Work and the author of *Meds, Money, and Manners: The Case Management of Severe Mental Illness* and co-author of *Qualitative Methods for Practice Research*. His clinical practice focuses on adolescents and adults.

Russel Healy, BA (Drew University), MSW (Rutgers University), and DSW (Rutgers University), has over 25 years of clinical experience. He has worked along the continuum of care from in-patient treatment to outpatient counseling. Currently, he maintains a private practice and teaches for the Rutgers School of Social Work's Office of Continuing Education on LGBTQ issues. Russ's most recent work is in research and advocacy for transgender youth. He has been a consultant and writer for social work textbooks.

Miriam Jaffe, MSW, PhD, is the director of the Rutgers University Doctorate in Social Work Writing Program. She specializes in issues of autobiography, life-writing, and the case study method. Her publications, including the textbook *Social Work and K–12 Schools*, focus on pedagogies that de-silo academic disciplines. She practices with clients ages 7–80 through the lens of attachment theory.

Marisol Lado, BA in Sociology (William Paterson University), MSW (New York University), and DSW (Rutgers University) is a licensed clinical social worker in the state of New Jersey and a published writer on topics related to military deployments, life, culture, poetry, and end-of-life care in the *Journal of Palliative Medicine*. She is the family and trauma therapist at the Secaucus Vet Center, Department of Veterans Affairs, directly providing psychotherapy to combat veterans (from every combat era), victims of military sexual assault and trauma, and their families. Primarily working with individuals with combat trauma and post-traumatic stress disorder (PTSD), she also provides bereavement and complicated grief counseling for surviving family members of military services members, couples counseling, family counseling, and sexual assault/trauma treatment, and conducts groups on an ongoing basis. She also partakes in clinical presentations regarding military culture to community organizations, including working with the New Jersey Child Welfare Training Partnership, and trains New Jersey police officers in crisis interventions and how to engage and interact with veterans.

Jeffrey Longhofer, LCSW, PhD, is associate professor of social work at Rutgers University and the author of *A-Z of Psychodynamic Practice* and co-author of *On Being and Having a Case Manager*. His clinical practice focuses on children, adolescents, and adults.

Ruthie Norman, BA in Sociology (University of Massachusetts, Amherst), MSW (Springfield College), and DSW (Rutgers University) is a licensed clinical social worker providing trauma-focused and sexual abuse recovery treatment. Her research interests focus on trauma, sexually exploited youth, and the prevention and treatment of sexual abuse, and she is trained in cognitive behavioral therapy for post-disaster distress (CBT-PD), trauma-focused cognitive behavioral therapy (TF-CBT) for children and parents, and preventing the commercial sexual exploitation of girls. Her clinical experience includes extensive experience working in the prevention and recovery treatment of child sexual abuse, PTSD, and intensive family therapy. She currently provides recovery treatment to child sexual abuse survivors and their non-offending caregivers, and also provides intensive in-home family therapy. In addition, she provides consultations and education to area medical staff, schools, and community organizations regarding childhood trauma, trauma-informed practices, and sexual abuse prevention and recovery treatment.

Stephen Oreski, LCSW, MSW (Fordham University) and DSW (Rutgers University), has been involved in the sexual violence movement for over 20 years. His professional background includes leadership positions in social movements, policy, advocacy, and community organization. As the program development coordinator for the New Jersey Coalition Against Sexual Assault, he collaborated with other state and local program professionals and government agencies to plan and develop statewide policy and program initiatives within the sexual violence field. He has served on the New Jersey Governor's Council on Sexual Violence, the US Department of Health and Human Services Trauma Group, and NASW-NJ Continuing Education Committee. He is a contributor to the *Encyclopedia of Sexual Violence and Abuse* and has spoken to both local and national media regarding the effects of sexual trauma on the individual and society. Currently, he is the clinical director for the YWCA Bergen County—healingSPACE, New Jersey's largest sexual violence program, and maintains a private practice in Paramus, specializing in long-term counseling for survivors of sexual violence and their families.

Alan Oxman, BA in English (Amherst College), MFA (American Film Institute), MSW (New York University), and DSW (Rutgers University) is a clinical social worker and documentary filmmaker. After completing his MSW, he worked as a child and family therapist at the Postgraduate Center Child Clinic, where he used trauma-focused cognitive behavioral therapy and worked from psychodynamic and family systems perspectives. Recently, he worked in the clinic of a New York City psychoanalytic institute helping a diverse population of patients dealing with various issues, including trauma and addiction, using a psychodynamic and psychoanalytic approach. As a filmmaker, he specializes in social issue documentaries. He co-produced the Academy Award–nominated documentary *Children Underground*, an intimate portrait of homeless children living in a subway station in Bucharest, Romania, and *Assisted Living*, a film about the residents and staff of an assisted living home, which received the Elderserve Award for Eldercare. Most recently, he produced the Sundance Film Festival Official Selection, *Hot Coffee*, which explored issues of citizen rights and tort reform by taking a closer look at the famous case in which a woman spilled hot coffee on herself at McDonald's and sued.

Kim Stolow, LCSW, MSW (Rutgers University) and DSW (Rutgers University), has worked in the field of child abuse since obtaining her MSW. She currently works at the Dorothy B. Hersh Child Protection Center where she provides services to abused children and their families. She is also a private therapist who specializes in grief and loss and the treatment of sexually abused children and their non-offending parents. She co-facilitates groups for non-offending parents and children who have been victims of sexual abuse. She is a member of the Multidisciplinary Team in Mercer and Monmouth Counties and has provided numerous trainings on the signs and symptoms of sexual abuse, child sexual abuse treatment, working with the non-offending parent, and vicarious trauma. As a Finding Words faculty member, she teaches the mental health portion of the curriculum and facilitates small groups in order to critique the participant's child interviewing skills. She is also in the process of creating a training curriculum on the topic of child sexual abuse for the Institute for Families at Rutgers.

INTRODUCTION

Using Case Studies of Sexual Trauma in the Classroom

Megan Conti, Miriam Jaffe, Jerry Floersch, and Jeffrey Longhofer

Sexual trauma is one of the most horrific forms of interpersonal violence experienced by all manner of people in our society. Experiences of sexual trauma transcend socioeconomic, ethnic, political, and national boundaries. In the United States alone it is estimated that between 12 and 14 million individuals (adults and children included) are victims of some form of sexual violence each year (Waechter & Van, 2015). The prevalence of sexual trauma in our society almost guarantees that social work practitioners in every setting will encounter individuals who have been victims of sexual trauma at some point over the course of their careers. That being said, listening to stories of sexual trauma can be difficult and traumatizing in unique ways, making work with traumatized individuals some of the most challenging work we encounter. As such, conceptions of trauma must be flexible and complex enough to account for the many nuances of people's experiences of sexual trauma and the varied environments in which social workers will encounter traumatized individuals.

The Social Work and Sexual Trauma Casebook: Phenomenological Perspectives addresses two key components of the complex nature of treating sexual trauma. First, given the nuanced nature of sexual trauma, it is an understatement to call sexual trauma a challenging concept to articulate. The faces of sexual trauma victims and perpetrators are diverse, often different than those depicted in the media. Additionally, sexual trauma is manifested in a variety of ways. As such, this book aims to diversify and complicate the reader's understanding of who is victimized by sexual trauma, what sexual trauma is, and how that trauma is experienced and processed. That being said, the second concept, phenomenology, is integral to the case study approach to understanding sexual trauma. The phenomenological lens that informs each case study encourages readers to understand the distinctive and personalized nature of trauma experiences, thus fostering an appreciation of the unique, and inherently human, quality of each person's story.

In our work as social work supervisors, educators, and practitioners, one of the most invaluable tools we have in our arsenal are our experiences with clients from which we have developed practice wisdom. Additionally, as many social work practitioners might agree, our social work practice has imbued us with a deep appreciation for nuance and the knotty, challenging reality of working with human beings. By using human stories, we truly appreciate the dynamic and difficult nature of social work practice. The case study method, with its emphasis on narration and experience-near analysis, illuminates many of the important intricacies that emerge when working with traumatized and marginalized individuals, and it serves as an invaluable teaching tool to help students grasp complicated concepts and challenging situations.

Individuals who either teach social work or who supervise young social workers can appreciate how case studies, which elevate the points of intersection between our social work practice and the theories/concepts that often underpin our work, provide us with essential tools and opportunities to break down complicated ideas into clinical scenarios. Students are often full of questions about how to deal with different situations, and students are hungry for concrete experiences of individuals who have gone before them. Having clinical examples that serve to demonstrate different concepts facilitates and augments the learning process, as these clinical examples help to elevate our discussions with these young professionals from one that focuses on academic or theoretical material to one that reflects the challenges of the profession and the skills we want them to develop. This is especially important given the aforementioned fact that probably all of our students and supervisees will encounter victims of sexual trauma. Developing clinical and practical skills grounded in practice experience helps students to think of their academic material in a way that is related closely to the people they will serve and the scenarios they will encounter. Education, too, becomes experience-near.

Additionally, students often present to class or supervision with questions about the real-life applicability of the material they are learning in class, or with difficulty understanding how to conceptualize cases in a clinical way. Case studies provide students with an opportunity to see the concepts and assignments they encounter in school at work in a practice-focused, clinically developed way. Using case material can be inspirational to students who are looking to get a sense of how social work education will inform their practice moving forward. In this way, case studies are a tool for supervision and courses that aim to encourage students to learn how to frame cases and think clinically.

Thinking clinically is enhanced by critical thinking skills, as it enables providers to see past surface-level analyses toward a deeper appreciation of the human experience. A central limitation of textbooks and other teaching tools is their tendency to generalize and oversimplify complicated concepts, giving the lessons a hollow feeling devoid of genuine detail. Using case material does the opposite—case studies give space to the complications implicit in each clinical encounter. Furthermore, although case studies as a method are not generalizable, the value in using case studies as teaching tools lies in their transferability. Reading case material provides students with an appreciation of tough moments, potential impasses, and seemingly impossible moments that can be transferred across scenarios. By encouraging students to think differently about cases, to identify nuance, to consider systemic factors and influence, and to challenge their assumptions, students become self-reflexive practitioners engaging dynamically with important concepts and their clients.

Furthermore, the complicated nature of the material covered in case studies provides educators and students with examples of difficult, uncomfortable scenarios that arise when practitioners encounter work with human beings. The human face (of both the client and the practitioner) that case studies put on clinical practice scenarios allows for myriad emotions to emerge in students and young practitioners in a way that is unique to the case study method. When working with victims of sexual trauma, this human aspect is especially relevant. Sitting with the discomfort elicited by the experiences of such patients is an essential tool. As practitioners working with traumatized individuals, which one might argue is generalist practice, we often have to sit with challenging situations that simply do not make their way into textbook-like educational materials due to the necessary level of nuance required to adequately portray any given situation. Case studies enable us to have that level of nuance, grounded in theory, so as to challenge our students and ourselves to sit with discomfort and to embrace the ambivalence that might be triggered when working with such clients.

The real life experiences that are utilized as the point of knowledge generation in case studies help to identify crucial intersections—the areas where we can readily recognize how our practice as social workers can epitomize, complicate, or challenge theories and models of practice. As such, case studies encourage students to think critically about the material we are covering, to reconsider the ways in which certain ideas are framed, and to push back on the dominant practice narrative. This is especially important when learning about instances of sexual trauma, which require that we have a keen awareness of the socially constructed nature of trauma, the meaning making that is involved in trauma recovery work, and the stigma that is placed both on victims and perpetrators of sexual trauma. Trauma work requires a healing that inherently involves challenging and questioning our assumptions.

Social workers have an important perspective that needs to be taught more overtly and articulated more fully in conversation with dominant practice and teaching paradigms. As practitioners and as scholars, social workers have to do more to develop our unique perspectives on care and ethical practice. Furthermore, social workers need to be open about their thoughts and experiences working on the front lines with some of the most vulnerable in our society, especially when traditional theories and paradigms do not speak to the reality facing our clients. Case studies enable social work students to see how to challenge central tenets of practice and education in the interest of making notable contributions to the field. Developing our clinical voice, case studies empower students to see areas where they can push back against theories that are often taken for granted in both our education and practice.

In encountering human beings at some of the most vulnerable points of their lives, we as social work practitioners are positioned uniquely to speak to the reality of human suffering. That unique positionality also calls us to use those experiences to further knowledge about practice. Utilizing the case study method as a teaching tool provides social work students and practitioners with the opportunity to see the contributions we as social work practitioners can make to the greater body of knowledge regarding treatment and practice. In so doing, we can work toward the development of social work theories and practices that reflect core social work values and ethics, rather than relying on those developed by other disciplines. When considering sexual trauma, the case study method helps us to challenge our practice wisdom, to push back against the formal theories of treatment, and to evolve as practitioners in how we understand trauma in general. Ultimately, case studies demonstrate the value of the social work voice in the conversations about how we understand illness, how we approach treatment, how we categorize victimhood and perpetrators, and how we honor the person-in-environment perspective.

Using our voices as social work practitioners to further a theory of social work practice also involves identifying systems of power and challenging whose voices are being heard and elevated and whose voices are being disregarded and oppressed. As such, when working with social work students, supervisees new to the field, and even seasoned clinicians, it is essential to use our common humanity as a form of activism; social work is inherently on the side of the powerless, the vulnerable, and the injured. The case study method enables us to give voice to the voiceless, to validate and elevate one person's story, and to note how everyone's experience is valuable and important to us in our understanding of humanity and the human experience. Social workers regularly identify the unique and important value in each individual story, and the case study method gives students and practitioners the platform through which they can continue to develop this important work.

Megan Conti, co-editor, sets the stage for this volume in Chapter 1, "Thinking Critically About Sexual Trauma in the 21st Century," by examining the social construction of trauma against the backdrop of managed mental health care. Conti's brief outline of trauma therapies serves to contrast her presentation of two case vignettes, in which she challenges the diagnostic model of the privileged mythical norm: white, male, heterosexual, cisgender, and class dominant. First, we learn about Ava, 17, an immigrant from Mexico. Ava's grandmother casts her as a seductress and sinner for the childhood abuse she endured at the hands of her uncle; Conti demonstrates how Ava has been affected by a larger socioeconomic system of maternal migration that left Ava vulnerable to abuse, and she goes on to show how these socioeconomic conditions intersect with a gender-biased religious upbringing and Ava's self-concept as a dark-skinned emerging adult. Then, we learn about Brad, an American-born white heterosexual male who was sexually assaulted in childhood by an older man; Brad resists acknowledging the roots of his pain in fear of labels that would mark him as "sick" or somehow at odds with hegemonic masculinity. Conti's therapeutic intervention is based on her contention that

> we have to raise our own awareness of the systems in place that contribute to an individual's trauma narrative and that may, or may not, influence the extent to which their healing is an individual journey or an indictment of larger, social forces.

Ultimately, Conti challenges readers to consider how the process of defining trauma and identifying oneself as traumatized are uniquely personal, and this consideration should inform clinical practice approaches.

In "Virtual Trauma: Social Work With Adolescents in the Online Era," Lauren Busfield offers another perspective on the danger of (mis)interpreting and (mis)labeling sexual trauma. Busfield presents the case of Olivia to argue that parental approaches to online sexual experimentation—and even evidence-based practices aimed at managing teens' online worlds—are developed by adults who are digital immigrants instead of digital natives. Digital immigrants, Busfield says, do not necessarily understand the newly developing sexual norms of the online era, and these new norms are changing accepted conventions of how adolescents experience sexual development. Busfield invents the word "virtual trauma" to discuss online encounters that would more solidly be classified as potentially traumatic had they occurred in the "real world." Although Olivia's symptoms may, on the surface, meet the criteria for Busfield's initial post-traumatic stress disorder (PTSD) diagnosis, Busfield finds Olivia resistant to trauma treatment because in Olivia's estimation, her online experiment was not traumatic. In contrast, Olivia, like so many adolescents, especially those outside of heteronormative boundaries, finds the internet to be a safe zone for experimentation. So, how do social workers know if someone has experienced a "virtual trauma"? Busfield presents a risk assessment tool for clinicians, one that dodges the victim blaming that can occur when digital immigrants do not fully grasp the online behaviors of adolescents.

Following this theme of victim blaming, we feature the work of Russel Healy, titled "Victim or Offender? Stigma and Justice in a Complex Forensic Case." Here, Healy brings readers along on his journey through an area of social work practice with which many clinicians may struggle: conducting therapy with a convicted sex offender, whose stigmatization overshadows his own struggle to confront the years of sexual trauma he experienced at the hands of an older sibling. Healy calls for social workers to engage in a new level of critical thinking about offenders who have also been victimized. His work challenges legal systems that do not take into account the full complexity of sexual trauma. Moreover, Healy's process of self-reflexivity is a model for social work practitioners as he reveals his commitment to treat his client with dignity and respect.

Stephen Oreski's chapter, "Sexual Abuse, the Therapeutic Alliance, and Therapist Self-Disclosure," exhibits the lengths to which a clinician will go to affect his client's dignity and self-respect. Oreski tells the story of his work with Kevin, whose sense of shame over the sexual abuse he endured by his uncle is not breached until Oreski makes a personal disclosure of his own history of childhood sexual abuse. While Oreski's self-disclosure is a controversial but important part of the therapeutic alliance he forms to help Kevin heal, self-disclosure is not the true focus of this chapter. More salient is Oreski's consideration of male survivors of sexual abuse and the specific conflicts they encounter in conjunction with the codes of masculine socialization in relational and intimate situations. From this chapter, we also get another glimpse into how sexual trauma plays out in the courtroom setting; part of Oreski's treatment of Kevin involves the therapist's presence and support as Kevin reads his statement aloud in court. This kind of social work is certainly not part of manualized treatment, but rather a model of humanity and empathy too often avoided in a field so full of countertransference and vicarious trauma that even the best clinicians find themselves establishing boundaries instead of breaking them down.

"Redefining Resilience in Children: A Story of Strength and Survival," by Kim Stolow, uses the idea of boundaries in a different way; Stolow recognizes that her client's boundaries and coping mechanisms are signs of her resilience. From age 5 to age 12, Stolow's client, Tonyah, was abused by a family member, and Tonyah coped by covering her body, dissociating, engaging in risky sexual behaviors, and cutting. Stolow helped Tonyah to understand that these coping mechanisms were bodily responses that encouraged Tonyah's survival and were, therefore, behaviors that showed her resiliency. Stolow argues:

> Clinicians, and frankly, society, owe it to survivors of trauma to find a new way to understand resiliency and to be careful how that term is applied. The labeling of one as resilient or not resilient carries a tremendous weight. The label of resilience fails to take into consideration the biological impact of trauma, as well as the adaptive mechanisms inherent in human beings. It also forces the clinician to make a choice between the mind and the brain, rather than creating an intervention that acknowledges the individual as a whole.

Stolow's aim, as one can read in her careful process recording, is not to cure Tonyah but to help her understand how an awareness of her own mind-body connection could help her to relearn how and who to trust.

For a clinician to establish a therapeutic alliance with a client in a case of sexual trauma is, in large part, about gaining trust. Kara Beckett, in her chapter "Social Work and Sex Trafficking: Therapeutic Intervention in the Commercial Sexual Exploitation of Children," learns that establishing a trusting relationship with Avani, a victim of child sex trafficking, is the only path to healing—and perhaps the only goal she could realistically achieve. Despite Beckett's deepest desires to treat the underlying causes of Avani's repeated return to "the life"—a lay term for the sex-trafficking industry—Beckett realizes that she must keep her expectations in check. Avani developed Stockholm syndrome, returning time and again to a brutal pimp, and no amount of suffering or therapeutic intervention, including hospitalizations for both of these reasons, could keep Avani from running away from home back to the streets. Beckett struggles with the fact that Avani trusts her enough to let her be a listener, to let her know the horror, without allowing Beckett, and the team dedicated to Avani's survival, to save her. Victims of child exploitation are not just victims of their pimps and johns; trafficked children are victims of a global system that makes children powerless against rape culture. Still, for some people, the question remains: if Avani returns to a life of prostitution, if she a victim or a criminal?

Jesselly De La Cruz faces this question in her case study of Sarah, "Social Work With an Adolescent Female Sex Offender." Because only 7% of juvenile sex offense arrests involve a female offender, De La Cruz takes a person-in-environment approach to understanding why Sarah was one of them. De La Cruz writes, "sexual trauma is weaved into a historical, cultural, and sociological discourse on the detrimental impact of the negative images and narratives that Sarah and other young girls receive from rape culture about what it means to be a girl." Without excusing Sarah's kidnapping and perpetration of rape against another young girl, De La Cruz establishes empathy for her client through a careful look at her client's context. In Sarah's surroundings, images of rape portray power, and De La Cruz takes up the idea that Sarah offended to gain power as a mode of self-protection in a rough neighborhood. Perhaps it was Sarah's exposure to rape culture that engendered her vicarious sexual trauma, thus leading her to take drastic measures toward her own self-protection. Again, we see that the lines between victim and perpetrator are sometimes more blurry than we would like to think.

And sometimes, as Ruthie Norman's chapter reminds us, the lines between victim and perpetrator are very clear—so clear that even a seasoned social worker loses her own sense of safety. "In-Home Treatment for In-Home Sexual Trauma: The Case of Becky" describes Norman's work to remove a child who was a victim of incest from the home where the child was being sexually abused. Whereas clinical readers will tune in to their countertransference while reading Becky's disclosure of abuse—as did Norman herself—Norman teaches us that a social worker's countertransference must sometimes be ignored as a self-protective mechanism. Norman focuses on the precarious nature of working with a victim in the presence of her ever-threatening perpetrator, revealing the many ways in which theories and systems meant to protect children sometimes fail to protect not only children from sexual trauma, but also clinicians from vicarious sexual trauma.

As difficult as it is to read a case of incest within the household, Marisol Lado, in "The Silent War Within: Military Sexual Trauma," describes institutional incest. Lado says, "military sexual trauma can be linked to the experience of incest in the civilian world" to point out that identification with the aggressor makes military sexual trauma (MST) perplexing to negotiate, especially when victims of MST are turned away from getting treatment by the very institution that tacitly enabled their abuse as part of military culture. Lado writes with curiosity about how and why MST is kept silent, but, moreover, she gives voice to the stories of victims as a way to advocate for change in military culture. Through case vignettes, Lado portrays how the military identity of victims becomes an identity that revolves around stigmatization and shame.

In that vein, we end with Alan Oxman's chapter on "Social Work, Sex Addiction, and Psychodynamic Treatment," where Oxman offers the case of Drew to explore sex addiction as a possible manifestation of childhood sexual trauma. Through his psychoanalytic lens, Oxman explains that the disease model of addiction

> decontextualize[s] the *subject* by using the *addict* label to dissociate individuals from their social context and place[s] all the pathology in the *addict's* brain. This model, which indelibly etches the abject label of *sex addict* onto Drew's self-identity, can lead to hopelessness and continued compulsive behavior.

Oxman challenges the entire approach to the treatment of sex addiction by noting that the real work involved making room for Drew's humanity as well as his own. Ultimately Oxman suggests that the clinician's use of empathy, especially in cases of sexual trauma, is far more effective than any other treatment of sexual trauma.

In order to achieve this kind of empathy, the clinician must—as we see throughout these chapters—be willing to ethically listen to each individual. Ethical listening is a kind of listening that considers context, the person-in-environment, the environment as socially constructed. This volume offers a range of empathetic approaches that involve "listening to" rather than "listening for." When we "listen for," we are entering the therapeutic relationship with a set of expectations for which we are seeking fulfillment. These preconceived notions get in the way of genuine connection with our clients, thusly closing the door on the possibility for true empathy. When we "listen to," we open up the possibilities for deep empathy because we allow our clients' understandings of themselves to guide our responses.

What may feel missing from this volume is a case study that deals directly with sexual trauma in the LGBTQ population. While some LGBTQ issues are obliquely manifest in the cases presented here, we decided that one or two cases dedicated to LGBTQ sexual trauma could only serve as symbolic and reductive. And although this collection thematically overlaps with sexual trauma in the LGBTQ population, we endeavor to present a volume of cases, like this one, with more space to draw out the connections between social work and sexual trauma with an LGBTQ population.

Our hope in presenting this volume is to encourage empathy as a response to individuals who have experienced sexual trauma. This human connection is the foundation for all social work practice, but empathy is a form of witness that is particularly important in cases of sexual trauma because it reveals to the individuals who come to us with their pain that they have not only been heard and seen, but also felt to the point that empathy's reciprocal energy can become a healing force. If we can use these case studies to teach empathy—to teach empathy as a part of ethical listening—in our classrooms, then we are enhancing social work practice through close reading and writing as acts of discovering own capacities for empathy.

Reference

Waechter, R., & Van, M. (2015). Sexual violence in America: Public funding and social priority. *American Journal of Public Health, 105*(12), 2430–2437.

1

THINKING CRITICALLY ABOUT SEXUAL TRAUMA IN THE 21ST CENTURY

Megan Conti

Pre-reading Questions

1. When you think of sexual trauma, what images or ideas emerge? Who are the victims? What are the circumstances?
2. What do you think might be different about how we conceptualize sexual trauma in the 21st century as opposed to the 20th century?
3. In what ways might structural elements and systems of power influence our understanding of sexual trauma?

Over the past 25 years, literature on defining and treating trauma has increased significantly. This development has been part of an open discussion in the media and in public forums about trauma and its various manifestations (Watters, 2010; Fassin & Rechtman, 2009; Kirmayer, Lemelson, & Barad, 2007). Most notably, the increase in trauma theory and research can be linked to a post-Vietnam War social consciousness and the increase in feminist theory about domestic violence and child abuse (Herman, 1992b; McNally, 2004). Such knowledge has undergone an identifiable spike since the early 1990s, as marked by the publication of Judith Herman's first edition of *Trauma and Recovery* and the emergence of Bessel van der Kolk's research on neuroscience and its relationship to trauma. This spike has resulted in what can now be identified as the "social phenomenon" of trauma, in which trauma has become an identified social problem that requires attention and, more often than not, empathy (Fassin & Rechtman, 2009). This increase has occurred amid the emergence of managed health care, in which mental health is increasingly reliant on diagnostics and psychopathology for the provision of care (Rosenberg, 2007; Kirschner, 2013). In tandem, diagnostic language and concepts have become part of contemporary discourse and identity development (Marecek & Gavey, 2013). With these developments come important considerations regarding the epistemological significance and social influence of trauma and its partner, complex trauma (Young, 1995).

Research has demonstrated that trauma responses can be considered on a spectrum (Kaminer & Eagle, 2017), and this spectrum includes proposed subsets of trauma, most notably Complex Post-traumatic Stress Disorder (PTSD; Herman, 1992a). Complex PTSD, with its recognition of the differing symptomatic, characterological, and relational presentations of victims of repetitive exposure to trauma, was a response to the limitations of a traditional trauma diagnosis of PTSD (Herman, 1992a; Newman, Riggs, & Roth, 1997; Pelcovitz et al., 1997; Cloitre et al., 2009; Sar, 2011; Hyland et al., 2017). Traumatic experiences captured by the frame of Complex PTSD include repetitive interpersonal violence perpetrated by close caregivers or important attachment figures (Herman, 1992b; Ford & Courtois, 2009), as well as other types of trauma that involve larger, structural and transnational forces (Hardy, Compton, & McPhatter, 2013).

Through the evolution of our understanding of trauma, treatment research has developed an approach to human suffering that has become an embodiment in and of itself, and has perpetuated key assumptions about the recovery process (Lester, 2013). In general, mainstream trauma treatment theories tend to follow a trajectory of steps that facilitate the healing process (Herman, 1992b; Foa & Rothbaum, 1998; Resick & Schnicke, 1992; Ehlers & Clark, 2000; Shapiro, 1995; Schauer, Neuner, & Elbert, 2005; Dorrepaal et al., 2014; DeJongh et al., 2016). Therapists are encouraged to develop a feeling of safety with their patients, at which point the patient is then guided on a journey during which they open up about their trauma, generating a narrative that leads them to an ultimate truth about their suffering (Herman, 1992b; Schauer, Neuner, & Elbert, 2005). Ultimately, the process is meant to empower patients and help them to reconnect with their world in a new way (Herman, 1992b). Other theorists rely heavily on brain imaging, citing that our advances in neuroscience will help us to pinpoint the changes in the brain that take place after a traumatic experience and, in doing so, will guide our way through the process of recovery (Van der Kolk, 2014; Elsey & Kindt, 2017; Zaleski, Johnson, & Klein, 2016; Rau & Fanselow, 2007; Bremner, 2007). The shift to neurobiology in the study of trauma mimics the larger shift in psychology toward reliance on neuroscience and carries with it significant implications for treatment (Kirschner, 2013). While these developments in our understanding of trauma and trauma theory are valuable and integral to our understanding of the etiology of and symptoms characterizing trauma, what is the extent of their influence on our approach to treating victims of significant trauma?

When considered from a perspective that is experience-near to a patient's narrative, questions regarding diagnostic relevance and treatment framing emerge. Rather than being, as Lester (2013), "carved out of the flow of everyday existence and . . . bracketed as a 'thing' that is discernible against the backdrop of a person's life" (p. 755), a patient's presentation can be messy and complicated. Furthermore, the patients' understanding of themselves can be subversive of our application of diagnostic and positivistic practice wisdom with its a priori approach to treatment (Guilfoyle, 2013), or the biological reductionism of the medical model (Kirschner, 2013). An individual's experience of trauma does not take place in a vacuum from which we can extract a trauma narrative and a healing trajectory. Instead, the experience of trauma is couched in a person's life experiences and informed by her understanding of herself and her world. As such, it becomes unique and distinctly harder to capture, and treatment recommendations should reflect this nuance.

When approached from a frame that is tied closely to a patient's experience of himself, and pushing back against the dominant, medicalized, scientific understanding of mental illness, clinicians are free to explore individual accounts of suffering from a phenomenological approach that honors the individual's right to understand and define the components of their experience and their meaning (Hornstein, 2013). A larger, phenomenological focus becomes particularly relevant when individuals who have suffered from what might be diagnosed as Complex PTSD present for treatment having developed an identity completely divorced from that of their victimhood. These are individuals whose experience of trauma is embodied on a daily basis due to structural and environmental influences or who have incorporated a trauma narrative into their identity in ways that are culturally informed and do not necessarily involve ideas such as truth or recovery. For such people, Burstow (2003) argues, psychiatric diagnoses "cannot do justice to the psychological misery of people's lives, never mind the social conditions that give rise to the misery" (p. 1300). These patients remind clinicians and researchers that experiences of trauma defy reductionism. In so doing, these patients caution us against an overreliance on positivist definitions of traumatic nosology, regardless of their presenting symptomatology.

In order to approach trauma from a perspective that honors a patient's relationship to his traumatic experiences (which is necessarily ontologically and epistemologically different than the dominant treatment paradigm), we must consider how each patient's experiences and his interactions with the world add up to his narrative and his understanding of himself and his trauma. In doing so, we are allowing for the true complexities of the human experience to illuminate for us the inherently layered nature of exploring trauma and trauma treatment. While concepts like Complex PTSD help us to better understand experiences of extreme and prolonged exposure to trauma, they do not necessarily translate to a helpful frame for all patients whose presentation meets the criteria for this diagnosis/formulation. When patients do not identify with their trauma, or do not identify their trauma as such, we are challenged to consider how to approach treatment from a lens that is both trauma-informed and respectful of our patients' development of the self.

Literature Review

The American Psychological Association's *Diagnostic and Statistical Manual* (DSM; 2013) and its categorization of mental illnesses serve an important purpose. The DSM has helped guide clinicians as well as individuals suffering from mental illness through the process of making sense of what can be frightening, uncomfortable, and life-threatening experiences (Hornstein, 2013). Specifically, Complex PTSD research has provided a helpful expansion of diagnostic criteria and framing for understanding cases where the nature of the traumatic experience is repetitive and prolonged, and where the patient's presentation tends to fall outside of the parameters established by a traditional PTSD diagnosis (Herman, 1992a; Newman, Riggs, & Roth, 1997; Pelcovitz et al., 1997; Cloitre et al., 2009; Sar, 2011; Ford & Courtois, 2014; Ford, 2015; Hyland et al., 2017). Complex PTSD refers to trauma that is developmental in nature, meaning that traumatic experiences are repetitive and additive, typically occurring over a period of time, and taking place in relational contexts that are influential to the victim's development (Sar, 2011; Gleiser, Ford, & Fosha, 2008; Courtois, 2004). The central contribution of Complex PTSD to the psychiatric nosology is the added attention to "disturbances predominantly in affective and interpersonal self-regulatory capacities" (Cloitre et al., 2009, pp. 399–400). In expanding the clinical focus to involve understanding a patient's mood and relational issues, Complex PTSD helps to guide the clinician to better understand how complicated traumatic experiences have the potential to have a pervasive effect on a victim's development and ongoing life experiences.

However, the authority, influence, and power with which the DSM operates (as well as concepts, like Complex PTSD, that emerge from DSM diagnostic categories) is problematic (Georgaca, 2013; Hornstein, 2013; Kirschner, 2013; Burstow, 2003; Marecek & Gavey, 2013; Cermele, Daniels, & Anderson, 2001). Feminist, poststructuralist, and antiracist theorists have noted that the dominant influence of psychiatry and the ongoing expansion of diagnoses and criteria have resulted in the "colonization" of mental health practices (Cosgrove & Wheeler, 2013). This colonization involves an increase in the number of people who qualify for diagnoses, a neurobiological reductionism that conflates symptoms with a biological origin that is largely unfounded, and the oversimplification of complicated human experiences (Cosgrove & Wheeler, 2013; Hornstein, 2013; Fee, 2000; Kirmayer, Lemelson, & Barad, 2007). Additionally, poststructuralists argue, the shift toward greater medicalization of mental illness reflects more of what is constructed as mental illness and knowledge than an objective truth upon which all practitioners can agree (Cermele, Daniels, & Anderson, 2001). As such, approaching mental illness from a psychiatrically informed position is fraught with clinical (and potentially ethical) concerns related to what constitutes truth and knowledge, whose experience is honored, whose agenda is served, and whose treatment is considered when creating labels and frames for human experience.

A limitation to randomized, controlled studies of treatment effectiveness is the way in which controlled environments fail to capture the real life circumstances of trauma treatment, particularly in community-based mental health facilities (Kaminer & Eagle, 2017). Despite its "scientific" validity, an understanding of trauma and trauma treatment that grows out of a psychiatric appreciation of human suffering is inherently limited in its scope (Burstow, 2003). Current diagnostic paradigms tend to focus on the interpersonal experience of trauma and fail to consider the larger, structural powers that contribute significantly to an individual's daily traumatization and polyvictimization (Quiros & Berger, 2013). In reality, diagnostic categories upon which research and evidence-based practice models are founded do not reflect the reality of daily trauma experienced by vulnerable members of society (Ali, 2004; Bryant-Davis & Ocampo, 2005). The impact of systemic racism, sexism, heterosexism, ableism, and cisnormativity are daily and powerful, resulting in systems of oppression and trauma that traditional approaches to trauma fail to capture.

Additionally, diagnoses emerge from a cultural embodiment that privileges the white, male, heterosexual, cisgender, dominant narrative and this narrative was used to conceptualize a PTSD diagnosis (Burstow, 2003; Georgaca, 2013). The culturally defined nature of diagnostic categories in general, and trauma and trauma diagnosis in particular, has been well documented (Young, 1995; Burstow, 2003; Kirmayer, Lemelson, & Barad, 2007; Watters, 2010; Fassin & Rechtman, 2009; Quiros & Berger, 2015; Georgaca, 2013). The American Psychiatric Association's approach to mental illness emerges from American social structures, privileging the dominant class—white, male, middle class, able-bodied, heterosexual, and cisgendered (Burstow, 2003; Brown, 1995; Cermele, Daniels, & Anderson, 2001; Quiros & Berger, 2015). The construction of mental illness that emerges from such a frame fails to recognize "how race, class, age, gender, and other forms of bias undergird many of the diagnoses," and fails to consider the nuance of individual experience (Cosgrove & Wheeler, 2013, p. 94). In addition, feminist scholars have noted, such models tend to pathologize gendered racial/ethnic responses to stressors in the interest of privileging power structures as normal (Cermele, Daniels, & Anderson, 2001; Brown & Ballou, 1992). Although the DSM is not intended to be a social commentary, it serves the function of reifying systems of power and significantly influencing how mental health practitioners and patients alike frame mental illness and human suffering (Guilfoyle, 2013).

Foucault's (1988) identification of the individual's resistance to being essentialized is particularly relevant when considering patients who present to treatment with identities that do not fit modern conceptualizations of mental illness or trauma (cited by Guilfoyle, 2013). Working with patients whose understanding of themselves and their life experiences embody this type of resistance to essentialism requires closer attention to their process of meaning making and the culturally informed embodiment of their experience. As such, there are instances when one's approach to complex trauma requires a discerning frame that honors feminist, postmodern, and intersectional conceptualizations of illness and treatment approaches. Although the evidence for treating PTSD supports approaching treatment with trauma-focused cognitive behavioral therapy (TF-CBT; Cusack et al., 2016; Schnyder et al., 2015), prolonged exposure (Foa & Rothbaum, 1998), or eye movement desensitization and reprocessing (EMDR; Shapiro, 1995), a relational, phenomenological approach to treatment is indicated. Such treatment allows for a patient's own process of meaning making and self-exploration to emerge free from the confines of the DSM or other diagnostic categories. In doing so, our use of case material as the point of analysis enables us to consider the ways in which nuanced clinical narratives can illuminate practice questions centered on the development of the self, honoring a patient's meaning making, and privileging a patient's narrative development.

Case Vignette: Ava

Ava made a strong first impression. Stunningly beautiful, she had a radiant and welcoming smile bracketed by deep dimples in her caramel-colored skin. Ava also had these dark, almond-shaped eyes that gave her a haunting look, communicating her emotional depth and underlying pain. When Ava appeared in my office for the first time for her intake appointment, she was visibly nervous and unsure, but somehow conveyed a deep commitment to the potential for this process to work. As we began to talk about her life and her experiences, I was impressed by how mature and articulate she was; she was wise beyond her 17 years. As the details of her life became intimately known to me over time, however, I began to understand why. Ava had suffered significant sexual trauma at the hands of her uncle. Additionally, her life story brought me on a journey that involved immigration, economics, power and privilege, and intergenerational systems of abuse that were quite remarkable. These experiences left Ava well versed in the evils of the world in a way that the average 17-year-old should not be, and caused her to be deeply pained and significantly emotionally damaged.

Ava had sought out therapy on her own, deciding that she wanted to talk about her feelings and her problems, despite significant cultural pressure to the contrary, which was mainly leveled against her by her mother, Camila. Ava was remarkably resourceful, reaching out to a family friend who she knew could connect her with services. When Ava came to me she was experiencing significant symptoms of anger and aggressive outbursts at home and at school. Prior to beginning treatment, she found herself becoming agitated upon the slightest provocation, often abruptly cutting people out of her life and thus losing friendships over things that she considered, ultimately, to be insignificant. Although she could reason with herself that these things were, in fact, minor, and that she had overreacted, she found it extremely difficult to let any of her anger go; she was unable to mend any of her broken relationships. Ava found herself losing friends, isolating herself, and feeling more and more depressed as time went on.

As our relationship developed, Ava began to share more and more about her relationship with her family—namely, her mother. Ava vacillated between extremes of idealized love and intense hatred for her mother, a tendency that was rooted in her early experiences with her mother in Mexico and her early childhood trauma. When she would reference her sexual trauma it was in terms of her own agency and her role as a victimizer (at age 8, Ava "experimented" with other children by showing them her nipples) rather than as being victimized. Additionally, her understanding of herself was complicated and, at times, hard to follow. In light of my attempts to weave together a story from her disclosures, it quickly became clear to me that in order to understand Ava's sexual trauma, I had to understand the intricacies of her experiences on a larger level.

Rather than grasping at disparate strands of her narrative, I began to realize that Ava's presentation was a complicated web of various threads that resulted in an overarching theme of traumatization. In many ways, Ava was an exemplar of how trauma is not equally distributed in the world and how "many seemingly unrelated problems co-occur because they arise from a common set of historical and social conditions" (Kirmayer, Lemelson, & Barad, p. 13). In Ava's case, her social location both in Mexico and the United States, her family's cultural and religious identity, her intergenerational family history of abuse, and her complex relationship with her mother all combined to form the young lady who sat before me, rife with guilt, shame, and anger.

Ava was born in a rural village in Mexico in the early 1990s as the Mexican economy was just beginning to feel the impact of international trade agreements like NAFTA on their rural economy. Ava's mother, Camila, unmarried and single (Ava's father was never involved in Ava's life) attempted to raise Ava on her own by getting various odd jobs when she could and trying to save enough money for her and Ava to live on their own (rather than staying with Camila's mother). However, the struggling economy in rural Mexico in the 1990s ultimately forced Ava's mother to immigrate to the United States to seek economic opportunities when Ava was only 3 years old. Ava was left in Mexico to be raised by Camila's mother—Ava's grandmother.

Camila's departure symbolized a significant shift in Ava's life. After her mother left for America, Ava became more vulnerable to the other members of her family who were not as loving to Ava as her mother had been. Ava's grandmother was reportedly very cold and distant from Ava, believing Ava to be a bastard undeserving of the same attention as her other cousins and family members. Ava's grandmother was a deeply religious Pentecostal woman who would assign any bad behavior demonstrated by Ava as a character flaw linked to her sinfulness from being a child of sin. Ava reported trying to get her grandmother's attention by being good and helpful around the house, but her grandmother would repeatedly point out what Ava did wrong and tell her that she needed to pray in order to be less wicked. Thus began an internalization of Ava's shamefulness and wickedness, her identity development as influenced by her relational trauma, as well as the seeds of her significant rage against her mother.

Ava's plight only worsened as time went on. When Ava turned 5, her uncle began to repeatedly rape her. He promised her gifts if she would cooperate with him, luring her into his bedroom. Ava was able to recall that her uncle started by touching her and having her reciprocate the touching. Ava often struggled with this part of her narrative, as she would remark that the touching felt good, and that she welcomed the attention her uncle was paying her. However, she would also share that her uncle was mentally ill, and he often scared her when they were together. These discrepancies in her memories caused significant confusion for Ava when later trying to piece together her understanding of her trauma. Even as the sexual abuse moved on to penetration and rape, which were painful and caused bodily harm, Ava struggled with recognizing how she could be considered anything but a willing participant. These messages were further validated when Ava, at age 9, eventually told her grandmother what was happening. Her grandmother blamed her for being sinful and enticing her uncle into sexual acts with her. Being young and believing that she was inherently sinful, Ava internalized this explanation. In Ava's young mind, this was what people like her deserved; this was what her life was going to be like.

When Ava was about to turn 10, her mother sent for her to come to the United States. Upon coming to the United States, Ava began to feel angry and out of place. Ava complained that her mother was not as affectionate with her as she used to be. Camila appeared cold and distant, which was reminiscent of Ava's grandmother and the rejection she regularly perceived in Mexico. Additionally, while in the United States, Camila had met and married a man with whom she was living. Although Ava recognized that her stepfather was a good, honest man who treated her like she was his daughter, Ava felt acutely aware that she did not belong in their family. When Camila became pregnant a few years later, Ava's anger amplified and resulted in her acting out.

Ava's younger brother was born when Ava turned 13. After the birth of her younger brother, Ava shared that she became deeply jealous of him and the love their mother showed him. Ava became argumentative and difficult with her family members, particularly her mother. When her mother asked her what was wrong with her, Ava angrily told her mother about the abuse, blaming much of her struggle on her mother leaving her behind in Mexico. In response, Camila told her to get over it, as rape was something every woman has to deal with. Ava's rage deepened, causing her to resort to self-harm and substance abuse to cope with her severe depression and feelings of self-loathing.

In addition to her familial struggles, Ava experienced racism and sexism in her community and her school. Ava shared that she experienced microaggressions and outright racism based on the fact that she was Mexican woman with a darker complexion than her classmates. Additionally, Ava reported being harassed sexually on the street by men who would catcall her or proposition her regularly.

Ava noted feeling like the world was hostile toward her, but always equated it with her worthlessness, her past sexual history, and her sinfulness. Despite her struggle, Ava's access to mental health treatment was limited; her family did not believe in therapy and did not provide her with the support she needed at such a young age. It was not until a caring family friend referred her for therapy that she was connected to services.

When Ava came to treatment and we began to discuss her trauma, there was an additional rupture in her understanding of herself. In the United States, the narrative about trauma is victim centered and medical in its understanding— symptoms add up to a syndrome that can then be diagnosed and treated. Ava's experience simply did not follow that course. Her memories were unclear, her assigned blame and anger were not directed at her abuser, and her role was as an active participant rather than as a victim. As a result, encouraging her to accept a narrative in which she was absolutely a victim was not productive for Ava. In fact, it was an entirely irrelevant approach that had no meaning in Ava's world.

Discussion

If we were to consider Ava's symptoms and presentation from a psychiatrically, diagnostically minded frame, she would most appropriately fit into a diagnosis of Complex PTSD. Ava's behavioral issues (i.e., her anger, her volatility and liability) and her interpersonal relationships (fraught with ruptures and cutoffs) reflect the pervasive impact of her trauma on her life. Additionally, her personality structure was one that was related to her trauma—her dissociation, her difficulty integrating her emotions and her cognitions, and her struggle with intimacy. Finally, as Herman (1992a) notes, Ava's "vulnerability to repeated harm, both self-inflicted and at the hands of others" (p. 379), was a continual theme throughout her development, culminating in her significant self-harm prior to entering therapy. Ava's suffering was profound, and Complex PTSD certainly can shed light on how her trauma influenced the development of her worldview.

However, Ava's understanding of herself ultimately undermined much of this framework. In order to remain experience-near with Ava in our work together, it was essential to watch for the use of language or concepts that indicated an ultimate truth or a larger lesson from which she could draw conclusions (Guilfoyle, 2013). Therefore, in order to begin to understand Ava's experience of trauma and polyvictimization, her story must be rooted in larger social and economic systems that inform her location in the world. In examining Ava's life history, we can embed her experience in a framework that reveals significant power structures that are at work in her life, all of which determine a great deal about her risk and her vulnerability. As medical anthropologist Paul Farmer (2009) notes, in doing so, we are better able to "[illustrate] some of the mechanisms through which large-scale social forces crystallize into the sharp, hard surfaces of individual suffering" (p. 12). Taking a feminist, poststructuralist approach helps us to examine larger structural questions that are posed when we consider the existence of victims of sexual trauma in our society and in our practice without having an expected set of truths or labels that our patients will eventually grasp.

Ava is the victim, in part, of the larger, transnational economic systems that forced her mother to immigrate in search of a job and better opportunities. Her social location in Mexico as the daughter of a poor, rural family resulted in her vulnerability to larger economic systems, which influenced significantly the trajectory of her young life. Economic trade agreements, Mexican domestic policies, and American immigration law all resulted in Ava's mother moving to the United States and her inability to return to Mexico or to send for Ava for more than seven years. These and other choices that immigrant families have to make impact their safety and the safety of their children significantly. Studies have demonstrated the particular impact of early, maternal immigration on the mental health of children left behind (Adhikari et al., 2014). In a study conducted by the Scalabrini Migration Center (2005), researchers have noted that maternal migration has been associated with children feeling "lonely, angry, unloved, afraid, and worried compared to children of non-migrants" (cited in Adhikari et al., 2014, p. 782). As such, identity development was influenced at a young age for Ava by her mother's departure. Ava's understanding of herself as unlovable started very early on, and resulted in what seems like an intractable, rigid, identity structure.

Ava's intersectional "social construction of risk" was in place largely before her sexual, interpersonal, and psychological trauma began (Olofsson et al., 2014). For Ava, her vulnerable socioeconomic location begot greater trauma, a cycle of victimization that is not unfamiliar for many individuals facing sexual trauma (Decker et al., 2016). More than a singular event, Ava's risk was complex and included multinational forces of power, religious indoctrination, and intergenerational family systems that combined and resulted in Ava's polyvictimization and the strength of her sense of self as someone who deserves maltreatment and disdain.

The trauma of losing her mother at a very young age was exacerbated by Ava's grandmother's increasing role in her life. From Ava's early years, when her grandmother would tell her to pray and repent for her mother's sins, up until the time when she accused Ava of luring her uncle into a sexual relationship with her, Ava's grandmother regarded Ava as a child who was the product of sin and who deserved the bad that came to her. The religious beliefs in Ava's household were reflective of a larger patriarchy within which her grandmother operated, one that would not allow for a man—Ava's uncle—to be wrong, and that resulted in the demonizing of Ava in order to preserve his image as the valued man in the family. The connection between Camila's departure and Ava's religious upbringing lies in the fact that "both mainstream Christian religion and capitalism perpetuate and entrench discrimination against women and the oppression of the needy" (Friebach-Heifetz & Stopler, 2008, p. 516). Although the extent to which Ava's grandmother abused her may be a reflection of some issues that Ava's grandmother may have had personally, the Christian themes of patriarchy, salvation, chastity, and sinfulness that ran through Ava's early childhood narrative were nevertheless very powerful, and had a lasting impact on both her identity and her narrative development.

The powerful internalization of the negative message that occurred for Ava early on in her development was crucial in understanding her narrative; her trauma was understood as an extension of her inherent wickedness. Ava's identity was the product of a rigid, pejorative, and patriarchal religious system in which she, in her essence, was sinful and wrong. When she presented for treatment, therefore, developing Ava's trauma narrative would be disrupted by our inability to divorce the experience of the trauma from Ava's understanding of herself as the cause of the problem. Her understanding of not only her trauma but of her entire selfhood could not be divorced from these early messages about her sinfulness. The overwhelmingly patriarchal, oppressive, and abusive environment in which Ava spent her young years had a tremendous impact on Ava, and the environment reflects the way that structural violence continued to influence Ava's exposure to risk and abuse.

Ultimately, Ava's embodiment was informed by her early cultural identity and could therefore not be separated from her understanding of her traumatic experiences. Relying on diagnostic categories and psychiatric frames that have emerged from a white, male, heterosexual, cisgender, and dominant culture-normative perspective inherently misses the more nuanced, cultural elements of an individual's experience (Burstow, 2003). Ava's very understanding of her life experiences was informed by her socioeconomic and cultural identity that was formed early on in her development with the influence of her social location in conversation with her grandmother and her internalized belief systems. Ava's social location as an immigrant and as a woman influenced her perspective in a way that was not captured by a DSM-driven, Western scientific conceptualization. Her daily experience of living in a white-dominated country in which she encountered microaggressions and overt racism, even in her predominantly Hispanic community for having darker skin, having migrated from a community and a family in which she was demonized and abused, and trying to make sense of her life experiences through the lens of her punishing superego/cognitive schema resulted in an identity that was layered and complicated, and that refused to find truth in a set of labels that did not speak to her sociocultural experience.

Ava's victimization and trauma were experienced on several levels, all of which influenced each other. As we came to understand Ava's trauma, we had to understand the influencing factors that made her experiences traumatic. As Lester (2013) argues, we had to understand "what makes the injury not only traumatic, but traumatic *in particular ways*" (p. 755). What was particularly traumatic for Ava was the multifaceted nature of her risk, the structural nature of her exposure to violence, oppression, and victimization. The pervasive and insidious character to Ava's victimization (and, arguably, many other victim experiences) made our approach to her struggle even more complex. Ava could not separate the role she was sure she had played in the traumatic events from her victimization, and the daily experience of racism and sexism that she experienced reinforced these messages. Ava's traumatic experience was not divorced from the rest of her life; it was a woven part of the complex tapestry of her story.

Posing questions that expand our understanding of the structural nature of Ava's experience of trauma ultimately requires that we examine our cultural narrative about trauma and shed light on the systems of power that are in place in our own work with trauma victims. There is a quality to Ava's experience of trauma that is not sufficiently captured by a perspective that is generated by the same system that oppresses her. As such, her narrative requires us to consider how we work with trauma victims, given their complex, layered traumatic experiences. In doing so, we have to "bring attention to the process of narrative construction, interpretation, circulation, and reception in order to demonstrate how all of these registers are imbued in power relations" (Chowdhury, 2015, p. 99). This challenge to our treatment modalities demands that we recast our theoretical conceptions in a way that allows for these complexities to emerge. That being said, we must not neglect those whose identity development does not fit into a diagnostic or conceptual frame of Complex PTSD, but also does not fit into a structural understanding of trauma. We must, therefore, assess how we understand the traumatic experiences of those whose demographics might seem to put them in the category of beneficiaries of this oppressive system, but who are, in fact, also victims of the dominant narrative regarding gender, privilege, and power.

Case Vignette: Brad

On the surface, Brad appeared to be a very high-functioning man. He held a job as a corrections officer for roughly 20 years, he was the father of four beautiful children, and he seemed to have relatively stable relationships with his friends and family. Brad came into therapy because he was feeling significant amounts of anxiety, although he did not readily identify it as such. Brad often struggled identifying his emotional experiences; he was unable to identify any emotions other than happiness and anger. His reasoning for coming to therapy was that things were "just off," that he wanted to work on "doing better." However, the generalities in which he spoke belied his deep pain and stress. Brad was, in fact, the victim of sexual trauma and structural violence that impacted his daily life and caused significant distress for him and insecurity in his interpersonal relationships. His difficulty identifying his feelings, ultimately, was linked to a larger discomfort perpetuated by a strong internalization of gender norms as well as a fear of labels that would mark him as "sick" or "traumatized."

Working with Brad's emotional limitations, we began by developing trust and establishing me as his therapist and the transitional object onto which he could begin to project his anger and, ultimately, his unmet emotional needs (Winnicott, 1953). As the transitional object, the therapist serves as the vessel through which the patient works on integrating emotional experiences (Winnicott, 1953). Brad's early phase of treatment was characterized by his overreliance on anger and rage as a means of communicating his feelings. As our relationship progressed, Brad began to open up about his childhood and the influence that his early childhood experiences had on his ideas about appropriate ways to express himself, which were linked ultimately to larger structures of masculinity and maleness. Brad often recalled that his parents would tell him to "be a man" and to "man up" whenever he was struggling, especially when it came to work or his family. Brad described his childhood self as sensitive and isolating; he played alone because he felt different from the other boys in his neighborhood. When his parents would ask Brad why he was playing alone, he would share that he did not like the rambunctious and sometimes violent behaviors of the other boys. Rather than supporting him or encouraging him, his parents told him to be more aggressive and to stand up for himself because that is how boys are supposed to act. Brad's rage would become apparent when he talked about these memories, especially in terms of masculinity and maleness, sharing that his parents made him feel ashamed of being who he was and made him feel embarrassed for not wanting to act a certain way.

Brad's vulnerability to the social construction of gender was exacerbated when he was sexually abused at the age of 9. When Brad was 9 years old, he was playing by himself in a local park when he was approached by a close friend of his family. This family friend asked Brad to come over and help to clean out his garage. Brad agreed to go, thinking that he would be respectful and thinking that his parents would be proud of him for being a dutiful son. However, upon reaching the garage, the family friend proceeded to become physically violent toward Brad, and forced Brad to fondle him and perform oral sex on him against Brad's will. The perpetrator then told Brad that he would kill him if he told anyone about their encounter. Brad then ran home, scared to stop for fear of anything else happening to him.

Brad immediately told his father what had happened to him, at which point his father refused to believe him, telling Brad that he was making things up to get attention from his parents. Brad's father refused to accept that a friend of the family would do such a thing and, additionally, he refused to accept that boys could be the victim of something like rape. After that, his father refused to speak to him and told his mother that she was not to believe Brad's "story" either. Brad's rage toward his parents, his father in particular, took on new meaning after this incident. Not only would his parents reject his personality traits as unmasculine, but they would also reject him and his experience, citing that men do not get raped and that he was just trying to get attention by being hysterical like a woman. Similar to Ava, Brad's caregivers did not come to his aid, exacerbating his traumatic experience.

Although Brad's anger was correctly directed at his parents, their refusal to recognize his emotional experience and their denial of his abuse resulted in his rage turning inwards and manifesting itself in self-loathing (Freud, 1953; Dyer et al., 2009). Additionally, Brad detached from friends and family and became even more isolated than he was before. Brad struggled with maintaining close friendships, and often found himself alone for even more extended periods of time. This reinforced his feelings of not belonging and his deep shame about being different and being victimized by this family friend/perpetrator.

Brad's fears about his masculinity deepened as he grew up in what he described as "the boys club," or what some theorists would characterize as a community predicated upon hegemonic masculinity (Connell, 2015). Brad shared with me that any signs of emotions would result in his friends making jokes about him being "gay" or "soft," and he reported feeling ostracized for being sensitive, even as an adult. Brad would discuss his anger at being treated like he was "weak," and would follow these moments of vulnerability with long discussions about how strong he is and how he could "take" (meaning beat in a fight) any of the men who teased him. Brad acutely experienced the pressure of being a masculine male in his daily interactions with his peers, his coworkers, his friends, and his family.

As Brad grew up, his inability to develop close, intimate relationships with people became more apparent. He would have relationships with girlfriends that he characterized as unfulfilling and meaningless. Despite getting married, Brad never felt truly in love with his wife, instead fulfilling a role determined for him by his familial and cultural pressures. Brad found himself isolating more and more from his relationships. Although many of them were fraught with issues, they were his only connection to the real world. As such, he sought comfort and solace online. He became preoccupied by social media, checking his Facebook account hundreds of times a day, and interpreting online behaviors as having a deep significance in his real-life relationships. If a friend did not like his posts, he would ruminate about it for days, convincing himself that his friend was acting out some latent hostility toward him.

Brad's most remarkable shift to online life was his obsession with online pornography. Brad shared with me that he would spend hours online, often staying up all night, watching porn and masturbating. He shared with me that he felt a sense of control and power in this online forum that he did not feel in his real-life relationships. Brad's experience of sexual trauma had left him feeling embarrassed of his vulnerability, leaving Brad unwilling to engage in loving, emotionally vulnerable relationships and sexual encounters. Brad had a history of relationships in which he could maintain a distance, not allowing anyone in or anyone to be too close to him. Although these relationships ultimately left him feeling unfulfilled and lonely, Brad struggled with identifying the root of these issues and instead shifted to online relationships that offered him the facade of control and protection that he so desperately clung to.

Additionally, Brad's relationships with women had been difficult for him. He described his mother as controlling and manipulative. He also reported that his ex-wife would question his masculinity and his virility (according to Brad, they had initially had trouble conceiving, which his then wife attributed to Brad). These dynamics reflected a pattern of revictimization, in which an individual who has experienced complex trauma repeats the cycle of unhealthy relationships in other areas of his life (Herman, 1992a). Although not an explicitly victimizing experience, the relational and emotional abuse Brad perceived from these interactions and dynamics had a profound impact on him. For Brad, this meant maintaining unhealthy relationships with his family and finding a woman who was psychologically abusive toward him. When he was watching online pornography, he chose women that were submissive, over whom he felt control. He would choose scenes that were denigrating to the woman involved. Brad would use the online world to protect himself and to act out his fantasies of control and violence that served as a psychological Band-Aid for the pain he was continuing to suffer in his daily relationships and in the wake of his traumatic experiences.

Discussion

Although Brad's experience of sexual abuse was an isolated event, his experience of victimization at the hands of his caregivers in light of his traumatization resulted in what can be considered symptoms of Complex PTSD. Some researchers have noted that Complex PTSD can include emotional and psychological abuse that is repetitive over time and perpetuated by caregivers (Kliethermes, Schacht, & Drewry, 2014). Additionally, Brad's anger and his difficulty trusting people are consistent with victims of Complex PTSD (Kliethermes, Schacht, & Drewry, 2014). Brad's personality structure emerged from his exposure to both his sexual trauma as well as his family structure that pervasively reified gender norms and expectations that were, ultimately, very traumatizing to Brad, and would, potentially, result in his being assigned a diagnosis of Complex PTSD. However, as with Ava, Brad struggled with identifying himself as a victim, or as seeing how his experience of trauma and his interactions in a larger system of male privilege influenced his emotional pain and his deep struggles with intimacy, which poses similar questions regarding how to approach his treatment.

Traditionally, research about childhood sexual abuse and other forms of sexual violence has focused largely on women (Gagnier & Collin-Vézina, 2016; Artime, McCallum, & Peterson, 2014; O'Leary, Easton, & Gould, 2015). However, as growing attention is paid to sexual trauma, researchers have begun to turn their attention to male victims of childhood sexual abuse and, in some ways, have begun to consider the practice implications of dealing with rape and sexual violence with male victims (Forde & Duvvury, 2016; Chan, 2014; Easton, Coohey, Rhodes, & Moorthy, 2013). Researchers have noted that male victims of childhood sexual abuse not only face the impact of dominant masculine ideals and

gender socialization that all men face, but that there are added "burdens of negotiating social expectations in the context of their traumatic past" (Kia-Keating, Sorsoli, & Grossman, 2010, p. 667). As such, closer attention to the interpersonal development of male victims of childhood sexual abuse is indicated, and understanding the role of important attachment figures is essential in understanding the resulting relationships adult survivors of childhood sexual abuse develop and maintain (Kia-Keating, Sorsoli, & Grossman, 2010).

Although the modern conception of masculinity has not always been in place and is being challenged by many different individuals and social movements, the contemporary, stereotypical narrative surrounding masculinity is one that continues to characterize men as strong, powerful, aggressive, competitive, and unemotional (Chan, 2014; Connell, 2005). Gender norms are further reinforced given an individual's culture, socioeconomic level, and education (McGuffey, 2008). For Brad, his working-class Scottish household reinforced the gender stereotypes that men were to be strong, dependable, and stoic, ultimately reinforcing the messages that Brad already received from mainstream society and some that he had already picked up on in his interactions with other boys. Brad felt different from other boys before his traumatic experience of sexual violence, and his internalization of those messages began at a very young age. The difference between Brad and the other boys only seemed to be exacerbated by the experience of sexual violence, generating a powerful reaction formation in which Brad became not only masculine, but hypermasculine. The trauma solidified Brad's internalized narrative about needing to man up and be more masculine so as to prevent any further division from his interpersonal, familial, and cultural world, and this trauma also exacerbated his complicated relationship with his father.

Brad's definition of masculinity and therefore his own identity became rigid and blurred—Brad could not distinguish between his true self and the image of maleness he had so intrinsically internalized. In doing so, his ability to engage genuinely with the world became compromised. Brad rejected outright any emotional expressiveness. The presence of masculine ideals in his family and in his cultural narrative "[obscured] and [limited] the active construction" of Brad's sense of self (Chan, 2014, p. 250). He presented to treatment with an extremely stunted emotional vocabulary (alexithymia). Brad was dissociated from his emotions, and his problematic relationships reflected how hard he struggled to connect with people.

Like Ava's trauma, Brad's trauma has a structural element to it that is not captured by the diagnostic categories and traditional treatment approaches. The extent of Brad's victimization was due, in large part, to the socialization of gender and the structural violence of maleness. Unlike Ava, however, Brad's social location would suggest that he was the beneficiary of the patriarchal system in which men are powerful and women are victimized. This narrative was in line with Brad's internalized understanding of his own masculinity, which is the crux of the problem, and central to this complication of our understanding of trauma. Rather than being in a position of privilege, Brad's social location as a white male in a hypermasculine job as a corrections officer (which is an interesting example of his reaction formation in the form of an occupation) served to marginalize him and keep him tethered to his deep internal suffering. In light of his experience of sexual violence, Brad's gender identity served as a source of heightened risk amid his adaptation to his environment and family dynamics. Assigning a diagnostic label to Brad's experiences did little to illuminate the insidious ways in which structural elements of oppression furthered his suffering. In fact, one might consider the ways in which he Brad was alienated from seeking help by his fear of being labeled.

After his complex experiences of sexual violence and the influence of his social construction of gender on his narrative and identity development, Brad was unable to enter into genuine, loving relationships with anyone. In line with his overidentification with masculinity, Brad began to rely heavily on extremes of male control and aggression in his interpersonal and intimate relationships. Brad's experience of sexual trauma and his rigid identification with masculine norms led to a distorted understanding of interpersonal and intimate relationships (Kia-Keating, Sorsoli, & Grossman, 2010). Furthermore, the access afforded to him by technology and endless amounts of online pornography hindered Brad's emotional development and his recovery. Brad played out in a virtual world his deeply troubled relational needs and fantasies, and found a way to cope with his trauma by detaching from the real world and real people.

The added external force of access to technology complicated Brad's treatment further. Although the access he had to online pornography might be considered privileged in and of itself (easy access to the internet, the access to pornography that can, arguably, be considered the product of a system of oppression of women), Brad's use of the internet and the pornography again served more to marginalize and alienate him than to give him power. Studies have shown the relationship between childhood sexual abuse and relationship aggression (Feiring, Simon, & Cleland, 2009), the relationship between masculinity and sexual aggression (Murnen, 2015), and the relationships between pornography and sexual objectification (Mikorski & Szymanski, 2016). For Brad, there is a confluence of all of these strands of thought—masculinity, relational aggression, sexual victimization, and pornography. The added element of technology made Brad's pathology significantly more severe, making his victimization that much more pervasive and chronic. His easy access to images that objectify women and his ability to remove himself from real relationships at any time further alienated him from his trauma and his emotions. Brad's resultant understanding of himself was one in which he was powerful and not victimized—further pushing him away from a narrative that would result in understanding his trauma as one of victimhood.

Ultimately, Brad's experience of sexual violence and his family and society's impact on his trauma is one that forces us to look at the various structural elements that plagued Ava in a different way. Rather than understanding the view from below, Brad's narrative demonstrates how a person of privilege "extracts dominant conceptions of gender, race, and class from the macro world to interpret their personal experiences of trauma" (McGuffey, 2008, p. 216). Brad's understanding of himself in the moment when he was victimized influenced his inability to understand himself as a victim as well as his ongoing understanding of himself as a man and as a man in relation to women. Brad's daily experiences of gender norms and social pressures that oppressed him and further victimized him added to his alienation from identifying as a victim, and made his treatment more complex.

For Brad, dominant social narratives about gender and power influenced his victimization in the sense that it marginalized him and made it more difficult for him to access help, his emotions, or vulnerability in any real way. Working with Brad required paying close attention to how he assigned meaning to his experiences. Had I not allowed Brad to define for himself what his experiences meant, our treatment would have resulted in my fulfillment of the role so many had filled before me—the rejecting (in the case of his parents), the minimizing or deriding (in the case of his friends), or the assumption of privileged understanding of what really was wrong (which would put into play a chain of reactions and understandable resistance to what would be perceived as my dominance of him). Brad's refusal to be labeled or minimized pushed us to exist in a place of complexity and ambivalence that provided a space for him to trust me and to open up more and more about his experiences.

Both Brad and Ava's stories illuminate how "a critical consciousness of oppression *and* privilege is central to understanding the ways in which our worldviews are shaped by our social positioning" (Pease, 2006, p. 15). Furthermore, this social positioning influences the ways in which clients develop their identities, and complicate the application of knowledge generated in a controlled environment to a person's real-life experience.

Conclusion

In her seminal ethnographic study and discussion of hunger, poverty, and infant death in northeastern Brazil in the 1980s, anthropologist Nancy Scheper-Hughes (1992) draws a compelling connection between human suffering and what she describes as "the medicalization of . . . needs" (p. 169). Through a complicated understanding of the social and political constructions of hunger in an impoverished Brazilian community, Scheper-Hughes identifies how hunger is translated into *nervos*, "a rich folk conceptual scheme for describing relations among mind, body, and social body," and ultimately translated into "a biomedical disease that alienates mind from body and that conceals the social relations of sickness" (p. 169). In this analysis, the newly medicalized syndrome is treated with tranquilizers and medication. For Scheper-Hughes, this is a reflection of how those in power are willing to treat the symptoms of hunger as a medical issue, rather than looking at it as a social problem that requires real, sociopolitical, and economic action. In doing so, Scheper-Hughes challenges the reader to understand how systems of power, privilege, control, and most importantly, a biomedical culture add up to allow for the perpetuation of significant human suffering.

Using the same theoretical framework, we are challenged to understand how our own constructions of sickness, in this case trauma, serve the same purpose. Particularly insofar as we rely on systems like the DSM to guide our assumptions about illness and its presentation, is there an implicit force at work in our construction of trauma and our PTSD-informed narrative? Is there a call for a Freirean critical consciousness on the part of clinicians, students, and sufferers? (Freire, 1970). For Scheper-Hughes, the existence of the hungry in Brazil carried with them a profound statement about the functioning of Brazilian society and governance. By shifting the attention to a medical issue, individuals in power and the systems they represented were able to remain in power without addressing the complexities of this human rights issue. Those who have been traumatized in our world make the same statement as the hungry in Brazil. The fact that our society generates traumatized individuals and larger systems of oppression and violence is an uncomfortable reality to which we have to attend, but from which we possibly would rather hide. Approaching trauma from a system that was born out of a system of oppression (i.e., the DSM, psychiatry, positivist knowledge generation) inherently misses the point of the larger social and structural questions we must ask ourselves when approaching human suffering.

The cases of Brad and Ava illuminate how there are larger issues to which we as social workers must be aware and against which we must position ourselves. The social work value of social justice requires from us a radical approach to the deconstruction of knowledge and the dismantling of systems that perpetuate power. Writing about these exact systems of power and oppression that are challenged by the existence of victims of trauma, Amartya Sen (2003) argues, "We have to look for a better comprehension of the social causes of horror and also of our tolerance of societal abominations" (p. xii, cited in Farmer, 2005). In doing so, we have to raise our own awareness of the systems in place that contribute to an individual's trauma narrative and that may, or may not, influence the extent to which their healing is an individual journey or an indictment of larger, social forces. Rather than relying on the knowledge generated for us by those in power, it is essential that we pay attention to the experiences of those who have been victimized.

As noted earlier, an analysis of trauma that is ontologically and epistemologically different is necessary if we are to appreciate the significant place that trauma holds in our human history. Moving away from a narrative that is narrowly focused on PTSD and its various machinations based on DSM criteria and psychiatrically based understandings of illness makes room for the greater issues of power, privilege, oppression, social construction, and human rights to enter the conversation. Furthermore, a phenomenological approach to treatment allows for patients to determine for themselves what carries meaning and what does not. As Kirmayer, Lemelson, and Barad (2007) argue, "The emphasis on PTSD casts a long shadow in current discussions of trauma, organizing experience, simplifying causal explanations, and directing attention to symptoms in ways that may . . . distort a complex human and social predicament" (p. 4). This distortion leads us away from an appreciation of the complexity of human suffering and ushers us further into the realm of minimizing human experience. The comfort of a medicalized definition of trauma and a manualized treatment approach appears to be too tempting to avoid, and the proliferation of PTSD-oriented treatment research indicates our desire to minimize, categorize, and understand something that is arguably so much bigger than all of us.

Close Reading Questions

1. In what ways do Ava and Brad meet the criteria for a PTSD (and more specifically a Complex PTSD) diagnosis? How does Conti challenge the concept of Complex PTSD using the nuances of each client's narrative?
2. How does the concept of structural violence contribute to a more modern, evolving understanding of sexual trauma?
3. According to Conti, how does a phenomenological understanding of sexual trauma and mental illness lend itself to ethical practice?

Prompts for Writing

1. In what way can social work practitioners utilize theoretical ideas like feminism, phenomenology, and postmodernism to inform decisions they make with clients in day to day practice? Do you think this is a helpful way to frame a case?
2. How does Conti challenge social work practitioners to reconsider dominant practice and knowledge paradigms? What is the purpose of this challenge?
3. In what ways might Conti's phenomenological, feminist, postmodern approach to sexual trauma in a clinical setting be expanded and applied to social work practice writ large and social systems in general?

References

Adhikari, R., Jampaklay, A., Chamratrithirong, A., Richter, K., Pattaravanich, U., & Vapattanawong, P. (2014). The impact of parental migration on the mental health of children left behind. *Journal of Immigrant and Minority Health, 16*, 781–789.

Ali, A. (2004). The intersection of racism and sexism in psychiatric diagnosis. In P. J. Caplan & L. Cosgrove (Eds.), *Bias in psychiatric diagnosis* (pp. 71–75). Lanham, MD: Jason Aronson.

American Psychiatric Association. (2013). *Diagnostic and statistical manual of mental disorders* (5th ed.). Arlington, VA: American Psychiatric.

Artime, T. M., McCallum, E. B., & Peterson, Z. D. (2014). Men's acknowledgment of their sexual victimization experiences. *American Psychological Association, 15*(5), 313–323.

Bremner, J. D. (2007). Does stress damage the brain? In L. J. Kirmayer, R. Lemelson, & M. Barad (Eds.), *Understanding trauma: Integrating biological, clinical, and cultural perspectives* (pp. 118–141). New York: Cambridge University Press.

Brown, L. S., & Ballou, M. (Eds.). (1992). *Personality and psychopathology.* New York: Guilford Press.

Brown, P. (1995). Naming and framing: The social construction of diagnosis and illness. *Journal of Health and Social Behavior, 8*(4), 34–52.

Bryant-Davis, T., & Ocampo, C. (2005). Racist incident-based trauma. *Counseling Psychologist, 33*(4), 479–500.

Burstow, B. (2003). Toward a radical understanding of trauma and trauma work. *Violence against Women, 9*(11), 1293–1317.

Carraway, G. C. (1991). Violence against women of color. *Stanford Law Review, 43*(6), 1301–1309.

Cermele, J. A., Daniels, S., & Anderson, K. L. (2001). Defining normal: Constructions of race and gender in the DSM-IV casebook. *Feminism & Psychology, 11*(2), 229–247.

Chan, S.T.M. (2014). The lens of masculinity: Trauma in men and the landscapes of sexual abuse survivors. *Journal of Ethnic & Cultural Diversity in Social Work, 23*(3–4), 239–255.

Chowdhury, E. H. (2015). Rethinking patriarchy, culture and masculinity: Transnational narratives of gender violence and human rights advocacy. *Journal of International Women's Studies, 16*(2), 98–114.

Cloitre, M., Stolbach, B. C., Herman, J. L., Van der Kolk, B. A., Pynoos, R., Wang, J., & Petkova, E. (2009). A developmental approach to complex PTSD: Childhood and adult cumulative trauma as predictors of symptom complexity. *Journal of Traumatic Stress, 22*(5), 399–408.

Connell, R. W. (2005). *Masculinities* (2nd ed.). Berkeley: University of California Press.

Cosgrove, L., & Wheeler, E. E. (2013). Industry's colonization of psychiatry: Ethical and practical implications of financial conflicts of interest in the DSM-V. *Feminism & Psychology, 23*(1), 93–106.

Courtois, C. A. (2004). Complex trauma, complex reactions: Assessment and treatment. *Psychotherapy: Theory, Research, Practice and Training, 41*, 412–425.

Cusack, K., Jonas, D. E., Forneris, C. A., Wines, C., Sonis, J., Middleton, J. C., . . . Gaynes, B. N. (2016). Psychological treatments for adults with posttraumatic stress disorder: A systematic review and meta-analysis. *Clinical Psychology Review, 43*, 128–141.

Dattilio, F. M., Edwards, D.J.A., & Fishman, D. B. (2010). Case studies within a mixed methods paradigm: Towards a resolution of the alienation between researcher and practitioner in psychotherapy research. *Psychotherapy: Theory, Research, Practice, Training, 43*, 128–141.

Decker, M. R., Benning, L., Weber, K. M., Sherman, S. G., Adedimeji, A., Wilson, T. E., . . . Golub, E. T. (2016). Physical and sexual violence predictors: 20 years of the women's interagency HIV study cohort. *American Journal of Preventive Medicine, 51*(5), 731–742.

DeJongh, A., Resick, P. A., Zoellner, L. A., van Minnen, A., Lee, C. W., & Monson, C. M. (2016). Critical analysis of the current treatment guidelines for complex PTSD in adults. *Depression and Anxiety, 33*, 359–369.

Dorrepaal, E., Thomaes, K., Hoogendoorn, A. W., Veltman, D. J., Draijer, & van Balkom, A. J. L. M. (2014). Evidence-based treatment for adult women with child abuse-related Complex PTSD: A quantitative review. *European Journal of Psychotraumatology, 5*, 1–18.

Dyer, K.F.W., Dorahy, M. J., Hamilton, G., Corry, M., Shannon, M., MacSherry, A., . . . McElhill, B. (2009). Anger, aggression, and self-harm in PTSD and complex PTSD. *Journal of Clinical Psychology, 65*(10), 1099–1114.

Easton, S. D., Coohey, C., Rhodes, A. M., & Moorthy, M. V. (2013). Posttraumatic growth among men with histories of child sexual abuse. *Child Maltreatment, 18*(4), 211–220.

Ehlers, A., & Clark, D. M. (2000). A cognitive model of posttraumatic stress disorder. *Behavioral Research and Therapy, 38*, 319–345.

Elsey, J. W. B., & Kindt, M. (2017). Tackling maladaptive memories through reconsolidation: From neural to clinical science. *Neurobiology of Learning and Memory*, Advanced Online Publication. https://doi.org/10.1016/j.nlm.2017.03.007

Farmer, P. (2005). *Pathologies of power: Health, human rights, and the new war on the poor.* Berkeley: University of California Press.

Farmer, P. (2009). On suffering and structural violence: A view from below. *Race/Ethnicity, 3*(1), 11–28.

Fassin, D., & Rechtman, R. (2009). *The empire of trauma: An inquiry into the condition of victimhood.* Princeton, NJ: Princeton University Press.

Fee, D. (2000). *Pathology and the postmodern: Mental illness as discourse and experience.* London: Sage.

Feiring, C., Simon, V. A., & Cleland, C. M. (2009). Childhood sexual abuse, stigmatization, internalizing symptoms, and the development of sexual difficulties and dating aggression. *Journal of Consulting and Clinical Psychology, 77*(1), 127–137.

Foa, E. B., & Rothbaum, B. O. (1998). *Treating the trauma of rape: Cognitive behavioral therapy for PTSD.* New York: Guilford.

Ford, J. D. (2015). Complex PTSD: Research directions for nosology/assessment, treatment, and public health. *European Journal of Psychotraumatology, 6*(1), 27584.

Ford, J. D., & Courtois, C. A. (2009). Defining and understanding complex trauma and complex traumatic stress disorders. *Treating Complex Traumatic Stress Disorders: An Evidence-Based Guide*, 13–30.

Ford, J. D., & Courtois, C. A. (2014). Complex PTSD, affect dysregulation, and borderline personality disorder. *Borderline Personality Disorder and Emotion Dysregulation, 1*(1), 9.

Forde, C., & Duvvury, N. (2016). Sexual violence, masculinity, and the journey of recovery. *Psychology of Men & Masculinity*, Advance Online Publication. https://doi.org/10.1037/men0000054

Foucault, M. (1988). An aesthetics of existence. In L. D. Kritzman (Ed.), *Politics, philosophy, culture: Interviews and other writings 1977–1984* (pp. 47–59). New York: Routledge.

Freire, P. (1970). *The pedagogy of the oppressed.* New York: Bloomsbury Academic.

Freud, S. (1953). Mourning and melancholia. In J. Strachey (Ed. & Trans.), *The standard edition of the complete psychological works of Sigmund Freud* (Vol. 14, pp. 237–258). London: Hogarth Press. (Original work published 1917).

Friebach-Heifetz, D., & Stopler, G. (2008). On conceptual dichotomies and social oppression. *Philosophy & Social Criticism, 34*(5), 515–535.

Gagnier, C., & Collin-Vézina, D. (2016). The disclosure experiences of male child sexual abuse survivors. *Journal of Child Sexual Abuse, 25*(2), 221–241.

Georgaca, E. (2013). Social constructionist contributions to critiques of psychiatric diagnosis and classification. *Feminism & Psychology, 23*(1), 56–62.

Gleiser, K., Ford, J. D., & Fosha, D. (2008). Contrasting exposure and experiential therapies for complex posttraumatic stress disorder. *Psychotherapy: Theory, Research, Practice, Training, 45*(3), 340–360.

Guilfoyle, M. (2013). Client subversions of DSM knowledge. *Feminism and Psychology, 23*(1), 86–92.

Hardy, V. L., Compton, K. D., & McPhatter, V. S. (2013). Domestic minor sex trafficking: Practice implications for mental health professionals. *Journal of Women and Social Work, 28*(1), 8–18.

Herman, J. L. (1992a). Complex PTSD: A syndrome in survivors of prolonged and repeated trauma. *Journal of Traumatic Stress, 5*(3), 377–391.

Herman, J. L. (1992b). *Trauma and recovery: The aftermath of violence—from domestic abuse to political terror.* New York: Basic Books.

Hornstein, G. A. (2013). Whose account matters? A challenge to feminist psychologists. *Feminism & Psychology, 23*(1), 29–40.

Hyland, P., Shevlin, M., Murphy, J., Elkit, A., Vallieres, F., Garvert, D. W., & Cloitre, M. (2017). An assessment of the construct validity of the ICD-11 proposal for complex posttraumatic stress disorder. *Psychological Trauma: Theory, Research, Practice, and Policy, 9*(1), 1–9.

Kaminer, D., & Eagle, G. T. (2017). Interventions for posttraumatic stress disorder: A review of the evidence base. *South African Journal of Psychology, 47*(1), 7–22.

Kia-Keating, M., Sorsoli, L., & Grossman, F. K. (2010). Relational challenges and recovery processes in male survivors of childhood sexual abuse. *Journal of Interpersonal Violence, 25*(4), 666–683.

Kirmayer, L. J., Lemelson, R., & Barad, M. (2007). Introduction: Inscribing trauma in culture, brain, and body. In L. J. Kirmayer, R. Lemelson, & M. Barad (Eds.), *Understanding trauma: Integrating biological, clinical, and cultural perspectives* (pp. 1–17). New York: Cambridge University Press.

Kirschner, S. R. (2013). Diagnosis and its discontents: Critical perspectives on psychiatric nosology and the DSM. *Feminism & Psychology, 23*(1), 10–28.

Kliethermes, M., Schacht, M., & Drewry, K. (2014). Complex trauma. *Disaster and Trauma, 23*(2), 339–361.

Lester, R. (2013). Back from the edge of existence: A critical anthropology of trauma. *Transcultural Psychiatry, 50*(5), 753–762.

Marecek, J., & Gavey, N. (2013). DSM-V and beyond: A critical feminist engagement with psychodiagnosis. *Feminism & Psychology, 23*(1), 3–9.

McGuffey, C. S. (2008). "Saving Masculinity": Gender reaffirmation, sexuality, race, and parental responses to male child sexual abuse. *Social Problems, 55*(2), 216–237.

McNally, R. J. (2004). Conceptual problems with the DSM-IV criteria for post-traumatic stress disorder. In G. M. Rosen (Ed.), *Post-traumatic stress disorder: Issues and controversies* (pp. 1–14). New York: John Wiley & Sons.

Mikorski, R., & Szymanski, D. (2016). Masculine norms, peer group, pornography, Facebook, and men's sexual objectification of women. *Psychology of Men & Masculinity*, Advance Online Publication. https://doi.org/10.1037/men0000058

Murnen, S. K. (2015). A social constructivist approach to understanding the relationship between masculinity and sexual aggression. *Psychology of Men and Masculinity, 16*(4), 370–373.

Newman, E., Riggs, D. S., & Roth, S. (1997). Thematic resolution, PTSD, and complex PTSD: The relationship between meaning and trauma-related diagnoses. *Journal of Traumatic Stress, 10*(2), 197–213.

O'Leary, P., Easton, S. D., & Gould, N. (2015). The effect of child sexual abuse on men: Toward a male sensitive measure. *Journal of Interpersonal Violence, 32*(3), 423–445.

Olofsson, A., Zinn, J. O., Griffin, G., Nygren, K. G., Cebulla, A., & Hannah-Moffat, K. (2014). The mutual constitution of risk and inequalities: Intersectional risk theory. *Health, Risk & Society, 16*(5), 417–430.

Pease, B. (2006). Encouraging critical reflections on privilege in social work and the human services. *Practice Reflexions, 1*(1), 5–26.

Pelcovitz, D., Van der Kolk, B. A., Roth, S., Mandel, F., Kaplan, S., & Resick, P. (1997). Development of a criteria set and a structured interview for disorders of extreme stress (SIDES). *Journal of Traumatic Stress, 10*(1), 3–16.

Quiros, L., & Berger, R. (2015). Responding to the sociopolitical complexity of trauma: An integration of theory and practice. *Journal of Loss and Trauma, 20,* 149–159.

Rau, V., & Fanselow, M. S. (2007). Neurobiological and neuroethological perspectives on fear and anxiety. In L. J. Kirmayer, R. Lemelson, & M. Barad (Eds.), *Understanding trauma: Integrating biological, clinical, and cultural perspectives* (pp. 27–40). New York: Cambridge University Press.

Resick, P. A., & Schnicke, M. (1992). Cognitive processing therapy for sexual assault victims. *Journal of Consulting and Clinical Psychology, 60,* 748–756.

Rosenberg, C. (2007). Contested boundaries: Psychiatry, disease and diagnosis. In *Our present complaint: American medicine then and now* (pp. 38–59). Baltimore, MD: Johns Hopkins University Press.

Sar, V. (2011). Developmental trauma, complex PTSD, and the current proposal of DSM-V. *European Journal of Psychotraumatology, 2,* 1–9.

Schauer, M., Neuner, F., & Elbert, T. (2005). *Narrative exposure therapy: A short term intervention for traumatic stress disorders after war, terror or torture.* Göttingen, Germany: Hogrefe & Huber.

Scheper-Hughes, N. (1992). *Death without weeping: The violence of everyday life in Brazil.* Berkeley: University of California Press.

Schnyder, U., Ehlers, A., Elbert, T., Foa, E. B., Gersons, B.P.R., Resick, P. A., . . . Cloitre, M. (2015). Psychotherapies for PTSD: What do they have in common? *European Journal of Psychotraumatology, 6,* 28186. https://doi.org/10.3402/ejpt.v6.28186

Sen, A. (2003). Forward. In P. Farmer, *Pathologies of power: Health, human rights, and the new war on the poor* (pp. xi–xviii). Berkeley: University of California Press.

Shapiro, F. (1995). *Eye movement desensitization and preprocessing: Basic principles, protocols and procedures.* New York: Guilford Press.

Van der Kolk, B. (2014). *The body keeps the score: Brain, mind, and body in the healing of trauma.* New York: Penguin Books.

Watters, E. (2010). *Crazy like us: The globalization of the American psyche.* New York: Free Press.

Winnicott, D. W. (1953). Transitional objects and transitional phenomena: A study of the first not-me possession. *International Journal of Psychoanalysis, 34,* 89–97.

Young, A. (1995). *The harmony of illusions: Inventing post-traumatic stress disorder.* Princeton, NJ: Princeton University Press.

Zaleski, K. L., Johnson, D. K., & Klein, J. T. (2016). Grounding Judith Herman's trauma theory within interpersonal neuroscience and evidence-based practice modalities for trauma treatment. *Smith College Studies in Social Work, 86*(4), 377–393.

2

VIRTUAL TRAUMA

Social Work With Adolescents in the Online Era

Lauren Busfield

Pre-reading Questions

1.   What do you think Busfield's term "virtual trauma" means? How might it relate to a term like "cyberbullying"?
2.   How do think the online era has affected adolescent sexual development?
3.   How might social work clinicians help their clients to safely navigate online spaces? In doing so, what assumptions or misconceptions might social workers have when it comes to adolescents' online experiences?

Introduction

As Olivia stared at me, unblinking and unmoved, I was quickly made aware that what I had said was wrong. She had finished telling me her side of the story, and I had finished informing her of what the problem was: she had been traumatized. My interpretation of her words, the ways she told me she had been violated, my attempts at attunement and empathic responses, and my professional training had all worked together to lead up to this moment, which was meant to be a breakthrough; but instead of acknowledgment, a nod of agreement, or the crying realizations I was prepared for, I was met with a stare, and not one of amazement, but of dismissive annoyance. "No," she said, "It's not like that. It's just something that happens. It's what kids do now."

Adolescents become the subjects of experimentation in the mental health profession, as we try to figure out new and effective ways to treat and understand the next generation of young adults coming of age. Even when attempting to use the most up-to-date, 'evidence-based' practice, by the time the evidence is gathered, adolescents living in a technological age have developed new ways of communicating and relating to their peers, and new ideas about themselves, always staying one step ahead of the research. In this rapidly changing environment, as we learn about their individual lives, we can be given a glimpse into the culture that they experience daily; some of it similar to our own, but often with vast differences from our own adolescent experiences, as well as differences from those who grew up only a few years before they did.

Some commentators, bloggers, and reporters have started delving into the concerns regarding issues of social media and teen sexuality; only recently has this become a focus of any type of writing. Meanwhile, 'official' research centers, if they are publishing on social media usage at all, seem to be focused on outdated safety measures and statistics concerning "how often" teenagers go online. While these statistics are interesting, the analysis and the discussion of what they mean—for parents, for teens, for practitioners, and for a new generation—seems to be very lightly trodden territory. 'Cyberbullying' is a trendy and often-discussed subject, both casually and intellectually, but not all experiences online can be interpreted to fit into the definitions of 'bullying,' and online relationships by no means can be simplified to bullies and victims. Much like 'real life,' online relationships are complex; they offer the opportunity for depth and understanding from others, and they open the door for negative, potentially harmful relations.

In this chapter, I will explore the relationship between the technology utilized by adolescents and traditional conceptions of trauma. Using the case of Olivia, an adolescent young woman who went through what many professionals would consider a traumatic experience within the context of an online chatroom, I will highlight the intersection of trauma with technology and the dilemmas facing professionals treating adolescents and dealing with this brave new (virtual) world. The 'traumas' that are experienced online, which I will call 'virtual traumas,' may result in some of the same traumatic symptoms as interpersonal violence, but are often considered to be a 'normal' experience by adolescents, who have negotiated a new set of rules for online interactions, which often include virtual sexual exploration in an increasingly virtual world. Professionals treating those experiences as traumatic are constructing a narrative to fit in with current mental health theories, addressing these experiences as virtual sexual traumas rather than adapting the mental health theories to treat the daily experiences of adolescents who have grown up as digital natives and view these experiences as part of their identities.

Automedia will also be explored as a means of exploring online relationships to develop skills for relating in 'real life.' As it is not uncommon for adult relationships to begin online and develop further after meeting later in person, it is likewise not uncommon for adolescents to explore and test the boundaries of relationships in an online environment before trying them in a physical relationship. The concept of automedia may also play into the experiences of adolescents when they are interacting on social media, and it may impact how they integrate potentially 'traumatic' experiences as they write, often literally, their stories online.

Case Material

Olivia came to me for therapy with many of the 'typical' adolescent complaints— she was depressed, school made her anxious, and her friend group was a limitless source of stress. She was 16, and a recent move had complicated her social and family lives, leaving those she was closest to thousands of miles behind her. A naturally thin, beautiful girl, she dressed to show off her body and played with her long hair during every session, especially when she said she was feeling more anxious. She was fine with coming to therapy: she had been in therapy before, and in the hospital multiple times after expressing suicidal thoughts, so this was nothing new to her. She knew how to talk about her triggers, her coping skills, and her negative thoughts. We developed a good rapport, and week after week she would come to therapy to discuss things going on in her life: her arguments with her family and friends, her sadness about moving and leaving behind her social group, her desire to go back, her anxiety about and struggle to perform perfectly in school, and her uncertainty about her future. She was always candid and came across as an open person, never leaving me feeling like she had been anything but truthful. She did, however, tend to downplay negative things that had happened in her life; she liked the idea of things rolling off of her without giving them a second thought, although they rarely did, and they would come back to haunt her thoughts later. We worked on ways that she could express her-self and her feelings without turning to the use of self-harm to do so.

After months of treatment, Olivia was much the same. Despite her participa-tion in therapy and her willingness to talk, it always seemed to me that there was something other than the safe answers of 'school' and 'friends' that was causing her anxiety—that under the surface of makeup and hair and boys, there were places she would not go, things she would not address. Still, she continued to come and talk, and I contented myself with working on the surface issues she was ready to deal with—her relationships, managing her school stress, and her behaviors at home that caused so much conflict with her family—figuring that if nothing else, it might be possible to keep her from yet another hospitalization. Hospitalizations for her were a point of contention between her and her family members; her mother believed that she would use suicide threats as a tool to get attention. When I explored her history with her, she always identified relatively minor triggers as the causes of such threats; she convincingly denied any history of abuse, and although it was discussed, never revealed any traumatic events in her past that would lead to such behaviors.

One day, Olivia and her mom came in together. This was not unusual: mom was respectful of her daughter's space in therapy, but was also involved in her treatment, and we would meet to discuss any issues Olivia had been having at home or at school. Usually, this revolved around the fact that she neglected her schoolwork and was failing several classes as a result, or that her attitude and snapping at her brother and sister was causing tension in the house again. This time, however, mom wanted to talk about Olivia's behaviors online. Mom told me that Olivia had been making "poor decisions" online, and that week she had come to her mom after she got involved with a stranger online, and had taken her shirt off for him on her webcam, then panicked when he threatened her. Mom casually mentioned that this was not the first time her choices of how to spend her time online had ended badly; before they moved, she said, they had even needed to call the police to be involved with someone Olivia had connected with online.

Olivia spoke to me privately, and finally I felt we had something to work with. We had cracked that surface of school and friendships, and could talk about something going on in her life that had more significance and effect on her emotional well-being. Surely, I thought, a girl seeking attention by getting naked for strangers online has more to discuss now than her grades and her annoying brother. So we started a conversation about her activities online. This 'incident,' as she called it, was not the first thing that had happened. Previously she had been approached by someone online, but said she was 'over it' and did not see how it related to what had happened that week. Her mom, she said, begged to differ, and saw it as a cycle of negative behaviors—behaviors that Olivia was refusing to control out of spite for her family, and spite for things she was unhappy with. Her mom frequently referred to her 'acting out,' and saw many of her actions as attention-seeking, often expressing to me how exhausted she was by her 'behavior' and 'attitude.'

When I asked Olivia about what had happened that week, she told me about someone she had met online. She said that she was feeling 'upset' after school— something she told me often, to describe any uncomfortable feelings that she was having, ranging anywhere from annoyed at a friend to suicidal. She had been on the latter end of this scale, she said, and she wanted someone to talk to. Feeling that she could not turn to her friends from school, and afraid that her family would be tired of hearing the same old narrative of her suicidal thoughts, she decided to go online and find someone to talk to at random. She utilized a video-chat website, one that connects users randomly, regardless of age, gender, or interests. Olivia told me that she used this website frequently, and that she often had positive conversations and interactions with others on it. This was also the website that had connected her to the person her mom was referring to, however; she admitted that she received threats from someone after an unwanted sexual conversation had occurred, and that she had received unsolicited pictures from a man much older than she was. She said that they were of a sexual nature and that she was upset by them at the time, but she talked about this experience in passing as insignificant. I was aware of her tendency to downplay negatives, however, which I kept in mind as she told me about her more recent online experience.

That week, Olivia had connected with four people, three of whom she had short but positive conversations with. She said that the fourth described himself as a teenage boy—one who lived near her, but because she was new to the area and they attended different schools, she said that she had never met him. They had a friendly conversation, but it quickly went from platonic to sexual in nature. After a few minutes of chatting, the boy claimed to be able to "guess her bra size," if she would only lift her shirt for him over the video chat. She said that she was enjoying the attention that he was paying to her, that she was willing to do so, and that she did not see any harm in playing along. After she had taken off her shirt, instead of providing her with her guess and continuing with their conversation, the boy on the other end of the chat informed her that he had recorded her lifting her shirt, and that he would share the video with classmates if she did not agree to performing sexual acts for him over the chat. Olivia said that they had talked about their schools; he knew where she went, and he talked about other teenagers that she knew went to her school, and those were who he was threatening to share this incriminating video with. She said that she was scared, angry, and embarrassed; not seeing another way out, she performed other acts for him as he requested. He stopped threatening her and the interaction de-escalated, at which point she signed off from the chat for the night. She told me she felt guilty and ashamed immediately afterwards, but did not talk to her parents about it for several days.

The immediate response to this situation by both parents and other family members, upon discovery, was to attempt to minimize the potential damage by removing her from the websites she had been using and restricting her internet usage. I initially agreed with her parents about this method, hoping that limiting use would protect her and to leave her with little opportunity to make 'poor decisions' on websites. During the initial phases of the discussion of the 'incident,' we discussed the effect that she was having on her family and herself but making these choices. It was a continuation of the same discussions we had been having—her behaviors, her choices, her friends, and her family—but expanded to include her safety and her decisions online. We talked about what she had done, and what she should do differently, much like we did with other aspects of her life. Through these conversations, I started to question how I was working with her, and whether it was fair to hold her responsible for all of the things that had happened to her. After reflection, supervision, and conversations with Olivia's mom, I attempted to use a different perspective to explore Olivia and her case, and to expand the context of the situation online. This interaction took place online, but had similar characteristics to situations that take place in the physical world every day. Olivia was certainly not the first adolescent girl to report to me that she had been unwillingly involved in sexual activities with a boy or man. I asked myself how I would have responded to the same situation had it been one that took place in person instead of online. Olivia is a teenager, and she was taken advantage of, threatened, harassed, and even exploited by a man who was a stranger and who may or may not have been a teenager himself. She was forced into sexual acts, although not physically, and was uncomfortable with the entire situation but felt she had no way out. If Olivia had told me that she had been forced to perform sexual acts by a boy at her school, the lines would have seemed clear; she would be a victim, and she would likely have been traumatized by the interaction. Most professionals and parents would have an easier time recognizing the lines that were crossed in a real-life interaction: Olivia had not consented, she had attempted to leave the interaction, and when it was over she felt shaken, shameful, and scared, all of which would point to an unwanted sexual experience of which Olivia was the victim. However, because the interaction took place online, both her parents and professionals, myself included, were instead blaming Olivia for having put herself in that situation, for not controlling her 'behaviors,' and for seeking out attention in the wrong places. I failed to see how I could continue to address her behaviors when she was the one who had been exploited by a perpetrator online, when doing so was, with my newfound considerations, akin to blaming her for being victimized because of something she was wearing or where she was at the time of an assault.

I switched gears from my initial response. I started looking for symptoms of trauma that could be underlying in Olivia, fearing that I might have overlooked them while concentrating on her behaviors to be corrected and managed. I spoke to her mom, who agreed that since the first incident, Olivia had some symptoms consistent with trauma. She had trouble sleeping, difficulty concentrating, and changes in eating habits and social life. She had reported panic attacks, but always blamed school. All of these symptoms I had previously attributed to other factors in Olivia's life: she was also depressed and anxious, which could explain any and all of the symptoms she had been experiencing. Cautiously, I started to bring up some of the symptoms that she had experienced that might be connected to her online life. I asked about what she remembered feeling during the incident with the boy online, and she said she felt 'scared' and 'afraid,' that she 'panicked,' and that she was feeling unsafe and insecure during the interaction. This fear response confirmed what I had been thinking—that this had been a trigger point for her. When asked about her previous experience, she shrugged it off, saying she did not remember well what she had felt. After her initial reaction to being threatened online, Olivia identified many feelings that victims often name after assaults; she blamed herself for the event, saying that she felt 'stupid' and 'slutty' and that her friends would judge her if they found out, things I had heard from other girls around her age when they had felt pressured or forced into sexual acts. Feeling validated in my assumptions, I brought up trauma with her and talked about how her responses were normal after the traumatic event she had been through; the fear, the blame, the panicked responses. I started to talk to her about how we could start to work through the trauma, to process it and manage her symptoms, which was when I was informed that "It's not like that."

Olivia did not view the incident as traumatic. To her, it was a normal, adolescent interaction that went in a way that she did not want, but that was "just something that happens." She did not identify feeling victimized, and my instinct in this situation was to explain this as her not acknowledging her feelings, downplaying events, or that she was simply not ready to cope with them. After all, she had identified symptoms that were clear indications of trauma, and had been through an event that I deemed traumatic—as her therapist, I felt more capable to identify trauma than Olivia was. As she continued to insist that she was not traumatized, I was frustrated with her. This was the first time she had been 'resistant' to treatment, which eventually I realized was not the right treatment for her, simply because she was not traumatized. She told me very clearly that she believed that it was a normal adolescent experience—one that she had experienced before, one similar to the sexual experiences of her friends, and that I was the one who was making it into 'a big deal,' and she had nothing more to discuss about the incident. I had to realize that rather than Olivia repressing trauma, I was attempting to rewrite her narrative as a traumatic one. She was the actor in this experience, and whether or not her symptoms lined up with what is recognized by 'professionals,' the context of the online world shifted the experience from one that was traumatic to one that was simply a part of teenaged life for Olivia. To understand what is and is not trauma in the virtual world, we need to understand the context of the new reality that adolescents are currently living and growing up in.

Accessing Information and Support

The internet has changed the ways in which the world accesses information but it has changed different groups of people in different ways. Adolescents raised as 'digital natives' are perhaps the greatest benefactors and sufferers of these changes, as information has been readily and easily available to them, about virtually any topic, for all of their formative years. The term 'digital native' originates in John Palfrey and Urs Gasser's book, *Born Digital*, and refers to the generation born after 1980 that has continuous access to digital technology and the knowledge base to use it, both of which were non-existent in the generation preceding them (Palfrey & Gasser, 2008). All teens are now digital natives, beginning earlier and earlier in life. The access to and use of technology has only increased with time, as it always has. In studies conducted by the Pew Research Center, researchers found that the percentage of teens reporting accessing the internet was 95% as of 2013 (Madden, Lenhart, Duggan, Cortesi, & Gasser, 2013). It would be a safe assumption that this percentage has only gone up in the last few years, with the increasing accessibility of smartphones putting internet access into the pockets of nearly all adolescents. Although the high numbers are indicative of the prevalence of information technology and social media in the lives of adolescents, what is more important is not how often it is used, but what the motivations are for its use (Seidman, 2013). As information has become more readily and easily available, adolescents accessing this information have found ways to make it useful in their personal lives.

Far from being just an easier way to conduct research, teens use the internet to develop their identities, interact with others, and explore topics that might be considered 'taboo' by the adults in their lives. Information, a great deal of the time, comes in the form of social interactions online. Interconnectedness and the ability to find someone going through a similar experience—physically or mentally—no matter what that experience is, has allowed for firsthand experiences to be shared worldwide, with major impacts. One study found that personal experiences of other people, found online through social media, was one of the most important factors in making healthcare decisions (Entwistle et al., 2011). Support groups are not a new phenomenon, but the context of the online world in which support groups are now forming is. Why is this significant? While a limited number of people in the same geographical area might feel comfortable identifying as having a potentially stigmatizing problem, the online world allows for safety as well as increased connection with people experiencing something similar to them. One article discusses social media as a "non-threatening medium" in which those suffering from a severe mental illness feel comfortable connecting and gaining advice and information (Naslund, Grande, Aschbrenner, & Elwyn, 2014). This perceived threat could be the stigma that those suffering from a mental illness, or any illness, face when seeking help or even information. The internet allows for exploratory information-gathering in such a way that going to a physical support group would never be able to; by going to a support group, someone has to first identify that he or she needs that support, and identify what is 'wrong' with them, whereas the internet allows for searching and discussion before that identification and association needs to occur. In their article discussing internet use and some stigmatized illness, Berger et al. posit that "The informality of the internet diminished the extent to which a person has to self-identify as having a stigmatized illness, before looking for information" (Berger, Wagner, & Baker, 2005, p. 1822). Support on the internet does not stop at stigmatized illness. As adolescents carry their access to boundless information in their pockets, they also carry their support network. Teens use not only the contacts on their phones for support, but those that they connect with online through social media, whom they may or may not know in the 'real world.' Barak, Boniel-Nissim, and Suler (2008) posit that support online decreases social isolation in both online and offline settings, allowing people to feel more comfortable with social interactions in general after exploring them through online support groups. In a report put together by Common Sense Media, teens reported positive increases in social interactions, such as feeling less shy and more connected to those with common interests with people online

(Rideout, 2012). These interactions allow for conversations that might not happen in the physical world, by allowing teens to explore information without the fear of stigma and judgment. Adolescents who feel that they may face unwanted consequences by going to parents, teachers, or friends to discuss a stigmatizing topic could avoid the self-identification process by seeking out information and clarification online. Specifically, teens often have questions about sexuality and sexual experiences that they may not have had that they feel uncomfortable discussing with those whom they 'really' know, and can turn to their online groups for help. These topics can be a difficult one to breach between generations, but approaching peers may additionally result in a stigma being attached to the adolescent asking. Fear of being the only one in a peer group without experience with or knowledge of sexual topics can be avoided via the anonymity provided by the internet.

Professionals working with teenagers need to be aware of the ways in which they are accessing information about health and sexuality, as well as how they are seeking support. Accessing information online is not the same as research methods of past generations primary due to the social aspect of information-gathering. As Berger et al. conclude in their study, those most likely to turn to the internet for health information are those with psychiatric stigmatized illnesses. Often, this practice is overlooked, downplayed, or even criticized among the medical community, who do not want their patients searching for health conditions before being seen and self-diagnosing. Regardless of whether or not this practice is the best thing a patient could do, therapists working with those who have psychiatric illnesses need to be informed of where their clients are gleaning their information and how they are using it. This can be seen as a strength; Gray, Klein, Noyce, Sesselberg, and Cantrill (2005) report that in their study, information found online enabled adolescents specifically "to avoid a visit to a health professional, or find empowerment from online information within the medical encounter" (p. 1474). In either case, the adolescents are taking a more active role in their healthcare, but by connecting with others online and exploring anything from health questions to curiosities about sex, they are also developing their opinions about how they want to be seen by others.

Developing the Online Self Through Exploration

As adolescents use the online world for communication, with peers and as part of a larger community, they in turn develop ideas about themselves. Several articles and studies have focused on adolescent participation on social media websites (Lenhart, Purcell, Smith, & Zickuhr, 2010; Bargh & McKenna, 2004), although the websites and means of accessing them have changed drastically from those reported on in the studies in the last several years. Technology advances at a rate that makes it improbable, if not impossible, for research about its use and users to remain current. Jessica Ringrose (2011) discusses "how digital representation impact teens' relationships to themselves and others" (p. 101), and argues that the development of adolescent identity is much the same as it has always been; the only thing changing is the medium through which they develop and explore these identities. Sue Ziebland and Sally Wyke conclude from their study that the internet allows for separate sets of relationships, which in turn is helpful for maintaining two separate identities—one online and one "everyday identity" (Ziebland & Wyke, 2012, p. 233). In order to maintain two identities, adolescents are faced with the challenge and privilege of creating an online 'self'—one that allows for many more choices than the self that they present in their everyday world. The online self can be created and developed in many ways, and adolescents are able to change, experiment with, and adapt online selves to fit their desired online personas.

Exploring what it means to have an online identity can be accomplished through social media use, and through the use of automedia, a term that was adapted by Julie Rak to mean a way of enacting life stories in an online, digital environment (Rak, 2015). She writes about the use of the game *The Sims* as a way in which players can write the lives of virtual selves, thereby impacting their own identities and own stories. In other words, it allows experimentation with new and different identities that can be 'tried on' by those playing the game. Even the catchphrase for *The Sims Online* on the official strategy guide to the game is indicative of the desire to use their software to develop a new identity: "Be somebody. Else" (Kramer, 2002). Knutzen and Kennedy claim in their article that "the internet as a social milieu has greatly expanded the forums for identity experiments and feedback on the self" (Knutzen & Kennedy, 2012, p. 3). This supports the point that identity experiments, while taking place in a world unfamiliar to non-digital natives, have always been the norm. This new atmosphere, I believe, has unique qualities that have never existed before in human interactions, not the least being that the level of control that a user online has over any given interaction has been greatly increased. This can provide a level of safety while forming an identity, as "a user can access self-help groups whilst controlling their level of disclosure of their identity" (Gray, Klein, Noyce, Sesselberg, & Cantrill, 2005, p. 1475). This concept of control can be applied to various forums across the digital world. Unlike interpersonal, 'real-life' interactions, the online world allows for a level of control by the user, including removing herself from the interaction at any time. I would argue that this has a positive impact on the development of adolescent identity, as the adolescent has a range of options and unlimited choices about how he or she wants to be perceived, and can try on and adjust these identities through a controlled environment.

Identity online, although not widely recognized as an important aspect of adolescent development, has been looked at by researchers discussing the use of avatars online. Through the presentation of the self online through avatars and automedia, positive outcomes on self-image have been studied and reported. One report found that when people were able to 'try on' different identities first online, even if they carried out those identities later in the 'real world,' their contentment with that identity was likely to be higher (Knutzen & Kennedy, 2012). The concept of developing a 'self' online can be applied to experimenting with and 'trying on' specific aspects of an identity. In addition to developing a general sense of self online, adolescents have the opportunity to explore their sexual identities as well. Villani, Gatti, Confalonieri, and Riva (2012) posit that online, adolescents can often feel

> more distant from the real body, leading the adolescents to feel free to add elements, in particular related to sexual characterization . . . it becomes a tool to experience their self in a flexible way and create their own image.
>
> *(p. 5)*

A private, often tumultuous issue for teens can be explored in a less threatening way online, through the use of online identities. This exploration does not stop, however, with the development of an identity, but leads to further exploration online, now involving peers and others in this online world.

In addition to developing the self, the virtual world can be a place where adolescents explore and negotiate sexual relationships and experiences. Manago, Greenfield, Kim, and Ward (2014) discuss the change in types of relationships with teens, from exclusive relationships to more casual sexual encounters with their peers. As this change has taken place, there seems to be a series of events following it in a chain reaction. As there has been more concern about the risks involved with these sexual behaviors, there came a push for abstaining from risky sexual behaviors, which in turn led to teens focusing on 'technical virginity' (e.g., abstaining from only intercourse), and then studies discussing the risks of noncoital activities as a consequence. Lindberg, Jones, and Santelli (2008) report on the sexual behaviors of adolescents who are not having intercourse; but, like many other similar studies, their focus is on the physical risks of sexually transmitted infections (STIs) from noncoital activity. Their focus on the sexual lives of teens does not include any virtual sexual experiences, which is increasingly a major part of the lives of adolescents. In fact, while 'technical virginity' seems to be highly studied and discussed, even in recent articles, the online sexual lives of adolescents appear, as far as research is concerned, to be underacknowledged or unnoticed (Bersamin, Walker, Fisher, & Grube, 2006; Boekeloo & Howard, 2002; Schuster, Bell, & Kanouse, 1996; Remez, 2000; Brückner & Bearman, 2005). With 95% of adolescents regularly accessing the internet, their virtual lives can no longer be ignored. As relationship standards have changed, the online world can be a place in which sex is more recreational and casual, without the risk of pregnancy or STIs. Online spaces allow teens to explore their sexuality without the fear of physical consequences, while still connecting with others, or as Manago et al. put it, they are "places for adolescents to explore and socially construct their sexuality with peers, outside the supervision of parents" (Manago,

Greenfield, Kim, & Ward, 2014, p. 213). This exploration, however, brings up new questions and concerns about adolescents' safety as they explore in worlds new to the generations before them.

'Internet Safety' and Online Victimization

A major concern when discussing adolescents in the online world is their safety and the potential for victimization. Parents desperate to protect their innocent children from the vast and ever-evolving dangers of the digital world search for answers to the question that parents in all times have likely struggled with: how can I keep them safe? Despite the changing dangers, this question has been present in parents with all new developments and technologies throughout the ages. In *The Culture of Fear*, Barry Glassner discusses the practices of media and policy makers indoctrinating children and parents with the ideas that the world is a dangerous place, full of potential kidnappers and deviants waiting for any opportunity to snatch their next victim (Glassner, 1999). The ideas of fearing for safety are not new; but the perceived reach and means of the victimizers is all too new, and for most, unknown. I would argue that with the access to information, the widespread use of social media for news, and the sheer numbers of those connected to each other online who would have had no contact a decade or two ago has only increased the culture of fear that we have developed.

A search on Google for "keeping kids safe online" turns up some 60 million results—if parents were unsure of the risks their children might be facing before they searched, they certainly have no doubt that those risks are imminent threats by the time they are done. After reading articles claiming that they need to install apps and programs to block unwanted information from breaching the boundaries of their computer, monitor their child's every move online to ensure that they are not talking to strangers or that they are not potentially at risk for 'cyberbullying,' and police releases, warning parents of the 'latest' apps to check their children's phones for (as well as the names of some apps that those 'children' will use to hide those apps they do not wish their parents to see), it would be hard to not fall into the trap of fear. The well-known antivirus company, Norton, has a page on its website dedicated to "Ten Tips to Keep Kids Safe Online," on which it warns that "statistics vary, but at least 20 percent of kids will receive harassing, hateful, or insulting messages via social networks, emails, instant messages, videos, and texts" (Merritt, n.d.). Any parents reading that their child is at greater risk for receiving 'hateful' or 'insulting' messages would feel that they have reason to panic, and to read all of the messages their child sends and receives to prevent this atrocity from happening. As parents and practitioners working with digital natives, however, I would propose that before this reaction occurs, we need to ask ourselves: have *we* ever received a hateful, insulting comment from someone, in 'real life'? Is it realistic to prevent children and adolescents from having this experience if this is their new world, the new 'real life' online?

Adolescents conduct much of their social lives online; this comes with many positives, but not all aspects of human interactions are going to be positive, and it is unreasonable to expect them to be able to avoid any negativity. Perhaps, instead of a valid desire to protect children, this response is a gut reaction to consequences in a world mostly unknown to us; seen as avoidable by some, but not by the adolescents who have now grown up in and exist in it. For them, perhaps, these communications are a part of their everyday and need to be dealt with as such, as we would encourage them to deal with any types of negative social interactions—which is not to avoid social interactions altogether.

At times, the safety advice for monitoring the online lives of adolescents appears to be little more than a blind, outdated panic. The FBI's internet safety report, currently online, contains laughable suggestions for parents, such as how to access and monitor their child's AOL account, and to have the incoming calls to their home phone lines forwarded to their pagers (Freeh, 2005). Meanwhile, adolescents are developing and using applications on their smartphones at such a pace that by the time a 'guide' comes out for parents to warn them of the dangers, those applications are outdated to the adolescents. One of the main concerns that seems to appear often is the sexual victimization of youth online. Although it is a new area of research, one set of researchers (Ybarra & Mitchell, 2008) calls for pediatricians to educate their patients "about what does (and does not) increase the likelihood of online interpersonal victimization" (p. 356), focusing on what they think are risky behaviors of youth online, such as meeting new people online and talking about sexual topics with others. I would contest this assessment of risk; talking about sex online does not necessarily mean that an adolescent is engaging in risky behaviors, and to assume that they are being victimized if they do so is to ignore the changes in culture and development present for digital natives.

Adolescents in the current generation explore their identity and sexuality in realms that are new to their elders, but in ways that are similar to how humans have explored their sexuality across generations. Adolescents are curious about sex by nature; now, they have more access to explore and delve into that curiosity, but some question the safety of that access. In her article on sex play in a virtual realm, Robin Wilson (2009) discusses the legal implications of children engaging in 'virtual sex play' with adults in adult online communities. The discussion is focused mostly on the laws surrounding a changing climate of child abuse, but she also delves into opinions about the harm to a child in virtual worlds. She concludes from her review that sexual acts in an online world have the potential to "corrupt the minor's innocence, change her own mental view of sex and sexual relationships," and that this serves as support for the concept that noncontact still poses a risk to the child involved (Wilson, 2009, p. 1147). I will not diverge into the exploitation of children by adults in this chapter. While this area certainly needs more research, especially as the culture we live in rapidly becomes more and more virtual, what I am most concerned with are not the legal ramifications of online 'sex play,' but the psychological effects when these interactions are sought after and found by adolescents. Wilson's comments provide an interesting insight into the current opinions of youth engaging in sex play online; that they are innocent, that their views of sex or sexuality may change from the experience, and that this is a negative occurrence. In fact, the 'child' in this scenario, whether engaging with an adult or another legal 'child,' has knowingly lied about his or her age to be able to access the areas of the site that Wilson refers to, where the sex play occurs, and has sought out partners with which to engage in sexual virtual acting, and continuously consent to the play. Whether they should legally be able to consent to such an activity is a topic beyond the scope of this chapter, but the children seeking out these activities are far from passive participants absolved of all responsibility. In their article discussing digitized sexual identities of adolescent girls, Ringrose and Barajas (2011) observed that the sexual behaviors displayed online by adolescent girls were demonized by media and parents, but within peer groups was considered normative. Perhaps we should consider that their motivations for seeking sex play online are exactly for the reasons that the legal experts fear—that they would desire not to be so innocent, and that they wish to change their knowledge or view of sex, and that this is the 'norm' for teens growing up in a digital world. If we consider this, we have to question what it is that we are so afraid of, and what we are trying to protect adolescents from. Are we concerned for the moral and societal implications of our children seeking to sexually experiment in a world to which we are so unaccustomed, or that those experiences will leave them with more than new opinions of sex, so that we instead traumatize them?

Social Construction of Trauma

Social constructivism is a lesser-discussed means of looking at trauma. Theories about trauma, what it is, where it comes from, and how we should address it seem to change with each passing generation. It is important to recognize that these changing perspectives mean that trauma is not a concrete, particular thing that always holds the same meaning, but a fluid and developing term, developed by each society defining it. In their book *The Empire of Trauma*, Didier Fassin and Richard Rechtman discuss the changes that have occurred in the conceptions of trauma since it was introduced as a term. From hysteria to 'shell shock,' trauma has been shaped by changing theoretical viewpoints and the acceptance (or non-acceptance) by the society in which those theories were presented (Fassin & Rechtman, 2009). As popular psychiatrists and the public alike moved away from a negative view of those experiencing trauma symptoms, the creation of the DSM criteria for post-traumatic stress disorder (PTSD), according to Fassin and Rechtman, "effectively affirmed that any normal individual might suffer such distress if he or she were exposed to an event deemed traumatic" (Fassin & Rechtman, 2009, p. 77). However, they continue to posit that the societal factors impacting viewpoints of trauma may have been more significant in the shift than the writings of the DSM-III.

Fassin and Rechtman are not the only ones writing about how society constructs a trauma narrative. Jeffrey Alexander (2016) writes of what he calls 'culture trauma,' and applies his concepts to the atrocities of World War II, claiming that societies participate in "constructing and broadcasting the tragic narrative of the Holocaust" (Alexander, 2002, p. 34). He does not make the claim that the events of the Holocaust were not horrific, or that they were not often traumatic, but rather discusses the dramatized (often literally, through books, plays and movies) responses and retellings of events that the majority of people did not have any firsthand experience with, and in doing so, bringing that majority into the trauma narrative and making the experience their own. He goes on to say that "symbolic extension and emotional identification are both necessary if the audience for a trauma and its social relevance are to be dramatically enlarged. I will call the effects of this enlargement the 'engorgement of evil'" (Alexander, 2002, p. 44). Following this line of thought, if the 'evil' of events are dramatized and 'enlarged' for the purpose of social relevance, we should consider what other aspects we as a society intentionally or unintentionally enlarge or dramatize in order to make them socially relevant as well. While the Holocaust is certainly a large-scale example, perhaps this concept could be applied to the fears that cripple parents and societies at different times, making the fear response disproportionate to the actual threat. Common fears of children being kidnapped or victims of a school shooting, for example, are fears based on statistically improbable and terrifying, but very few, instances. The threat is seen as more relevant through the production of fear-based media, which in turn impacts the society's view of an experience. When told at every turn that their children are in danger, the adults in a society, for the most part, respond in wanting to protect them from that danger— but in doing so reinforce the idea of the threat and the concepts of potential victimization, instead of exploring what may be a part of normal adolescent development in digital natives.

Virtual Trauma

Discussions of trauma usually focus on times of war, or cases of abuse that seem more clear-cut: to our understanding of trauma, how could a person escape these events without the mental scars that mark a 'traumatic' event. When the lines become blurred, however, we may have more questions. What happens when the same event can happen to two different people and produce two different responses? When we are responding from a place of fear and possibly constructing the narrative of trauma for those who are the first to have these experiences, we must be sure that we are not falling into the trap of dramatizing otherwise normal experiences. As adolescents who are digital natives are the first to form their identities online, are the first to experience sexuality in a virtual world, and are among the first to be potential victims in this world, we must consider first that they have the only knowledge in existence on those subjects.

If adolescents are expected to gain health information online, prevent sexually transmitted infections (STIs) and pregnancy, and they foster more peer support a positive self-image through the creation of their online selves, why are we insisting that they need to be 'safe' online, and that virtual predators are waiting to traumatize them at every turn? We are telling them that they need to protect themselves from the 'threat' that exists online, when that threat exists primarily from our fear of the new identity of digital natives, which is created in part by their experiences in a virtual reality. We construct the trauma through this narrative, without consideration for individualized responses to events that may or may not actually be traumatizing for that person.

Olivia turned to people online for support. She had been criticized for her overuse of some of her support networks; her parents were tired, her friends were tired, *she* was tired of speaking her feelings when it landed her in a hospital stay or on a suicide hotline. Instead, she turned to the less threatening option: the internet. Like many teens, she found the use of social media to be a forum of positive, supportive interactions, and a place where she felt she could go to explore herself and her identity without judgment. She had a negative experience while exploring, but it was not until the reactions of the adults in her life that she considered that this experience should have been a traumatic one. She saw it as a normal, minor risk of interacting with people who are strangers.

Rather than focusing on the elimination of social media use, what might have been more helpful in Olivia's case would have been to discuss what changed that made her feel more comfortable taking control of the interaction and logging off. This is where there is a distinct difference between 'real life' and virtual trauma: the control that a user has over their situation. I would argue that if the trauma occurs online, and the interaction stays in the online realm, the implications are that the trauma should be lessened because of the control that a user has and maintains throughout a potentially traumatic interaction. In the case of Olivia, even when she felt threatened, she maintained control of the situation in that she had options that those who might be victimized in 'real life' would not necessarily have. This put her in a position of power, although it seemed to take her a while to exercise it. Eventually, when the interaction was upsetting her, she made the choice to sign off, and could have done so at any time during the conversation.

Blaming the Victim

While the user has control over an online interaction, I would like to distinguish between crediting the user with control and the common practice of using victim-blaming language to discourage the use of online interactions that seem to be common in any 'internet safety' literature. I would assert that allowing space for someone to control their online interactions should be seen as separate from victim-blaming practices seen in interpersonal situations. While there are similar 'tips' for 'staying safe' in both the online and the 'real' world, the online world cannot be viewed in the same way without risk of applying concepts that only work in face-to-face interactions. Ideally, we as a society would never blame victims of crimes; however, until we reach that ideal, we can acknowledge that while there are cases in the physical world where a perpetrator cannot be stopped, this is not the same online. In a virtual world, each user has control of his or her participation in the world. An individual can choose how to present himself, how to develop her online identity, and how long he wants that interaction to last. In this world, then, the same rules that may govern a physical interaction need not apply; there is not physical threat, and verbal or emotional abuse can be ended at any time, *by the user being targeted*, an option not readily available in the 'real-life' realm. In Olivia's case, the parents and professionals in her life reacted by asking her to control her behavior. While this is a form of control, perhaps it would have been more effective to ask her about the power and control that she already has in an online situation, and to encourage her to use that when she felt she needed to. This would allow space for her to be in control without blaming her for any interactions that happen online. Those interactions can be normalized, and the space for an adolescent to decide how they feel about it can be given.

Virtual Trauma Risk Assessment Tool

Perhaps, rather than teaching children and adolescents that there are places that they cannot go and things that they cannot do because they will surely become the victims of online pedophiles looking for a target, we should focus our attention and education efforts on reinforcing the control that a user has when online. Empowering adolescents with the knowledge that they can sign off any interaction at any time that is making them feel uncomfortable, or options for if they are feeling threatened would ultimately give them more resources than telling them that perhaps they should not have been on that part of the internet and they could avoid the threat. As with real-life interactions, virtual ones cannot always be avoided, but they can be responded to appropriately.

I have created a questionnaire (Appendix I) for use in evaluating social media use with adolescents, but more importantly, to open a discussion in therapy about what roles social media plays in an individual adolescent's life, and to help assess the risk that they might be in for experiencing virtual trauma. This could be used as part of an evaluation or brought up at any time during treatment to talk about online lives. If we need to rethink our relationships to ourselves and our identities with the addition of the virtual world, and if trauma is something that has a major impact on our identities, now confused by the online world, then perhaps we need to rethink our conceptions of trauma in interpersonal relationships to allow for this complication. Virtual trauma, I would argue, is something that can occur and then lead to trauma symptoms, or it can be processed as a normal developmental occurrence, depending on the experiences and the attitudes of the individual adolescent. Therefore, the only way to assess the types of effects that virtual trauma would have on the lives of an adolescent is to open the door for conversation, without preconceived notions of what trauma looks like in a virtual realm, and to listen to whether online experiences that go badly are traumatic—or are just something that happens.

Appendix I   Virtual Trauma Risk Assessment Tool

1. What is your primary reason for using social media? (to meet new people, to stay in touch with friends, to share pictures, etc.)
2. Do you engage in conversations with people whom you have not met 'in real life'?

    a. If so, what has this experience been like for you? What relationships have come from it?

3. Do conversations online sometimes turn sexual when you do not want them to?

    a. If so, how do you respond?

4. Are you comfortable ending a conversation if it makes you feel uneasy in any way?

    a. What ways could you do this?

5. Do you use dating apps, and if so, do you use them for purposes other than dating? (to meet new friends, to find hookups, etc.)
6. Do you share personal photos of yourself through messaging apps or through social media?

    a. If so, what influence has this had on you, positive or negative?

7. Do you play games online that connect you to other players?
8. Have you felt threatened online, either physically or psychologically?

    a. If so, what did you do about it?

9. What are things that you do to make sure that you are safe online?

Appendix II   Clinical Use of Virtual Trauma Risk Assessment Tool

Guidelines for use:

This tool is intended for use by the clinician, not as a self-directed form to be completed by an adolescent. The questions are guidelines to help direct conversation in such a way that an adolescent would feel comfortable discussing his or her online experiences, and to open a dialogue about what effect those experiences have had on him or her.

This tool should not be used as a scale in which a certain number of negative answers would equal a risk for virtual trauma; rather, the clinician should assess from the severity and impact of negative experiences expressed through use of the tool whether or not a particular adolescent is at greater risk for virtual trauma.

A clinician using this tool should be open to hearing about other ways that an adolescent engages with the world through the internet; this tool does not begin to encompass the vast array of activities that a digital native may participate in. Allow the client to lead this conversation: it is his or her narrative and native world, and he or she is best able to inform the clinician.

Engage parents in a discussion, if relevant, after the tool has been used and online life has been discussed individually. Educating parents about ways in which an adolescent uses the internet and whether or not his or her use is within the realm of normal activity for digitally native adolescents can help them to be more involved and understanding of their adolescent's virtual life.

Close Reading Questions

1. Why did Busfield initially suggest a trauma-related diagnosis in Olivia's case? What symptoms had Busfield convinced that Olivia's issues were trauma related? Do you think "virtual trauma" could cause these symptoms?
2. What do you make of Olivia's "virtual trauma," considering, in her words, it is "just something that happens"?
3. How is developing a sexual identity online safer than developing one in the real world? In what ways is it more risky?

Prompts for Writing

1. How would you counsel an adolescent client whose parents or guardians thought that the adolescent was making "bad decisions" online? What is your opinion of Busfield's approach and her assessment tool?
2. How does Busfield's conceptualization of a double identity—the "online" self and the real world self—relate to the subject of Alan Oxman's case study on sex addiction?
3. How might the expanding "culture of fear" that Busfield discusses be related to "victim blaming" and/or a world in which adolescents are too scared to engage in their own development?

References

Alexander, J. C. (2002). On the social construction of moral universals: The "Holocaust" from war crime to trauma drama. *European Journal of Social Theory*, *5*(1), 5.

Alexander, J. C. (2016). Culture trauma, morality and solidarity: The social construction of "Holocaust" and other mass murders. *Thesis Eleven*, *132*(1), 3–16.

Barak, A., Boniel-Nissim, M., & Suler, J. (2008). Fostering empowerment in online support groups. *Computers in Human Behavior*, *24*(5), 1867–1883.

Bargh, J. A., & McKenna, K. Y. (2004). The Internet and social life. *Annual Review of Psychology*, *55*, 573–590.

Berger, M., Wagner, T. H., & Baker, L. C. (2005). Internet use and stigmatized illness. *Social Science & Medicine*, *61*(8), 1821–1827.

Bersamin, M. M., Walker, S., Fisher, D. A., & Grube, J. W. (2006). Correlates of oral sex and vaginal intercourse in early and middle adolescence. *Journal of Research on Adolescence*, *16*(1), 59–68.

Boekeloo, B. O., & Howard, D. E. (2002). Oral sexual experience among young adolescents receiving general health examinations. *American Journal of Health Behavior*, *26*(4), 306–314.

Brückner, H., & Bearman, P. (2005). After the promise: The STD consequences of adolescent virginity pledges. *Journal of Adolescent Health*, *36*(4), 271–278.

Entwistle, V. A., France, E. F., Wyke, S., Jepson, R., Hunt, K., Ziebland, S., & Thompson, A. (2011). How information about other people's personal experiences can help with healthcare decision-making: A qualitative study. *Patient Education and Counseling*, *85*(3), e291–e298.

Fassin, D., & Rechtman, R. (2009). *The empire of trauma: An inquiry into the condition of victimhood*. Princeton, NJ: Princeton University Press.

Freeh, L. J. (2005, June 3). A parent's guide to internet safety. Retrieved May 2, 2016, from www.fbi.gov/stats-services/publications/parent-guide

Glassner, B. (1999). *The culture of fear: Why Americans are afraid of the wrong things*. New York: Basic Books.

Gray, N. J., Klein, J. D., Noyce, P. R., Sesselberg, T. S., & Cantrill, J. A. (2005). Health information-seeking behaviour in adolescence: The place of the internet. *Social Science & Medicine*, *60*(7), 1467–1478.

Knutzen, K. B., & Kennedy, D. M. (2012). Designing the self: The transformation of the relational self-concept through social encounters in a virtual immersive environment. *Interactive Learning Environments*, *20*(3), 271–292.

Kramer, G. (2002). *The Sims online: Prima's official strategy guide*. Roseville, CA: Prima.

Lenhart, A., Purcell, K., Smith, A., & Zickuhr, K. (2010). Social media & mobile internet use among teens and young adults: Millennials. *Pew Internet & American Life Project*. Retrieved from http://pewinternet.org/Reports/2010/social-Media-and-Young-Adults.aspx

Lindberg, L. D., Jones, R., & Santelli, J. S. (2008). Noncoital sexual activities among adolescents. *Journal of Adolescent Health*, *43*(3), 231–238.

Madden, M., Lenhart, A., Duggan, M., Cortesi, S., & Gasser, U. (2013). *Teens and technology 2013*. Washington, DC: Pew Internet & American Life Project.

Manago, A. M., Greenfield, P. M., Kim, J. L., & Ward, L. M. (2014). Changing cultural pathways through gender role and sexual development: A theoretical framework. *Ethos*, *42*(2), 198–221.

Merritt, M. (n.d.). Ten tips to keep kids safe online | Norton. Retrieved May 1, 2016, from http://us.norton.com/kids-safe/article

Naslund, J. A., Grande, S. W., Aschbrenner, K. A., & Elwyn, G. (2014). Naturally occurring peer support through social media: The experiences of individuals with severe mental illness using YouTube. *PLOS One, 9*(10), e110171.

Palfrey, J. G., & Gasser, U. (2008). *Born digital: Understanding the first generation of digital natives.* New York: Basic Books.

Rak, J. (2015). Life writing versus automedia: The Sims 3 game as a life lab. *Biography, 38*(2), 155–180.

Remez, L. (2000). Oral sex among adolescents: Is it sex or is it abstinence? *Family Planning Perspectives, 32*(6), 298–304.

Rideout, V. J. (2012). Social media, social life: How teens view their digital lives. *Common Sense Media.* Retrieved from https://www.commonsensemedia.org/research/social-media-social-life-how-teens-view-their-digital-lives

Ringrose, J. (2011). Are you sexy, flirty, or a slut? Exploring "sexualization" and how teen girls perform/negotiate digital sexual identity on social networking sites. *New Femininities,* 99–116.

Ringrose, J., & Barajas, K. E. (2011). Gendered risks and opportunities? Exploring teen girls' digitized sexual identities in postfeminist media contexts. *International Journal of Media & Cultural Politics, 7*(2), 121–138.

Sales, N. J. (2016). *American girls: Social media and the secret lives of teenagers.* New York: Alfred A. Knopf.

Schuster, M. A., Bell, R. M., & Kanouse, D. E. (1996). The sexual practices of adolescent virgins: Genital sexual activities of high school students who have never had vaginal intercourse. *American Journal of Public Health, 86*(11), 1570–1576.

Seidman, G. (2013). Self-presentation and belonging on Facebook: How personality influences social media use and motivations. *Personality and Individual Differences, 54*(3), 402–407.

Villani, D., Gatti, E., Confalonieri, E., & Riva, G. (2012). Am I my avatar? A tool to investigate virtual body image representation in adolescence. *Cyberpsychology, Behavior, and Social Networking, 15*(8), 435–440.

Wilson, R. F. (2009). Sex play in virtual worlds. *Washington and Lee Law Review, 66*(3), 1127.

Ybarra, M. L., & Mitchell, K. J. (2008). How risky are social networking sites? A comparison of places online where youth sexual solicitation and harassment occurs. *Pediatrics, 121*(2), e350–e357.

Ziebland, S.U.E., & Wyke, S. (2012). Health and illness in a connected world: How might sharing experiences on the internet affect people's health? *Milbank Quarterly, 90*(2), 219–249.

3

VICTIM OR OFFENDER?

Stigma and Justice in a Complex Forensic Case

Russel Healy

Pre-reading Questions

1. How do you define stigma? How does the media contribute to the stigmatization and judicial treatment of sex offenders?
2. What are a social worker's ethical obligations when working with a sex offender? What are some barriers social workers face when working with sex offenders?
3. If you knew that a sex offender had lived a life of neglect and sexual abuse before committing an offense, would that information change the way you viewed the offense?

Prologue

Charlie committed his offenses just one day after his 18th birthday. During the course of an afternoon, he fondled two clothed boys in full public view in two different department stores. Technically they were clumsy forms of frottage, wherein the offender will grope someone over their clothes in a crowded place like a subway train. Charlie's first target was an 8-year-old boy. He was standing next to his mother when Charlie groped his buttocks. Charlie then went to another store and saw an 8- or 9-year-old boy in the pharmacy department. That boy was testing his blood pressure, seated, his arm in a cuff. Charlie groped the boy's crotch and then asked the shocked child if he would like to go with him to the men's restroom. Charlie saw that he was noticed, and he panicked. Instead of leaving the store he went into the men's bathroom where he was apprehended by security guards.

After Charlie was arrested, the police found surgical gloves, Vaseline, bungee cord straps and a large, serrated knife in the cab of his truck. Understandably, the police were alarmed. Somehow the media was alerted, and Charlie was on the 6 o'clock news. From this point forward, Charlie would have no control over his identity. He would be labeled a sex offender.

Before he would be sentenced, neighbors would vandalize his parents' home. He would be denied employment and lose friends and supporters. Travel across the state line would be prohibited. To make matters worse, the paraphernalia found in his truck made him appear like a sadistic, violent offender. I was skeptical that I could help him on a voluntary, outpatient basis. After a relatively long period of engagement, he become one of the most noteworthy clients of my career. I learned a lot from working on his case, and it changed many of my previously held beliefs. Hopefully, I will demonstrate in this chapter that a case narrative can yield new practice knowledge.

The Clinical Context

In the early 1990s many of my colleagues were working with trauma survivors such as adult sexual abuse victims. In his essay, "The Wave That Brought PTSD to Sri Lanka," Ethan Watters (2010) tells us, "if you were an ambitious researcher in psychology or psychiatry during the 1990s, PTSD was where the action was" (p. 72). My colleagues claimed to be seeing more and more clients with disorders along the dissociative spectrum. It became a mark of clinical distinction to be able to count clients with multiple personality disorder (MPD) among one's cases. Some believed in phenomena like recovered memory, which we now know to be a fallacy.[1] There was, in addition, a voyeuristic quality to their fascination. What seemed to me to be a sudden and popular surge in what was once considered a rare diagnostic syndrome further spurred my skepticism. So, when I had an opportunity to be trained to treat sex offenders, my curiosity took over where my skepticism left off.

This is a case study about the importance of critical thinking and ethical reasoning in clinical work with stigmatized persons. The subject is a pre-adjudicated sex offender whose individual case challenges conventional assumptions. He does not represent the typical offender who poses a clear threat to the community. At this point the reader might be asking, "why use a sex offender as an example? They are not a sympathetic population." My reply would be "why not?" Questioning the use of a sex offender in this study is tantamount to demonstrating my notion that people will use stigma automatically whenever certain language or labels are used. My argument is that, as clinicians, we ought not use stigma or participate in stigmatization because of the damage it does to a person's identity.

The dimension of stigma that sex offenders occupy is characterized as "controllability of causes" (Corrigan, 2000, p. 52). In short, many people believe that offenders are able to control their actions despite the fact that a number of them have a diagnosable sexual disorder, impulse control disorder or are re-enacting their own abusive traumas. Because sex abuse is aberrant and often harmful, most perpetrators—regardless of the facts of their crimes—are seen as dangerous. They are the only class of criminal offender who continue to be punished once their sentence has been concluded (Sample & Bray, 2003, p. 66). The stigma they endure is particularly toxic because the laws governing their management are harsher than those for any other criminal act.

Sex offender-specific therapy (SOST) is a cognitive behavioral, evidence-based, outcome-driven approach (Marshall & Laws, 2003). In many settings it is a manualized form of treatment (Mann, 2009). It evolved as a reaction against psychodynamic approaches to the treatment of sex offenders, which are largely ineffective. In keeping with the tenets of cognitive behavioral therapy (CBT), SOST clinicians do not concern themselves with transference or countertransference. Instead, they use a relapse prevention approach, which is a reasonably scientific and non-judgmental method. However, when G. Alan Marlatt and Judith R. Gordon edited the seminal text on relapse prevention (1985), the concept of relapse prevention was meant to apply to addictive behaviors, not aggressive behaviors that violate the rights of others. Techniques such as motivational interviewing are also utilized, which stress the importance of clinician empathy (Miller & Rollnick, 1991, p. 5). Motivational interviewing was developed for the treatment of addicts. Consequently, SOST needs a stronger foundation on which to claim efficacy.

SOST efficacy research is the product of randomized clinical trials (RCTs). Researchers of SOST defend the use of RCTs on the grounds that such research is scientifically sufficient (Seto et al., 2008). Detractors against the use of RCTs include William Marshall, one of the early proponents of utilizing CBT with sexual offenders (Marshall & Marshall, 2007). Within the field the debate appears to be one of good science versus good clinical work. If applied as designed, SOST is not a harsh or punishing therapy. But SOST in its pure form does sequester behavioral symptoms and does not address the whole person. Underlying dynamic issues become reduced to "triggers." Outside of that framework the offender's experience is far less relevant to the treatment.

The rate of sex offender recidivism is lower than or equal to that of recidivism for all criminal offenders (Sample & Bray, 2003, pp. 64–66). Yet the public believes that most offenders will offend again. Risk assessment instruments have been developed to predict risk based on actuarial factors (Hanson & Bussiere, 1998; Stokes, Berg, Cobbina, Huebner, & Valentine, 2006). Some instruments weigh fixed variables only, such as the age of the victim at the time of the offense, the gender of the victim, and the number of victims. Other instruments address both dynamic and fixed measures. Dynamic variables such as marital status, length of time since the last offense, and response to treatment are seen by some as important predictors of continued or reduced risk. Overall these actuarial scales are useful for clinicians as well as law enforcement. Many have been rigorously researched and are considered valid and reliable (Witt, 2000). But that may not be enough to reassure society. When science and good clinical work is not enough, society and its agents can employ stigma.

Therapy specific to sex offenders has been criticized as a "one size fits all approach" (Laws & Ward, 2006). Having facilitated this type of therapy, I would not argue against that perception. Simple approaches to solving complex, systemic social and public health problems may lull communities into a false sense of safety. For the clinician, the challenges are abundant. It is impossible to conduct SOST without also considering the safety of the community. Conversely, and for various reasons, some offenders pull for the clinician's sympathy. Because SOST does not utilize an analysis of countertransference, it is easy for an inexperienced clinician to fall to one or the other side of the dialectic arc that emphasizes a demand-for-work or overuse of clinician empathy that Marsha Linehan outlined in her approach to the treatment of borderline personality disorders (1993). As regards SOST, I think there exists an offender-victim dialectic. It is easy to have empathy for victims. Conversely, it is easy to have contempt for perpetrators of sexual abuse. Providers of SOST often struggle with this dichotomy. Most navigate it well. For the clinician working within the SOST context with a client who is both victim and offender, the demands are more challenging. The solution is critical thinking and ethical reasoning.

Charlie I

Charlie's parents found a competent, well-respected criminal defense attorney who sent him to my mentor, Dr. White, for an evaluation. The lawyer wanted to know what kind of risk Charlie might present to the community if he was released on bail. If the risks were acceptable, then treatment would be recommended.

Dr. White was puzzled by Charlie's case. Unlike most "stranger danger" offenses, Charlie's were crude, public, and verified by witnesses. On the surface, his offenses were negligible when compared to Dr. White's usual referrals. Charlie had no prior history of sexually deviant behavior and could not articulate any credible fantasies that focused on young boys. Instead, they were vague and impressionistic. If there is such a thing as a "deviant sexual fantasy narrative," then this one was not. Charlie insisted that he was heterosexual and explained the paraphernalia in a plausible fashion. The knife and bungee cords were for kayaking (he was an accomplished kayaker) and the gloves and Vaseline were for digitally penetrating his girlfriend. Charlie had a learning disability that made him a literal processor of information. When his health teacher said that preventing HIV transmission involved condoms and certain lubrications, Charlie understood that to mean he needed such protection on his hands, too.

My first session with Charlie was frustrating, despite his superficial cooperation. He appeared on time without his parents. He was dressed casually and was polite and friendly. He was a good-looking older adolescent, somewhat shorter than average in height, athletic but stocky. We began by reviewing Dr. White's report and the discovery material.

"So Charlie," I asked,

> you told Dr. White that you only like girls. If that's so, what sense do you make out of what you did? Many straight guys discover they like girls by messing around with boys when they are young. That's usually done in private. You groped two boys in full, public view. You know yourself better than I do. What do you think?

Charlie shrugged his shoulders, looked at me and flashed a disarmingly open and friendly smile. I asked, "Have you ever fantasized about young boys?," referring to the two fantasies he told Dr. White. Charlie offered the same vague, impressionistic fantasies to me. First he recalled a dream where he was on a beach watching a boy of 9 or 10 playing on the sand. He claimed the dream aroused him, but not enough to serve as a masturbation fantasy. The second fantasy was also from a dream, according to Charlie. There may have been a fantasy while awake, but he could not recall the details. When asked how often he masturbated to fantasies involving boys or men, his denial was adamant—well, adamant for him: "nope."

I asked him about his relationship with his girlfriend. How often did they have sex? "Never." How often do you mess around with each other? "Sometimes." When you do mess around, what do you do? "Just stuff. You know . . ." "No, Charlie—I really don't know. Is sex difficult for you to discuss?" "No, I don't mind talking about it." I found him elusive. Yes, he answered my questions but would not elaborate, even if I made my questions specific or encouraged him to tell me more. After several more rounds of questions I learned that his girlfriend broke up with him because of his arrest. "I'm sorry to hear that, Charlie—do you miss her? I mean, especially now with everything going on . . ." "No, we weren't very serious." Interviewing him was like trying to nail Jell-O to the wall. I made a point of trying to explore what it meant that his offenses occurred only one day after his 18th birthday. That also bore no fruit. "Just bad luck, I guess." I hunkered down for a slog, not yet aware of the prescience of his reply. I doubt that he recognized the implications of his response either.

Stigma, Briefly

Stigma as a method of social control dates far back. References to stigma may be found in Nathanial Hawthorne's *The Scarlet Letter*. Hester Prynne is convicted of adultery under Puritan law. She bears a child as the product of a single moment of desire with the revered local minister. She keeps the identity of her lover a secret in spite of intense pressure to reveal his identity. Part of her sentence involves wearing a scarlet-colored letter "A" on her clothes. In this passage, Hester is in the market-place following a particularly successful sermon given by her former paramour:

> While Hester stood in that tragic circle of ignominy, where the stunning cruelty of her sentence seemed to have fixed her forever, the admirable preacher was looking down from his sacred pulpit upon an audience whose very inmost spirits had yielded to his control. The sainted minister in the church! The woman of the scarlet letter in the market place! What imagination would have been irreverent enough to surmise that the same scorching stigma was on them both!
>
> *(1850/2003, p. 221)*

This passage reveals the inherent social violence that stigma confers to individuals. Hester's life, although an isolated one, can contain dignity because she has nothing left to lose. By refusing to reveal her lover's identity she chooses to retain some control over her life, thereby frustrating the community's effort to shame both her and unknown other person.

Sociologist Erving Goffman defines stigma as a term "used to refer to an attribute that is deeply discrediting" the stigmatized person "is thus reduced in our minds from a whole and usual person to a tainted and discredited one" (1963, p. 3). As stated in the title of his classic *Stigma: Notes on the Management of Spoiled Identity*, Goffman describes the various processes through which society and its agents use stigma to manage the unwanted other.

How stigma is bestowed is based on the historical setting in which it is used. The following passage tells that stigma is a cruel relic of an unenlightened pre-modern era:

> With knives and branding irons, the ancient Greeks would slice and burn criminals and traitors to denote their immorality or lack of fitness for regular society. Such a mark was called a "stigma," and an individual bearing a stigma was to be discredited, scorned and avoided. . . . To stigmatize an individual is to *define* in terms of (their) negative attribute. . . . Most researchers of stigma note that the process of stigmatization has a long history and is cross-culturally ubiquitous.
>
> *(Neuberg, Smith, & Asher, 2003, p. 31)*

In this passage, Neuberg, Smith, and Asher tell how the ancient Greeks used physical marks on offenders. Brutal and bodily stigma has no place in the ethos of our contemporary world. In the 21st century we do not use branding irons or tattoos to communicate stigma. We use information technology. Information about anyone's background is easily available online for free (if one knows where to look) or for a minor fee. We have the internet to tell us whom we can scorn and discredit.

Several decades prior to the emergence of the internet, Goffman (1963) describes how stigma is communicated through various forms of information control:

> Apparently in middle class circles today, the more there is about the individual that deviates in an undesirable direction from what might have been expected to be true of him, the more he is obliged to volunteer information about himself, even though the cost to him of candor may have increased proportionately. . . . Here the right to reticence seem earned only by having nothing to hide. It seems that in order to handle his personal identity it will be necessary for the individual to know whom he owes much information and to whom he owes very little—even though in all cases he may be obliged to refrain from telling an "outright" lie.
>
> *(p. 64)*

This places the offender in a double bind in which they are leveraged to participate in their own stigmatization. They cannot pass a routine background check; if they reveal their status on a job application they will not even get to the background check. The offender can be easily known because their identities are recorded on state and federal registration sites on the internet.

Sex offenders, however, are deviant. They engage in taboo-breaking criminal behavior that often harms those less powerful. The use of stigma against them is to be expected. Societal deviance results from collective social agreement. A pedophile may be secretly deviant as well as societally deviant if the community knew about his secret life. If urges are acted upon and he is apprehended, the pedophile (per psychiatric diagnosis) becomes a sex offender. At that point he is a situational deviant. The criminal act leads to prosecution, conviction, and the application of the label "sex offender." This is acceptable assuming a just and effective legal system. But what if the prosecution is false and leads to a false conviction? Or, what happens if the prosecution leads to a wrong or unjust, but not false, conviction? The label sticks, even if the person is acquitted or found to be innocent at a later time. Once the situational stigma exists, it becomes the property of society (Falk, 2001).

The question I want to address has to do with complexity and justice. As I will describe later in this chapter, not all criminal acts are volitional or committed by someone with the intent of exploiting another person or persons. In the introduction I made reference to the dimension of stigma called controllability of cause. What if someone's aberrant, taboo-breaking behavior could be understood in another, perhaps more humanistic context? Would that mitigate situational stigma or fine-tune it to take into consideration every aspect of the situational context? Or is stigma such a blunt instrument that contextual factors are irrelevant? Conversely, maybe we have become too civilized with respect to how we stigmatize. While it is true that internet registries do not maim or physically mark offenders, they do violence to their identity. This includes those who sincerely wish to reform as well as those who have been reformed. Information on the internet is permanent.

Because of sex offender registry laws, many sex offenders live under a panoptic gaze.[2] They never know who knows about them at any given time. Under federal law, all states must maintain an online internet registry that contain a photograph of the offender, the crime(s) committed and often the offender's home address. These registries are easily accessible to the public because they are intended for public use. In New Jersey, real estate agents are required to inform potential homebuyers if a moderate or high-risk offender lives in the neighborhood. All states require that offenders register with local police on a regular basis, and many states have some form of "supervision for life" that is administered by parole officers. These measures are of dubious utility to the community and hinder the offender's ability to find housing or employment (Levenson, 2007).

Offenders committed to preventing recidivism carry the double burden of having to monitor their own (potential) urges and their fear that they might violate some bureaucratic condition of their lifetime parole. People assume that once a sentence has been concluded, a criminal offender is allowed to return to his or her previous status, their debt to society paid in full. In principle, it is only fair to offer a second chance. But in practice, all sex offenders and ex-felons in general are subject to information control, especially when it comes to background checks and internet registries (Tewksbury & Lees, 2007). The effect of an invisible scarlet letter truly does violence to the life space of those who "wear" it.

The Role of Ethical Reasoning and Critical Thinking

Social work is a transdisciplinary profession. We study the humanities and the social sciences. Some work settings demand a mastery of legal or medical knowledge. I propose two additional realms of knowledge for clinical social workers. The first requires the study of biomedical ethics.[3] If a counselor, psychologist, or clinical social worker provides a diagnosis or a procedure code, they are working in the medical model. Therefore, biomedical ethics can come into play.

Biomedical ethics offer three major models of decision-making: deontology (principles based), consequential utilitarianism, or virtues. Each model addresses the four principles of biomedical ethics from their unique vantage. Those four principles are beneficence (do good), non-maleficence (do not harm), respect for autonomy, and justice. Ethical reasoning in clinical social work focuses on deontology, or the rules that determine what can't be done and what should be done. But I argue that ethics can help clinicians decide what can be done in equal or higher contrast to what should not be done. Everything a clinician does has ethical as well as clinical implications. Our ethics are reflected from the theories we practice to the populations we favor. Even our smallest interventions reveal our ethical philosophies.

Most clinical social workers begin their careers as deontologists. The problem with deontology, which assumes that an unwanted outcome can be countenanced if the rules were followed, is that it serves the clinician more than the client. Deontology, in short, is about professional practice risk reduction. Over time and with experience, many clinicians become consequentialists: the rules may be bent or even broken if in the end the right outcome ensues. Later in this chapter I will suggest another approach social work may want to embrace. For now I will state that when I began working with Charlie I leaned more toward deontology, but my work with him taught me the value of a consequentialist approach.

Social workers are familiar with the principles of justice and autonomy; however, in biomedical ethics justice has a broader meaning, as it emphasizes the importance of proportion. In some contexts proportion refers to the just distribution of healthcare resources; in others it refers to the just treatment of a person. Unlike law, justice in medicine is not blind. Some persons by virtue of the complexity of their case deserve care in a higher proportion—as long as the clinician's reasoning is consistent throughout all of her or his casework.

The second school of thought that should be part of clinical training is social psychology, which studies stigma and the phenomena of confirmation bias. Simply, confirmation bias is "the inappropriate bolstering of hypotheses or beliefs whose truth is in question" (Nickerson, 1998, p. 175). On macro (theory) and micro (practice) levels, confirmation bias can facilitate the labeling that drives stigma. Social psychologist Raymond A. Nickerson (1998) writes:

> The history of science contains many examples of individual scientists tenaciously holding on to favored theories long after the evidence against them had become sufficiently strong to persuade others without the same vested interests to discard them. . . . All of them can be seen as examples of the confirmation bias manifesting itself as an unwillingness to give deserved weight to evidence that tells against a favored view.
>
> *(p. 195)*

When clinicians practice with knowledge of confirmation bias, they are going beyond recognition of their subjective countertransference. They are working with a broader hypothesis that can raise questions as to whether or not stereotypes about certain persons are correct. Confirmation bias theory asks clinicians to consider whether or not their work contains double standards. The challenge for clinicians is how and when to recognize that they ought to examine their work. Reflexivity evolves with experience over time. Oftentimes, good supervision can help a clinician learn to recognize when to think critically. Such awareness can lead to an integration of ethical reasoning and clinical acumen. Sound clinical skills alone are not enough to make for good therapy. If incorporated with the ability to think critically then good therapy is enhanced. If I wanted Charlie's treatment to be as useful as possible for him, I realized that I had to

throw the SOST manual out the window. That was my first step toward con-
sequentialism. The next phase of his therapy changed the way I thought about
many things. What follows is how I learned to value critical thinking.

Charlie II

The subsequent few sessions with Charlie were uneventful unless we were talking about his interest in outdoor sports. Charlie was quite skilled at kayaking,
canoeing, and primarily mountain biking. He took pride in his capacity for measured, informed risk-taking. For example, he was able to handle a 6-foot drop
while pedaling his mountain bike at full bearing and land successfully. He had
won many awards for his cycling. Prior to his arrest he was working on getting
a sponsor so that he could compete on a higher level. I enjoyed getting to know
that part of Charlie, but I was concerned that I might be colluding with him
to avoid the unpleasant topic of his offenses. In an effort to get him to open up
more, I suggested that he join one of my offender groups. The members of that
group were much older than Charlie. None had young male victims. Like Charlie, some were still under investigation. They formed a very cohesive group of
nonjudgmental and accepting men. At 18, Charlie would be the youngest member. I wanted the group to be protective toward him, and maybe draw him out.
    One evening, after a few group meetings were under his belt, Charlie arrived
visibly distressed. He had just met with his attorney. The group feared that Charlie
was going to jail. This was an unstated but constant fear that hung over each group
member. One of the guys asked him what had happened. Charlie burst into tears and
said: "I told him the truth. He said he knew I was hiding something. I just couldn't
keep it in any more. So I told him everything." Assuming the worst, I thought that
Charlie had just confessed more offenses to his attorney. That would not have been
unusual: many offenders have hidden offenses and will shift into a confessional
mode under the right conditions. A group member asked Charlie, "What did your
lawyer think you were hiding?" With the prompt of a specific question Charlie
revealed to the group that his older brother (by four years) had been repeatedly
and aggressively molesting him since his earliest recollections. The abuse involved
penetration and was coercive. That was Charlie's secret, and he revealed it in tears.
    My reaction was immediate. It was an 'aha' moment, which, I suspect, is
what the experience of shedding confirmation bias must feel like.[4] All of my
resistance to believing that dissociation was a common response to sexual abuse
evaporated. Everything Charlie said made sense from what I had been told about
post-traumatic stress. He was recalling experiences that involved helplessness and
horror. He coped by dissociating. I wish I could report that his individual sessions became infused with new energy and that the prosecutor saw Charlie as
a victim and chose to investigate his brother instead. But that is not what happened. The catharsis had a momentary impact on Charlie that allowed him to
reveal his truth. Dissociation is a powerfully effective coping mechanism. I knew

that I had to change tack from the SOST model I was employing to something more dynamic. It was an ethical decision as much as a clinical one. I chose to see Charlie as more victim than perpetrator. This meant that I had to examine my own biases regarding dissociation and reconfigure his treatment plan. It also meant that I would have to be mindful of the offender–victim dialectic. I could give more weight to helping the victim-in-Charlie but not at the expense of minimizing that fact that he also offended. It would be in his best interest not to repeat what got him into this situation in the first place. If his dissociative coping triggered his offense, then addressing his personal history of abuse would be essential. Proportion would need to be the guiding principle, doing my best to strike a balance between the dual demands of his therapy.

Critical Thinking in Situ

In retrospect I realize that my skepticism, or my *reverse* confirmation bias regarding multiple personality disorders (MPD), caused me to reject the phenomenon of dissociation itself and how it could be used as a defensive mechanism or as a coping strategy. Charlie's revelation changed all of that. I saw firsthand that dissociation and its more metaphysical manifestation, MPD, were two very different phenomena. But, his case brought trouble to the way I had been trained to conceptualize and treat sex offenders. I sought out supervision from a psychologist who understood dissociation. He had treated a number of cases similar to Charlie's. He helped me to integrate SOST with an approach that addressed Charlie's post-traumatic stress disorder (PTSD).

Supervision taught me to examine my biases, not my countertransference. For one, I believed that if offenders had an exclusive history of homosexual offenses against minors, they could learn to be attracted to older males. If they targeted adolescents with secondary sex characteristics, that would especially hold true. At that time in my career I was interested in John Money's theory of "love maps" (1988).[5] Essentially, Money proposed that our patterns of arousal are either 'normophilic' (with love) or 'paraphilic' (cleaved from love). Arousal and erotic associations were shaped and conditioned by childhood experiences, both traumatic as well as random and idiosyncratic. I believed that what was learned could be unlearned. I saw arousal as a form of appetite and hypothesized that new appetites could be acquired. Once that was accomplished, I believed they could "become" gay; I was not ignoring the issue of orientation.

To test my hypothesis, I used standard relapse prevention and victim empathy strategies but integrated a gay affirming approach into the treatment. I had training in sexual arousal reconditioning and began to incorporate erotic homosexual material into the exercises. Also, I put offenders with male victims together in a separate therapy group from heterosexual offenders. This went against what other specialists did, but I was trying to remove as much homophobic bias as possible from the treatment of male target offenders.

At that time I believed that homosexual offenders could shed one stigmatized identity for another that at least offered community. Social psychologist Gerhard Falk might say that homosexuality, expressed as gay identity, would reflect simple societal stigma (2001). I thought that perhaps some of my clients were trying to avoid societal stigma by passing as heterosexuals. That passing gave them access to young males. Passing functioned to arrest their psychosexual development. By not acquiring a more age-appropriate sexual appetite they got stuck in an attraction to minors. Ironically, being apprehended earned them the worse, situational stigma—the form of stigma I assumed they wanted to avoid. In my mind I reasoned that their stigma could simply be reversed to the societal version, one that could be coped with more easily and reduce the risk of recidivism.

What I failed to grasp was that I was reasoning within the dimension of controllability of causes. When I realized that Charlie was not in control of the causes of his behavior, nor of his behavior itself on the day he offended, I began to see the complexity of his case. Charlie did not have a shred of homosexual or even pedophilic arousal. My naïve notions regarding sexual orientation withered on the vine when confronted with the power of dissociation.

Charlie III

Shortly after the group session, I reviewed the discovery material again. I noticed that there were about four hours in between the first and second offenses. I asked Charlie how much time he thought had elapsed between the two incidents. His response was "about a half hour." That got my attention. If he were dissociating, he would have lost track of time. I asked him again about the fact that his offenses occurred one day after he turned 18. Except this time I asked, "what happened in the day or two before you offended?" Charlie answered that he had just learned that his brother had flunked out of college and would be returning home soon to live with the family. He did not think he could reveal the incest to his parents, so by offending he functionally, albeit unconsciously, placed himself in a situation where the truth had to come out. He admitted that he was still afraid of the power his brother had over him.

Over time Charlie would tell me everything, but not immediately and not entirely before he was sentenced. He was still using avoidance and dissociation; confessional catharsis only works briefly. What I learned in the short term, however, was enough to build on. His was a tale of neglect and terror. I found some of the details gruesome. I did not want those images in my head. But in the sessions where he would reveal details of his abuse I practiced how to listen to a war story: sit still, don't lean backward or forward, avoid any expression of voyeuristic interest or repellence, and above all just listen and keep eye contact.

I characterize his tale as one of neglect because most of the assaults happened in the home while one or both parents were present. One of Charlie's early, clear memories was about something he witnessed. He recalled his brother and another boy his brother's age attempting to insert golf balls into the anus of a 4-year-old boy. In supervision I was taught the importance of pulling for details, the goal being to bring dissociated emotional memory to the fore, where it could be reprocessed and mastered. I asked Charlie if he was afraid it would happen to him, thinking he was ready to trust me enough to push through his haze and provide more detail. But he could not recall much more, and I was reluctant to press the issue. Another recollection was that his mother entered his bedroom when Chris and he were in flagrante. Nothing was ever said. Later, during a family session, his mother sadly whispered something to the effect of "boys will be boys." Charlie would report such recollections only when he was ready and without dramatic affect. Typically he would describe them in a superficial, matter-of-fact manner. He knew that he felt terror but could not recall what terror felt like. "I guess I felt numb," said Charlie. Like most people with PTSD, he split his emotional memory apart from his factual memory.

I continued to struggle with my biases, however. At times I was concerned about whether or not I was the right therapist for Charlie. I did not believe that I had in me what my colleagues who treated adult survivors of abuse had in them. For one, they felt a unique, singular empathy toward adult survivors of sexual abuse. My beliefs were more neutral and objective. During graduate school, I worked with World War II veterans who had been prisoners of the Germans. That exposure to post-traumatic stress was quite instructive. I easily could have adopted a belief that war-related imprisonment is the worst horror, but the POW camp survivors themselves taught me that there is no hierarchy of horror. While listening to these men describe their experiences in group therapy, I learned that no one category of trauma trumps another. Such beliefs impede healing.

Briefly I considered dropping his case, but I could not. The issue was Charlie's age. To me, 18 was still developmentally adolescent. I was unable to ignore his abuse history and its potential relationship to his offense. His memories were still fresh enough to be credible. As a therapist who worked with perpetrators, I did not doubt that the abuse itself was real. Ultimately I accepted the challenge to approach his therapy from the perspective that he was a victim who happened to offend reactively to his own history of abuse. Through supervision I learned his offense functioned as a cry for help. I wanted to give him that help, believing that addressing his own abuse history would reduce or eliminate a powerful relapse trigger.

I was also concerned about Charlie's brother, Chris. Allegedly, he was a serious repetitive perpetrator. A part of me thought that Chris should be my client, not Charlie. After all, Chris fit the profile of the kind of offender I had been trained to treat. Mostly, however, if I were treating Chris I would not have to care as much. Admittedly I was not allowing for the possibility that Chris too was a victim. But by then I had begun to feel protective of Charlie. I saw him as the victim. By allowing the breakthrough that challenged my skepticism and bias regarding dissociation, my experience of Charlie changed. I admired his willingness to trust, despite his own experiences being abused by an older male.

I conducted some family sessions, sans Chris, but it would be a few years before Charlie's parents could grasp what had happened. An immediate acceptance that one child harmed another is a lot to expect from parents. Also, the family sessions were just too difficult for Charlie, his mother, and his father. His parents were being asked, in effect, to choose one child over another.

In my individual work with Charlie, I focused on offering him a safe, therapeutic relationship. As our alliance grew, so did my confidence. In reviewing his case in preparation for this chapter, I was reminded of a theory from biomedical ethics. Good treatment involves comfort with power. In my experience, even experienced professional social workers seem uncomfortable with the idea that they have power. Yet, for many of our clients we are primary in their lives. They attribute us with the power to help. Physician and ethicist Howard Brody postulates in his book published in 2003, *The Healer's Power*, that physicians ought to feel confident to own their power, share it with the patient and aim it at the disease together. Many social work readers might think that Brody's concept is another way to describe the partnership between client and clinician. But I believe Brody is expanding the notion of partnership by acknowledging the power held by the healer.

Perhaps clinical social workers ought to hold the same notion. Confidence and power, when ethically utilized, can be an essential component of a therapeutic relationship. I maintain that without the confidence to acknowledge our power as clinicians, a vacuum is created that makes us vulnerable to confirmation bias. Instead of trusting our own experience, observations and wisdom, we may depend upon external variables such as zeitgeist and outcome-driven approaches to inform our treatment. This is one way in which our work becomes manualized. As my confidence in working without the manual grew, I think Charlie's self-confidence grew as well.

A Question of Justice

With work in individual therapy, Charlie was able to establish his own plan for safety and he overcame his fear of his brother. Meanwhile, his criminal case was stalled. Uncertainty and false hope of avoiding incarceration began to eat away at Charlie. The prosecutor had just lost two highly visible jury trials in which the alleged sex offenders were acquitted. He was not going to take a loss with Charlie, even though it could have been judicious to at least investigate his brother. There were other victims, albeit older by then, in the neighborhood. Once they learned about Charlie's offenses, they began vandalizing the family's home. The police would not respond. Still, no attempt was made to pursue his brother's alleged crimes. Moreover, there was a realistic possibility that a known offender who had lived in the neighborhood may have victimized Charlie's brother, but Chris was not talking. If the prosecutor wanted to protect children, how come he did not investigate beyond Charlie? I speculated that the prosecutor wanted a win so much that he failed to recognize his own confirmation bias.

Charlie's attorney made every attempt possible to mount an aggressive defense. The impact on Charlie was to feel tortured by hope. This compounded his trauma. It became difficult for Charlie to work on past traumatic injury while he was experiencing psychological and emotional trauma as a result of the glacial pace of the justice system. Charlie's mountain biking became more and more risky. He misjudged a jump, fell, and broke his collarbone. He admitted to a passive death wish and promised to ride more safely. By then we had developed a solid therapeutic alliance and our sessions were more about support and coping.[6]

Eventually, Charlie cracked under the pressure. He was caught smoking cannabis with a friend on public school property. With no other maneuvers (or funds) available, Charlie's attorney recommended that Charlie accept a plea bargain that assumed exposure to incarceration. The drug charges were dropped—a small concession.

I felt helpless and so did his attorney, who admitted to me that Charlie's case was the most upsetting defense in his career so far. He was a former prosecutor and a father. He understood what was at stake. After sentencing, Charlie was evaluated at a state prison that houses a sex offender–specific treatment program (SOTP). If Charlie met the criteria of "repetitive and compulsive," he would be eligible to serve his sentence there, where he would receive treatment.

Admission criteria to the SOTP are simple. Based on the fact that he groped *two* boys in one afternoon, he was found repetitive. Based on the interviewer's review of discovery materials—the House-Person-Tree Test, a standard psychological inventory and an interview—he found Charlie compulsive. Charlie served almost three years at the SOTP, followed by lifetime parole supervision and registration. He was more verbal and alert after his incarceration than I would have predicted. He said that he did listen to everything I tried to teach him about dissociation but just could not express how he was processing the material. He stated that he knew he had used dissociation in the past. After prison he simply could not employ that strategy any more. He replaced it with stoic resilience.

I continue to see Charlie. I can attest to the fact that he no longer dissociates, which is not always merciful. He feels everything he could not feel before. Charlie has bad luck. I believe in that the unconscious mind has a capacity to grant secret, self-defeating wishes. I also believed in randomness. Attempting to locate Charlie's problems on his subconscious desires, or even conscious ones, for that matter, is something I would have done in my more skeptical days prior to meeting him. Then I believed in controllability of cause. Faulting people like Charlie for having a life of misfortune is an attempt to distance ourselves from the horror we feel when we discover how little control we have over that which happens to us.

When compared to offenses perpetrated by fixated or serial offenders, I think Charlie's were nominal and that his punishment was excessive. I have struggled with the duality Charlie's case represents. As a clinician with experience treating perpetrators, I believe without reservation that the impact of sexual abuse should not be minimized. I am certain that the two boys he groped were frightened.

But, Charlie was caught before worse could happen, and consequently, his victims could be assured that justice would prevail and that they would be safe. More harm was done to Charlie than he ever caused to another person. From an ethical standpoint, I do not believe that the principle of justice was served. Justice requires proportion. In my view, the principle of proportion should carry greater weight in complex cases like Charlie's. By offering him a therapeutic alliance that was accepting, supportive and positive, I was trying to balance out the injustice he was facing and bring some proportion to his life situation. That exemplifies the way in which clinical and ethical reasoning intertwine. I believe that a just sentence would have allowed Charlie to remain in the community with probation supervision and continue treatment. I would also pose this question: is it even ethical to treat someone like Charlie as a sex offender, legally as well as clinically? I thought not, and so I did not.

Conclusion

When I began this case study, I wanted to make the argument that critical thinking and ethical reasoning could actually mitigate stigma. But the more I read about stigma and its history and the more I reflected on my work with sex offenders, it became clear that stigma as a social force is far more powerful than anything good clinical work can mitigate. Given how far back references to stigma can be found in the historical record, it occurred to me stigma may serve another function in addition to social control. Stigma might also result from a collective expression of fear of that which we believe we cannot manage as individuals. When the courts (the most authoritative body of society) are perceived to respond inadequately to heinous behavior, stigma takes charge. The social impulse to use stigma to manage those who frighten, confuse, or threaten us surpasses whatever technology we have at hand. In a postindustrial and postmodern world, we do not have to brand people or mark them. Information technology can accomplish that for us by keeping people out of the workforce or out of our backyards. I think we create technology whose use is beyond our moral grasp. I also believe that stigma itself is immoral. When combined, information technology and stigma devastates the individual.

As a method for informing the treatment of the stigmatized, I proposed that critical thinking and ethical reasoning are as useful as understanding countertransference or following a manual skillfully. As clinicians we are trained and expected to pay attention to our countertransference when working with people. I contend that such a task is easier than recognizing, acknowledging, and addressing confirmation bias. The latter requires that we look at whether or not we are wrong and then ask for supervision. That can be hard to do because it requires us to be aware of feeling dissonant in the first place. That has to be self-generated. In retrospect, the beliefs I held when I began seeing Charlie were naïve. I wanted to use my process with this client as an example of how to overcome confirmation bias. Although this may sound very basic to many readers, I hope to convince other clinical social workers to use ethical reasoning and critical thinking in their therapeutic work with all clients.

Finally, helping to reduce the impact of stigma on clients ought to be of particular concern to social workers. The National Association of Social Workers (NASW) *Code of Ethics* claims social justice as one of its principles. While NASW does not state explicitly that social justice requires proportion, the principle as written states that social justice efforts should be focused on discrimination, "equality of opportunity and meaningful participation in decision making for all people" (2008). This implies recognition of proportion, especially with respect to "equality of opportunity and meaningful participation." Few ex-offenders currently enjoy these basic human rights. In addition, NASW principles also emphasize the "dignity and worth of the person." Specifically, social workers should be "cognizant of their dual responsibility to clients and to the broader society . . . [and] seek to resolve conflicts between clients' interests and the broader society's interests in a socially responsible manner" (2008). To me, this sums up our obligation as social workers to the principle of justice. The challenge is to put those words into practice.

Close Reading Questions

1. According to Healy, why is biomedical ethics an important subject for social workers?
2. What do you make of Healy's use of *The Scarlet Letter* to help define stigma? What other definitions of stigma do you find important here?
3. Healy writes that "Faulting people like Charlie for having a life of misfortune is an attempt to distance ourselves from the horror we feel when we discover how little control we have over that which happens to us." What does this sentence mean to you? How does it change some of the thought you had before reading this case study?

Prompts for Writing

1. How does Goffman's (1963) definition of stigma change in the online era? How might Olivia, from Busfield's case study, be struggling with stigma in the online era? What is the relationship between how stigma affects Charlie's identity and Olivia's identity?
2. Describe a just ending to Charlie's case. What was particularly unjust about this case, if anything, in your opinion? And how does it compare to the outcome of Sarah's case as presented by De La Cruz?
3. Look up current statistics on whether or not most sex offenders report that they themselves have been victims of sexual abuse. How does the information you found relate to the case of Charlie?

Notes

1. Elizabeth Loftus's research has been credited with debunking the idea of recovered memory.
2. The Panopticon was a prison model influenced by philosopher Jeremy Bentham and the Quakers. It was designed to foster meditative self-reflection. Inmates were not permitted contact with each other. They were monitored from a tower built in the center of the prison called the Panopticon. Guards were stationed in the tower at various times looking at different sections of the yard and individual cells. If they saw violations to the no-contact rule, they would remove the inmates to even more solitary seclusion. In the end many inmates went mad. It seems that not knowing when they were being observed drove them over the edge. The power is in the hands of the watcher, not the watched.
3. A chapter of this length does not have the scope to adequately address the magnitude of what biomedical ethics can offer clinical social workers. Tom Beauchamp and James Childress offer a comprehensive source in their book, *The Principles of Biomedical Ethics* (2001). Readers simply have to generalize from a medical to a mental health context in order to tap their wisdom.
4. I include this critical incident in Charlie's treatment to illustrate how shedding a confirmation bias might be experientially different from a clinician's experience of countertransference. Typically, clinicians try to induce breakthroughs in their clients, not in themselves. Had I not allowed myself to consider what this new information meant, I would not have been able to offer him a true therapeutic alliance.
5. My interest in Money's ideas existed prior to the revelations that discredited him. That story, as told in John Colapinto's *As Nature Made Him: The Boy That Was Raised as a Girl* (2000), is a prime example of the dangers of confirmation bias.
6. Years later Charlie would tell me that his relationship with me helped correct his damaged relationship with his brother. He called me the "older brother he wished he had had." Had I stuck to the manual, I doubt that Charlie would have had such a corrective experience.

References

Beauchamp, T. L., & Childress, J. F. (2001). *The principles of biomedical ethics.* New York: Oxford University Press.

Brody, H. (2003). *The healer's power.* New Haven, CT: Yale University Press.

Colapinto, J. (2000). *As nature made him: The boy who was raised as a girl.* New York: HarperCollins.

Corrigan, P. W. (2000). Mental health stigma as solution: Implications for research methods and attitude change. *Clinical Psychology: Science and Practice, 7*(1), 48–67. Retrieved from http://webcast.und.edu/health-wellness/healthy-und/mental-health-stigma-fawn.pdf

Falk, G. (2001). *Stigma: How we treat outsiders.* Amherst, NY: Prometheus Books.

Goffman, E. (1963). *Stigma: Notes on the management of spoiled identity.* Englewood Cliffs, NJ: Prentice Hall.

Hanson, R. K., & Bussiere, M. T. (1998). Predicting relapse: A meta-analysis of sexual offender recidivism studies. *Journal of Consulting and Clinical Psychology, 66*(2), 348. Retrieved from www.csor-home.org/wp-content/uploads/2014/01/Predicting-Relapse-A-Meta-analysis-1998.pdf

Hawthorne, N. (1850/2003). *The scarlet letter.* New York: Bantam Classic.

Laws, D. R., & Ward, T. (2006). When one size doesn't fit all: The reformulation of relapse prevention. In *Sexual offender treatment: Controversial issues* (pp. 241–254). Chichester: Wiley.

Levenson, J. S., D'Amora, D. A., & Hern, A. L. (2007). Megan's law and its impact on community re-entry for sex offenders. *Behavioral Sciences & the Law, 25*(4), 587–602. https://doi.org/10.1002/bsl.770

Linehan, M. (1993). *Cognitive-behavioral treatment of borderline personality disorder*. New York: Guilford Press.

Loftus, E., & Ketcham, K. (1996). *The myth of repressed memory: False memories and allegations of sexual abuse*. New York: St. Martin's Press.

Mann, R. E. (2009). Sex offender treatment: The case for manualization. *Journal of Sexual Aggression, 15*(2), 121–131. https://doi.org/10.1080/13552600902907288

Marlatt, G. A., & Gordon, J. R. (1985). *Relapse prevention: Maintenance strategies in the treatment of addictive behaviors*. New York: Guilford Press.

Marshall, W. L., & Laws, D. R. (2003). A brief history of behavioral and cognitive behavioral approaches to sexual offender treatment, part 2: The modern era. *Sexual Abuse: A Journal of Research and Treatment, 15*(2), 93–120. https://doi.org/10.1177/s107906320301500202

Marshall, W. L., & Marshall, L. E. (2007). The utility of the random controlled trial for evaluating sexual offender treatment: The gold standard or an inappropriate strategy? *Sexual Abuse: A Journal of Research and Treatment, 19*(2), 175–191. https://doi.org/10.1007/s11194-007-9046-3

Miller, W. R., & Rollnick, S. (1991). *Motivational interviewing*. New York: Guilford Press.

Money, J. (1988). *Lovemaps: Sexual/erotic health and pathology, paraphilia, and gender transposition*. Buffalo, NY: Prometheus Books.

National Association of Social Workers, Washington, DC. (2008). *Code of ethics of the National Association of Social Workers*. Retrieved from www.socialworkers.org/pubs/code/code.asp

Neuberg, S. L., Smith, D. M., & Asher, T. (2003). Why people stigmatize: Toward a biocultural framework. In T. F. Heatherton, R. E. Kleck, M. R. Hebel, & J. G. Hull (Eds.), *The social psychology of stigma* (pp. 31–61). New York: Guilford Press.

Nickerson, R. S. (1998). Confirmation bias: A ubiquitous phenomenon in many guises. *Review of General Psychology, 2*(2), 175. Retrieved from http://psy2.ucsd.edu/~mckenzie/nickersonConfirmationBias.pdf

Sample, L. L., & Bray, T. M. (2003). Are sex offenders dangerous? *Criminology & Public Policy, 3*(1), 59–82. Retrieved from http://heinonline.org.proxy.libraries.rutgers.edu/HOL/Page?handle=hein.journals/crpp3&page=59&collection=journals#67

Semple, J. (1993). *Bentham's prison: A study of the Panopticon penitentiary*. Oxford: Oxford University Press.

Seto, M. C., Marques, J. K., Harris, G. T., Chaffin, M., Lalumière, M. L., Miner, M., & Quinsey, V. (2008). Good science and progress in sex offender treatment are intertwined. *Sexual Abuse: A Journal of Research and Treatment, 20*, 247–255. https://doi.org/10.1177/1079063208317733

Stokes, S. D., Berg, M., Cobbina, J., Huebner, B., & Valentine, D. C. (2006). Sex offender risk assessment. *Public Policy Publications (MU)*. Retrieved from https://mospace.umsystem.edu/xmlui/bitstream/handle/10355/2608/SexOffenderRiskAssessment.pdf?sequence=1

Tewksbury, R., & Lees, M. B. (2007). Perceptions of punishment how registered sex offenders view registries. *Crime & Delinquency, 53*(3), 380–407. https://doi.org/10.1177/0011128706286915

Watters, E. (2010). *Crazy like us: The globalization of the American psyche*. New York: Free Press/Simon and Schuster.

Witt, P. H. (2000). A practitioner's view of risk assessment: The HCR-20 and SVR-20. *Behavioral Sciences & the Law, 18*(6), 791–798. https://doi.org/10.1002/bsl.420

4

SEXUAL ABUSE, THE THERAPEUTIC ALLIANCE, AND THERAPIST SELF-DISCLOSURE

Stephen Oreski

Pre-reading Questions

1. Do you have any assumptions about how sexual abuse might affect children differently based on their genders or sexuality? How might factors of gender and/or sexuality influence the way victims of sexual abuse narrativize their traumas and identities?
2. What is therapist self-disclosure? Can you think of an example from your fieldwork or from your other experience when you wanted to self-disclose in order to help a client? What amount of self-disclosure is appropriate, if any?
3. How do you imagine healthy and/or professional boundaries between a social work clinician and a client in creating a therapeutic alliance? Why do you think that establishing a therapeutic alliance would be especially important when dealing with cases of trauma? Give an example from your experience.

Sitting on the courtroom bench, I am suddenly aware of the beating of my heart. Not the normal beat, not even the one you feel when you have just barely missed hitting the car that comes out of nowhere, or when you trip and toss a carton of eggs into the air, deftly defying the laws of physics by catching them with one hand while balancing on two toes. But the heartbeat that is so loud, it feels like it is coming out of your ears and forces all your other senses into the background. I turn and look around, half expecting those nearby to have heard it, and I find myself reaching for the edge of the bench. I glance down and notice that the bench has a comforting smoothness, a velvety roundness where the varnish has been worn away. That worn oak bench bears witness to those who have come to this courtroom seeking justice, a hand-tooled memorial that anchors the insecurity of these moments, and is somehow consoling in this time of uncertainty.

The judge enters and my comfort is gone, as I am forced to stand and release my hold on that oak bench. I look toward Kevin, having worked with him as his psychotherapist these past 18 months; I can gauge his affect. He is scared. The presence of his mother Lisa, and his aunt and uncle, as well as myself, do little to ameliorate the intensity of this moment. It is the moment he would come face-to-face with his cousin, Manny, who had sexually abused him for 5 years. Two uniformed court officers, guns holstered at their sides, enter the courtroom and are immediately followed by a short, overweight, and unkempt man wearing orange prison garb. Hands and feet shackled, he shuffles slowly toward the lone seat in front of him. He sits down as the clang of the metal punctures the silence. Looking toward Kevin, I can see him looking at Manny from the corner of his eye. He is frozen, not even blinking his eyes; gripping his hand, white-knuckled, his breathing quickens, as he begins to tremble. Somewhere in the courtroom, I hear someone sobbing. It's Kevin's mother, Lisa, who has collapsed onto the bench, unable to stand, her face turned into her sister's shoulder. It is a tearless sob. She no more tears to cry, so Kevin cries for her, tears streaming down his cheeks without a sound.

The judge begins to read the charges. He finishes and turns toward us, asking if the victims want to make a statement prior to sentencing. Lisa stands, and begins to respond to the judge's request, but cannot find words to adequately express the pain of a mother who could not protect her child. She lives with that demon daily. As a survivor of sexual violence herself, it is all she can do to hold it together, so she shakes her head no, unable to read her statement, and remains silent. I look toward Kevin. Slowly he rises from the bench, and with the weight of uncertainty strapped to his shoulders moves toward the microphone. Alone with a piece of ruled loose-leaf paper crumpled and held tightly in his left hand, he looks all the more younger, as if Manny's presence had somehow transformed him into that vulnerable 8-year-old who just wanted to learn how to fish. I can feel the heaviness of his silence—everything has stopped except the ticking of the clock, taking me back to my first meeting with Kevin, almost two years ago, and how I came to be part of his story and his truth.

As a psychotherapist working in a private practice setting, I have come to recognize that telling one's story is an important aspect to developing a secure and organized sense of self. McAdams (2011) views psychotherapy as a major venue for the telling of stories, stating:

> Therapists work with clients to re-story their lives, often aiming to find more positive and growth-affirming ways to narrate and understand emotionally negative events . . . through repeated interactions with others, stories about personal experiences are processed, edited reinterpreted, retold,

and subjected to a range of social and discursive influences, as the story-teller gradually develops a broader and more integrative narrative identity.

(p. 236)

Developing a narrative of one's life allows an individual to piece together threads of experience into a pattern, weaving together groups of discrete experiences with all their complexities into a cohesive tapestry of self. However, creating this tapestry of self-truths is a complex and multifaceted process, and spinning the thread of life is not without difficulty, particularly for those with experiences that are not so easily incorporated into the design of their lives (Vilenica, Shakespeare-Finch, & Obst, 2013; Tuval-Mashiach et al., 2004). Against a back-drop of an ever-changing world, greatly influenced by consumerism, technology, and a world full of many truths, traumatic experiences shatter narrative and one's sense of self in ways that are profound and life-changing. For the male survivor of sexual violence, these traumatic experiences disrupt the coherence of the dominant masculine narrative, and complicate the healing process for these men.

So What Do You Know About Football?

I moved my head down a few more inches, trying to catch a glimpse of the 14-year-old boy who sat before me slumped in the chair. It was my first meeting with Kevin, and I was hoping to at least make eye contact. Kevin slid even lower, ensuring I wouldn't see him as he pulled his black hoodie down almost to the end of his nose. He was determined. There was no way this man, this therapist, was getting in. After sitting with both him and his mother for the past 45 minutes, intently listening, as she explained the circumstances that led her to seek counseling for her son, all I could think was, *he would rather be anywhere but here.* Kevin had not moved or uttered a word as his mother shared all that had occurred over the previous 9 months, since the day that he disclosed his sexual abuse, perpetrated by his older cousin Manny. Once she had finished, I asked her to leave Kevin and me alone for a few minutes so we could speak with one another. I wanted to hear *his* story.

As I sat facing Kevin, I wondered where to begin. How could I help him tell his story? This barely 14-year-old young man who had learned that silence was a survival skill did not want to talk with anyone. *Your mother filled me in on the events of the past month.* Silence. *It must have been difficult for you to talk about those things.* Silence. *I'm glad you are here.* Silence. He pulled his black hoodie down further over his head. Silence. The only sound was the ticking of the clock, cruelly reminding me that I was getting nowhere with Kevin. I struggled. *How's school going for you?* Silence. He sat there frozen, emotionally closed, and locked. I sat there putting the pieces together in my head; more questions than answers, unsure whether I had that key. *What did you think of the Super Bowl?* He looked up—finally a response. *So what do you know about football?* This was my way in, the bridge to Kevin sharing his experience. I sat and thought for a minute about all of this, then walked through the door that Kevin had opened between us. *Did you watch the Super Bowl?* He said as he reached up and pulled the hoodie over his head, revealing a young teenager with brown hair and green eyes. A fine of layer peach fuzz covered his cheeks, interrupted by a few pimples, which had been squeezed, one too many times, in a desperate attempt to banish them from his teenage reality. He wore a Baltimore Ravens jersey, baggy sweats, and sneakers. I noticed that he was biting his nails.

As we continued to speak, I could sense a distance in our interaction and made a mental note of it. He had a blank expression. It was that state of numbness I recognized from working with other survivors of sexual violence. It is almost as if he could not allow himself to feel, to smile, to cry, because if he did, then all of *it* would come out—laid bare on the floor in front of me, this stranger, this therapist, and I would be privy to those feelings, those emotions, and those thoughts, the ones that he worked so hard to keep buried deep within. This was hard. Men aren't supposed to get hurt or talk about feelings, or challenges. So he kept it in, he kept all of it in. All in all, we spent about 30 minutes together alone that day, with Kevin agreeing, despite his initial resistance, to attend sessions weekly, every Tuesday at 4 p.m. He left the way he came in—in silence—leaving the door open behind him.

Numerous studies have shown that survivors of male childhood sexual abuse are at an increased risk for a variety of psychological impacts such as suicide, depression and anxiety, addiction, post-traumatic stress disorder (PTSD), dissociative disorders, overdeveloped avoidance response, somatoform disorder, tension reduction behaviors, and challenges with sexual identity (Alaggia & Millington, 2008; Briere & Spinazzola, 2005; Cushman, 1990). Clinical presentations can vary, and while not present in every case of sexual violence, clinicians should remain aware of the ways in which these adaptations to trauma can manifest themselves in the daily lives and coping skills of their clients. It is important for clinicians to educate themselves regarding the impact and challenges surrounding assessment and treatment of those impacted by sexual violence. As we sat across from one another, Kevin with his hoodie pulled down and me struggling to engage him, my clinical assessment might have been something other than PTSD. Kevin's initial clinical presentation was one of a defiant youth, a young man disenchanted with society and yearning for the independence, and control of their environment, that teenagers in American culture often deem as the ultimate goal of adolescence. A clinician assessing an individual challenged with addiction, eating disorder, self-injury, or compulsive or unsafe sexuality should make note of these behaviors as a possible indicator of a trauma history, often involving sexual violence (Alaggia & Kirshenbaum, 2005; Cromer & Goldsmith, 2010; Little & Hamby, 1999). Clinicians working within managed care environments, or those clinical settings that require a quick assessment, are at risk of missing those individuals, such as Kevin, who have been impacted by trauma and present with a complex array of behaviors and symptomology.

At this early stage of treatment, paramount within the clinician's mind should be the development of the therapeutic relationship. This therapeutic relationship is the foundation of the treatment, without which no healing can occur (Antoniou & Blom, 2006). Indeed, the cornerstone of treatment with a survivor of sexual violence is establishing and maintaining a safe therapeutic environment, "a major factor in ameliorating the negative effects of abuse" (Hunter, 1990). For the survivor of sexual violence, the development of a safe therapeutic relationship with a knowledgeable clinician is paramount for effective engagement and a successful outcome to treatment. The engagement process for the client, such as Kevin, can be more complex and nuanced, and require an awareness surrounding sensitive issues that might complicate or sabotage the course of treatment. These are individuals who have experienced violence, often by a person in a position of power, or perceived position of power. Therefore, this power dynamic figures greatly into the therapeutic relationship as the "experience of betrayal of trust by someone in a position of authority is so germane to their abuse" (Beutler & Hill, 1992, p. 20). As the very nature of the therapeutic relationship has a power differential in its structure, recognizing and remaining vigilant to this underlying dynamic is key. This requires the clinician to work through engagement in a conscious and deliberate way, to address the process challenges inherent within the therapeutic process and the therapist client dyad (Koehn, 2007; Mandell, 2008).

For Kevin this process involved a loosening of the locus of control within our initial sessions. From a clinical perspective, I made a conscious decision to let Kevin dictate the direction and content of our initial conversations, thus allowing him the experience of being in control of interactions with another male, something that had become unfamiliar to him after several years of abuse. Several sessions were spent engaging Kevin in discussing what interests him: his favorite sports teams and his challenges as a teenage boy. For the next month, that's all we talked about: football. But through these ongoing football discussions, Kevin began to feel safe enough to share some of his stories and what he had experienced in his 14 years of life. I came to learn much about Kevin, about who he was and how he viewed the world. Through this process he came to know me as a male who was safe, an individual who would not hurt or exploit him, someone he could relate to, and most importantly someone he could trust, thus allowing for development of a solid therapeutic relationship.

Did I Ever Tell You How My Dad Left the House?

During the second month of treatment, Kevin decided to share some information regarding his relationship with his father. I wasn't expecting this conversation; it had been several weeks since our first meeting, and talking about his father was something that Kevin avoided, quickly changing the direction of the conversation whenever I approached the topic. *No, I don't think you ever told me about that . . .*

There wasn't a time that Kevin could remember a peaceful Sunday morning. The routine was always the same, lying awake in his bedroom, looking up at his superhero posters; he would hear the front door open. Julio, Kevin's father, would try to sneak into the house without making too much noise, an almost impossible feat after a night of drinking. Julio, the youngest of seven children, was a slight man, with coarse black hair and deep brown eyes. Standing five-foot-one, he had a slender build, and unassertive demeanor, preferring to remain in the background. Emigrating from Puerto Rico as a teenager, Julio never felt at place in his new country unless he had a bottle of rum at his side, which according to Kevin was often a daily occurrence. The turn of the key in the door was all it took to wake his mother, Lisa, from her fitful sleep; after another night of waiting for Julio to return home, she had little patience left for his drinking or his women.

More often than not, Kevin witnessed the violence. He remembers his father intoxicated and fighting with his mother, he remembers plates hitting walls, and his mother sobbing on the kitchen floor. He remembers bruises on arms and legs, tears on faces, and one too many trips to the emergency room. During these fights Kevin would not leave his room. Retreating into his world of superheroes, he felt safe. Able to escape into this world of powerful figures, with their superpowers, strong sense of right and wrong, and their ability to fight back, Kevin felt a sense of safety and escape that was sorely needed.

But on this particular Sunday morning, that wasn't working. Kevin recognized the tone of his father's voice and knew it was coming. It wouldn't be long now. The cursing had started. He jumped up in bed as he heard the first slap across his mother's face. He felt the house shake as his mother struggled to get out of the path of Julio's drunken tirade. He tried harder to escape his reality, placing his head under the pillow. He said a prayer. Two prayers. Nothing was working. He rose from the bed. Taking a deep breath, he looked up at his posters and stepped out of his room and into the kitchen—right in between his parents—first with his words, then with his fist. Julio lost two teeth that day, along with his pride, and his marriage. He moved out that Sunday and life changed dramatically for Kevin and his mother.

Raising Kevin alone was a struggle for Lisa. She worked full-time as a radiology technician and overtime as a mother. Lisa was the only daughter of first-generation immigrants from Italy. A vibrant young woman with full brown wavy hair, she had bright blue eyes that had begun to lose some of their sparkle, a result of one too many years spent arguing with Julio. She was emotional and would break into tears frequently when discussing anything relating to Kevin. Coming from a traditional Italian background, family was very important to her. As the oldest of three children, she maintained a close relationship with all her family members, including her father and brother, who struggled with alcoholism. Every week the family would gather together for Sunday dinner, and Lisa would make sure that she and Kevin always attended. She worked hard to ensure that Kevin maintained his relationship with his father, although that, according to Kevin, was Saturday afternoons at a fast food restaurant, either McDonald's or Burger King, and on the rare occasion when Julio had some money, a movie. But Julio was not as consistent with his parenting obligations as he was with his drinking. Lisa would often find Kevin waiting on the front porch for his father, who more often than not was still sleeping off the previous night's binge, so she was particularly excited when Julio's father took an interest in teaching Kevin how to fish. Kevin remembers those fishing trips with his grandfather fondly.

Kevin's grandfather, a reserved, hard-working man, had moved himself, his wife, and his seven children to New York City from Puerto Rico, a promise he had made to his wife the night he asked her to marry him. A reserved man with traditional values, he took great pride in his ability to support his family, often working two or three jobs. He always found time to spend with Kevin. A churchgoing man, he never approved of Julio's love of women and rum, and often chastised him for his lack of consistency in parenting Kevin. Kevin would often reminisce about those afternoon fishing trips with his grandfather, who had become the primary male figure in his life, offering both stability and love, an attachment without the emotional turmoil Kevin had come to know as family life. Several months into the fishing lessons, Kevin's grandfather developed pancreatic cancer. The cancer progressed quickly and within four months had taken his life. Kevin grieved for months after his grandfather passed away. The following spring, a cousin of Kevin's father, Manny, offered to continue the fishing trips, and Lisa agreed, thinking it was a positive interaction with a male.

After that session when Kevin finally spoke about his father, I began to recognize the importance of my relationship with Kevin. Not only was I his psychotherapist, an individual with whom he felt he trust this information, I had become one of the primary male figures in his life, an individual Kevin could rely on and trust with his secrets.

He Made Me Try Beer

Kevin: I never liked it but Manny always tried to get me to drink it. I took a few sips, but never more than that. It was nasty. And he used to smoke this stuff. I'm not sure what it was—but he always asked if I wanted to try it but I hated smoking—so I never did. He knew I liked to watch movies—you know—I used to go with my Dad all the time—so we would do that a lot. He (Manny) had all these movies we used to watch.

Me: What kinds of movies?

Kevin: He had lots of videos for kids—you know—like Power Rangers, Anime, Harry Potter movies . . .

Kevin: One day the Power Ranger video busted, so he put on a video that freaked me out.

Me: Which video was it?

Kevin: There was no name—it was just little kids—you know . . . I mean you know of kids. Like kids doing it—fooling around . . .

Me: Doing it?

Kevin: Yeah—you know—doing it . . . like . . . sex. It was little kids having sex.

Manny began sexually abusing Kevin. This lasted for four years.

Kevin couldn't remember how many times the abuse occurred with Manny. He did remember the scenario, one that was repeated over and over again. Manny lived in the basement of his parents' home. During visits to his aunt and uncle's home, and when Manny would "take him fishing," he would find a reason for them both to go down into his basement apartment. The ritual was always the same. They would sit on his bed and talk about the day. Manny would drink beer and smoke marijuana. He would ask Kevin if he wanted to try it. He would tell Kevin he wanted to show him something, and turn on his computer, forcing him to watch child pornography. Then he would pull down his pants down.

Placed in a powerless position by the perpetrator of the violence, stripped and objectified, their sense of control and agency gone, the act of sexual violence has profound consequences for the individual, calling into question a host of questions. As Herman (1997) states,

> Traumatic events call into question basic human relationships. They breach the attachments of family, friendship, love, and community. They shatter the construction of self that is formed and sustained in relation to others. They undermine the belief systems that give meaning to human experience. They violate the victim's faith in the natural divine order and cast the victim into a state of existential crisis.
>
> *(p. 51)*

No longer assured of safety, the individual is called to renegotiate his relationship with the world, with others, himself and his own concept of truth. This upheaval, by its very nature, shatters the sense of self, causing a rupture in the cohesive quality of the individual's narrative (Lev-Wiesel, 1999; Sorsoli et al. 2008; Sorsoli, 2010). The known quality of truth and reality is altered as sexual violence shifts perspectives, moves boundaries, and narrows horizons. For the male survivor of sexual violence, their perspective of the self shifts, challenging traditional concepts of masculinity. Trying to contextualize these experiences is challenging: "Male survivors face particular challenges in resolving the conflicting experience of their childhood sexual abuse histories with the tenets of masculine socialization and expectations of relational intimacy" (Kia-Keating, Grossman, Sorsoli, & Epstein, 2005, p. 179).

Indeed, there is no metanarrative for male powerlessness, much less one that that includes sexual victimization (Platt & Freyd, 2012; Sinclair & Monk, 2005). The current construct of traditional American masculinity consists of power, physical strength, aggression, a sense of control, sexual prowess, mastery of one's environment, and a rejection of anything feminine (Trembley & Turcotte, 2005, p. 133). Gender roles reinforce these concepts, and while both the feminist and LGBTQ rights movements have shifted some gendered stereotypes, the American masculine narrative remains firmly entrenched in our culture. In order to heal and move forward, male survivors of sexual violence must somehow navigate unchartered territories and loosen the constrictive and rigid stereotypes, which have come to embody the ideals of masculinity. "Revisiting confusing, disempowering, 'feminizing' experiences may present an especially strong threat to men. Reinforcing that all children, regardless of gender, are vulnerable to victimization is an important message" (Alaggia & Millington, 2008, p. 273).

This was particularly important for Kevin. As an adolescent, Kevin was at a pivotal moment in the development of his masculine identity. Influenced by popular culture, the media, and advertising, Kevin would need to challenge the images and concepts of masculinity that personified his ideals surrounding what it was to be a man. His recovery process would require him to traverse the cultural landscape of gender as he struggled to renegotiate his masculinity as a male survivor of sexual violence. As David Lisak (2005) states, "the path to recovery winds straight through masculinity's forbidden territory: the conscious experience of those intense, overwhelming emotional states of fear, vulnerability, and helplessness" (p. 262). These emotional states fly in the face of the traditional concepts of masculinity, thereby presenting a complex endeavor to the male survivor who is called to deconstruct the masculine narrative and recreate a narrative that challenges the hegemonic masculinity that has become the dominant form of male expression in the American culture.

> Faced with such an intense conflict between the emotional legacy of abuse and the emotionally constricting dictates of their gender socialization, male victims must find some pathway to a resolution. One pathway entails the rigid adherence to masculine gender norms, a resolution which requires the forceful suppression and repression of abuse-related emotions.
>
> *(Lisak, 1996)*

Within the social construct of American masculinity, the male survivor of sexual violence has two responses to the disempowerment resulting from his experience of sexual violence. The male survivor begins to view life through these opposing contexts, thus causing a rupture in his perception of the world and forcing a change in his reality. West (2013) views this dichotomy from a Jungian perspective and states that there is a duality created from victimization, a schema that include an "element of being both the passive, 'victim,' as well as the aggressive, traumatizing, abuser" (p. 75). Lisak (1996) has shown that a significant number of abused men react by becoming hypermasculine; in other words, "over controlled, unemotional, action oriented, and abusive to others" (Kia-Keating et al., 2005, p. 170). These individuals identify with anger, aggression, bullying, or other behaviors they view as powerful. This behavior allows the individual to protect himself from the overwhelming emotional states that accompany the trauma, channeling it through traditional masculine behaviors. This overcompensatory adaptation allows the affected male continued identification with the male narrative, thus preserving his narrative coherence within the construct of the dominant male narrative, although it does not lend itself to processing the trauma as seeking assistance and speaking of feelings is not part of this narrative.

During the initial few months of treatment, Kevin experienced several instances of aggressive behavior in school and some additional behaviors surfaced while participating in male team sports. He was assigned detention for ongoing behavioral challenges with a male teacher. An active participant in after-school sports, Kevin began having a difficult time with teammates and was often benched after not backing down from an argument or altercation. Kevin's mother, Lisa, and his school seemed perplexed by his behavior. Both were aware of his disclosure of abuse and the ongoing court case, yet neither made the connection between his behavior and the struggle to integrate his experience of sexual abuse. Although Lisa was in psychotherapeutic treatment with another clinician, I met with her several times during this process in order to provide psychoeducation regarding some of the challenges that Kevin was experiencing. These meetings provided an opportunity to gain perspective on Kevin's functioning outside the therapeutic milieu while also allowing for work on the family communication and dynamics.

Six months after our initial meeting, it became evident that Kevin was beginning to withdraw from the external world. Once the outgoing and engaged teen, he started to avoid most social contact, preferring the safety of his own internal world. Kevin stopped playing baseball, once his favorite sport, and his grades in school markedly declined. The impact of the sexual violence filled his daily reality with an expectation of danger and distrust. Cloaked in feelings of powerlessness, the world was no longer a safe and wondrous place, but one wrought with fear and danger, nuanced meanings, and hidden agendas. Kevin had internalized the powerless persona, the other response to an experience of sexual violence. This internalization of powerlessness moves the male survivor away from identification with the perpetrator of the violence, and rather than externalizing his feelings of anger and betrayal, focuses them inward toward themselves (Grossman et al., 2006; Howard, 1991; Simon et al., 2010). It is not uncommon for those impacted by trauma to develop challenges with addiction or other self-medicating behaviors. Clinicians may observe behaviors such as lack of social interaction, a decreased interest in activities outside the home, and an increase in time spent alone.

I Saw His Face Laughing at Me

During one session, almost a year after our initial meeting, Kevin came in visibly upset. He sat on the couch, pulling a pillow onto his lap, as he shared his experience of the weekend. The previous Saturday night he had a date with his girlfriend and decided the time was right for a kiss. I listened intently as Kevin described the immense anxiety that accompanied his decision to kiss Charlene. Sitting on a bench, at the park. Looking into her eyes. Smelling her perfume. Leaning in to kiss her. It all was going just as he planned. As his lips touched hers, he opened his eyes. There above her left shoulder was an image of Manny.

Kevin: I just froze. It felt like I wasn't even there anymore. Then I blinked my eyes and looked again, but he was still there and he was laughing at me. Why did that have to happen? No one understands. Just when I think that I'm OK—something like this happens. I just want to feel like a normal kid.

Me: You are a normal kid Kevin—though it might not feel like it right now.

It is not uncommon for survivors of sexual violence to experience a flashback to a traumatic scene. Often triggered by a sensory event, these flashbacks create a bridge to unwanted and unwelcome memories of the trauma.

> Experiences of trauma become freeze-framed into an eternal present in which one remains forever trapped, or to which one is condemned to be perpetually returned through the port keys supplied by life's slings and arrows. The sense of one's own continuity, of the stretching along between past and future is collapsed.
>
> *(Epstein, 2013)*

These flashbacks are the mind attempting to make sense of experience. It is the interaction of the implicit and the survivor's narrative. The collapse of temporality is particularly disruptive to the survivor of trauma, as it interferes with the coherence and continuity of the individual's narrative. For the impacted male, this shattering of narrative has the effect of causing a disruption of one's sense of self in relation to the world around them. Unable to place their experience into a form where it can be better understood, this disruption of known reality can cause a re-experiencing of the traumatic event. Forced to relive the traumatic event not only through memory, but through somatic experience, the survivor of sexual violence struggles to place these experiences into a world in which there is no fit, no story, no narrative that can help explain away the unexplainable, creating an ongoing sense of danger and instability that can interfere with one's ability to fully enjoy life.

The content of Kevin's flashback speaks to the profound effect that sexual violence has on the individual (Culbertson, 1995; Van der Kolk et al., 2005). A first kiss, for a teenager, is an important step in gaining confidence with oneself and one's sexuality. That the flashback occurred during a moment of intimacy, a moment of vulnerability when Kevin felt confident enough to lean over and kiss his girlfriend, speaks to the incongruity of the experience of sexual violence, as contextualized by the dominant narrative of masculinity. However, it also indicated that Kevin was beginning to process the trauma of his sexual abuse. As Baljon (2011) states, "posttraumatic growth also correlates with intrusions of trauma-related thoughts or images, an important characteristic of posttraumatic stress symptoms, but not with fear and depression" (p. 157). Rather than viewing these instances as pathological, I viewed as part of the healing process and worked with Kevin to help him see them in that way. Reframing the flashbacks is a way to help regain mastery of one's experiences, allowing the individual to process them in a safe way—something that could not have occurred for Kevin while the abuse was occurring.

My work with Kevin continued for the next several months. He began to progress with minimal intrusive thoughts and flashbacks. Lisa reported that his social interaction had increased and he was participating in more school activities. I noticed the improvement in his affect. No longer hidden under his hoodie and silent, Kevin was engaged and talkative during our sessions. That changed quickly once he received the phone call.

The prosecutor called to inform Kevin that Manny had accepted a plea bargain. In exchange for his admission of guilt, Manny would be classified as a convicted sex offender and be required to register as such for the remainder of his life. The length of the jail sentence would be decided by the judge and could range from 6 to 12 years in prison. Both Kevin and his mother would have the opportunity to address the court to express the impact of the crime on themselves and their family. Lisa was adamant about sharing her perspective with the court and with Manny. Kevin wasn't sure, but agreed to at least work on writing a statement. Manny would be present for the sentencing.

I Keep a Baseball Bat Under My Bed

We worked on that statement for the next few sessions. It was difficult for Kevin. The thought of coming face-to-face with Manny, of challenging the narrative that had begun to settle in his mind regarding powerlessness, began to take a toll on Kevin. He began to feel like Manny was watching him, knew his thoughts, and was going to seek him out when he regained his freedom, ready to jump him, to again render him powerless. "I keep a bat under my bed," Kevin told me, "just in case he got out of jail and is waiting for me."

At times, I began to feel like we were moving backwards and started to doubt the benefit of working with Kevin to craft this statement and take action against the wrongs that were committed against him. Perhaps reporting it the police was enough. That alone took tremendous courage. Since that phone call from the prosecutor, Kevin seemed to regress to a younger age, becoming more careful and less independent. His affect changed. He once again began to seek the safety of his room and exhibited a diminished interest in socializing with friends. His mother became concerned and asked for a session with Kevin, and I agreed to meet with them both to discuss her concerns. The following Monday, I met with both of them, just two weeks prior to Manny's sentencing. There are powerful moments in psychotherapeutic treatment. This was one of them. Lisa expressed her sorrow and Kevin expressed his love and forgiveness. I remained silent, letting the intensity and the healing of that moment speak for it. A few moments had passed and I spoke—*it wasn't anyone's fault but Manny's.*

Kevin's anxiety began to increase as the court date neared. He shared several times that he felt he would not be able to adequately express the impact that Manny had on his life. He wasn't even sure that he would want to make a statement. I sat with him while he listed the reasons why he didn't want to do it—why he didn't want to stand up and face this man; the man who betrayed his trust, stole his innocence, and destroyed relationships within his family. I recognized the struggle in his eyes. I had seen it many times before, having worked with many individuals impacted by violence. It is the existential struggle between right and wrong, good and evil, between silence and speaking up. I have witnessed the impact of this struggle on those individuals who have remained silent. That silence, after so many years, begins to take its toll. One can see it in the eyes, weariness, as the weight of bearing witness without taking action begins to chip away at the psyche, lowering self-esteem, increasing a sense of isolation and depression, and creating challenges with love and intimacy.

As I sat there with Kevin, I recognized the immensity of this opportunity. Kevin had the ability to face the individual who had caused so much upheaval within his life, the opportunity to begin to dismantle the narrative of powerlessness that he had begun to feel so familiar to him. I recognized the profound impact that this might have on Kevin, this young man who struggled to regain his sense of self. As his psychotherapist, I sat and bore witness to that struggle over the previous year. For a 15-year-old teenager without much perspective or experience in life, there are not many alternatives. There is no path, no narrative of healing to follow. So, it is much easier not to stand up for yourself, to remain silent. How many times did Kevin lay in his bed, staring up at his superhero posters, silent, as his father physically abused his mother? How many times did Manny reward him for his silence? How many times did Manny threaten him— causing him to remain silent? The one time that Kevin spoke up, that he took action, caused his father to leave the home. The second time he did not remain silent, reporting Manny to the police, caused a rupture in his family. No, in his mind there was only one alternative: stay silent, don't speak up, don't draw attention to yourself, don't make yourself a target. Protect yourself. I knew what to say to say to Kevin. It wasn't the textbook response, or the generic; well let's weigh the alternatives. In my mind, there was only one alternative. That was to speak up.

I took a deep breath, as both anger and tears filled the room, cognizant of the dynamics at work in that moment. I was keenly aware that there was an innate power differential between us. Although I tried to empower Kevin, by the very nature of our client–therapist relationship, Kevin was placed in a powerless position. I had thought about this over the previous few months. How does this power differential influence the therapeutic relationship? Does it impact the therapeutic relationship in a way that can inhibit growth and healing? Despite all my efforts at minimizing the impact of these power differentials, was there any other way I could assist Kevin? I knew that this was a pivotal moment for him, a pivotal moment for us and our work together. It was a moment that might impact his life for many years to come. *Kevin, there is something I want to share with you.* For the next ten minutes I shared my own personal experience of sexual violence. He didn't ask details, or ask why I wanted to share that information; the walls didn't collapse around me, nor did my license fall off the wall. But I let him know that I understood his feelings and challenges, that I had felt similar feelings. The sharing of my experience helped give him hope in that moment of darkness by opening that door into our shared experience, the power dynamic in that room, in that space, and within the therapeutic relationship was changed. He wasn't the only one anymore, and I wasn't the other, and that could work toward empowering him. Kevin only asked one question—*So, you were able to get over it?* I told him I was.

The traditional psychoanalytic perspective states that disclosure in and of itself, regardless of the motivation, is a boundary violation and should be avoided at all costs. It is viewed as taboo or destructive to the therapeutic process. Freud (1958) instructed clinicians to view themselves as a mirror for their clients: "The (therapist) should be opaque to his patients and, like a mirror, should show them nothing but what is shown to him" (p. 118), in the hopes of fostering an environment conducive to transference. However, other perspectives espouse a differing view. Within the school of humanistic psychology, "self-disclosure is both expected and desirable as a means of exhibiting congruence" (Rogers, 1961) and transparency (Jourard, 1971). Additionally, feminist empowerment therapy recognizes the value of "judicious self-disclosure in reducing the power imbalance between therapist and client" (Hanson, 2005, p. 96).

For male survivors of sexual violence, these power imbalances can interfere with treatment (Glass, 2003). Already challenged with stigma and an experience of abuse that disrupts the coherence of the masculine narrative, these individuals are sensitized to their perceptions of powerlessness (Bertrandoa, 2000). Clinicians should be mindful that these dynamics greatly impact the therapeutic relationship with individuals such as Kevin, who have experienced powerlessness and are struggling to renegotiate their view of the world. The corrective emotional experience with the therapist will involve acknowledging, addressing, and revisiting these dynamics throughout the course of treatment. If the therapist is untrained or unaware of these dynamics, the probability is greater that there will be a rupture in the therapeutic relationship leading to a possible retraumatization of the client due to a re-enactment of the dynamics of the abuse (Middle & Kennerley, 2001).

Indeed, the configuration of the client–therapist dyad, in and of itself, has an inherent power differential within its configuration:

> Therapists must always assume that they are participating in domains of power and knowledge and are often involved in questions of social control. On this view, therapists must work to demystify and unmask the hidden power relations implicated in their techniques and practices.
>
> *(Besley, 2002, p. 134)*

My decision to disclose my own personal experience of sexual violence was important on a variety of levels. Beyond the opposition of varying perspectives, I consciously made a clinical decision to address the power dynamics within our relationship, through my use of self.

> Disclosure is not really a choice. It lurks in the co-construction of experience to be formulated and interpreted. It is interpreted through itself. By formulating an experience, one discloses that which has already been (in some unformulated way) disclosed. To disclose does not mean to tell but, rather, to open. The unconscious is not made conscious as interpreted by an expert on mental structure. The emphasis is not on mental structure but on mental structuring.
>
> *(Hartman, 2006, p. 281)*

Kevin may have already known implicitly that we shared this experience. Based on the books in my office, the depth of my knowledge, and my level of empathy, as well as what he interpreted from searching for my name online, Kevin had formulated inferences and judgments based both on his peripheral knowledge of clinical skills and online identity, as well as his experience of us.

Whether a therapist discloses or refrains from disclosure, they are making a statement. Indeed, the influence of the therapist does not disappear by failing to acknowledge or choosing not to speak, or by renaming it something else (Audet, 2011; Barrett & Berman, 2001; Bonovitz, 2006; Knight, 2009).

My choice was to either continue to perpetuate the power dynamic within the therapist–client dyad, or thoughtfully and mindfully intervene in a way that transformed those dynamics, and brought into the conversation, that which had been co-constructed both consciously and unconsciously, thereby allowing for a restructuring of the therapeutic relationship based on a more egalitarian foundation, aimed toward demystifying the person of the therapist and allowing Kevin to experience therapy as an interchange between two males rather than between expert and patient (Gibson, 2012; Prokopiou et al., 2008). Gillon (2008) views men as actively constructing the meanings of masculinity on a moment-by-moment basis, and suggests that psychotherapy can be viewed as a political act, a pathway for creating new masculinities that challenges the oppressive effects resulting from the dominant forms of masculinity: "Therapists can take on the role of helping men to see their experiences in the context of traditional expectations of masculinity, to critically assess gender roles, and to learn how to reformulate traditional codes based on their own provisions" (Kia-Keating et al., 2005, p. 183). Indeed, the creation of meaning is a dialectical process, one that Kevin and I had entered into through our psychotherapeutic work together. Through this process Kevin was able to begin to change his perspectives and masculinity, thereby challenging his masculine narrative. I believe that reconstructing a new masculine narrative is particularly important for male survivors of sexual violence. That moment in treatment when I made the decision to share my own experience of abuse was the beginning of that reconstruction for Kevin. It presented him with a template, allowing for development of a new masculine narrative that included his abuse experience (Pembecioglu, 2012; Penuel & Wertsch, 1995).

The following week was the last session prior to Manny's sentencing. Kevin, while nervous, had decided to attend the sentencing with his family. We had worked together on the victim impact statement that he would read for the court to use as consideration when sentencing Manny.

Kevin: Did you ever go to court when this happened to you?
Me: I didn't. I wasn't able to talk about the abuse until I was much older, so I did not have the opportunity to go to court or go to the police.
Kevin: Could I ask you one more thing? Would you come with me to court on Tuesday? You have been there with me through all of this and it would seem weird if you weren't there for this.

A week later, I found myself sitting there in court, as Kevin stood and moved toward the microphone. The court was silent as he stared down at the paper in his hands. It seemed as if he was frozen, unable to move, unable to speak, waiting for the words to magically jump off that crumpled loose-leaf page and into his mouth. Then he inhaled, taking a deep breath that seemed to break the moment, as he looked toward me. I exhaled and nodded as he cleared his throat and began his statement.

Kevin and I have continued to work together these past 4 years. He no longer wears a hoodie over his head or fails to shave for 2 weeks. He isn't afraid to go out of the house, nor is he afraid of Manny. After a lower than expected score on his Scholastic Aptitude Test (SAT), he found himself a tutor, and retook the exam, scoring 400 points higher than his original test score. Perhaps even more indicative of his progress in treatment, Kevin incorporated his experience with sexual violence into his admission essay for college. Kevin now speaks of the future and of a career. Through his hard work, he has been able to begin to live again, learning to place his experience of sexual abuse within the context of his life and not as the defining moment of his life.

For males such as Kevin, who have experienced sexual violence, the disruption of masculine narrative coherence is profound. Feelings of powerlessness and isolation challenge the construction of the post-traumatic masculine identity. Masculinity, abuse, and seeking help are interrelated in complex ways. There is a dichotomy between the masculine narrative and the victim narrative. Working with male clients to recognize this dissonance and challenge the traditional views on masculinity is paramount to the success of treatment with these individuals. The importance and impact of the therapeutic relationship cannot be underestimated. The therapeutic use of self, as well as the sharing of my own narrative of trauma and healing provided Kevin with an example of a cohesive masculine narrative that included trauma, masculinity, and healing, thereby providing a template that allowed him to begin to reconstruct his masculine identity in a way that engendered post-traumatic growth.

As psychotherapy moves into the new millennium, the continued impact of technology on the human experience calls for novel perspectives addressing the impacts of these challenges of the human psyche. Whether challenging the masculine narrative of sexual victimization or the narrative of self-disclosure within the psychotherapeutic milieu, both the therapeutic process and the content of conversation are changing in profound ways. Psychotherapists need to recognize these shifts have challenged the dominant discourse and look for ways that confront these assumptions and allow for the expansion of ideology in ways that expand horizons. Working with clients to find new ways to connect, grow, and achieve their potential require a self-reflexivity that challenges the status quo and looks toward the emergent themes embedded within our culture.

Close Reading Questions

1. Which details in the case study support the following quote: "Male survivors face particular challenges in resolving the conflicting experience of their childhood sexual abuse histories with the tenets of masculine socialization and expectations of relational intimacy"? (Kia-Keating, Grossman, Sorsoli, & Epstein, 2005, p. 179). Do any of the details you found seem like they might also apply to female survivors of sexual abuse? Why might the researchers cited in the case study feel the need to make a distinction?

2. What techniques did the therapist in this case study use to "demystify" the power dynamics of the therapist–client dyad? Why was it so important for the therapist to acknowledge his position of power?

3. Refer to specific passages in the case study to discuss how the therapist's self-disclosure helped his client to open up the client's definition of masculinity. Do you have the sense that Kevin's ideas about masculinity changed over the course of treatment? How would you describe what the therapist learned?

Prompts for Writing

1. Oreski uses Margaret F. Gibson's article, "Opening Up: Therapist Self-Disclosure in Theory, Research, and Practice," in conversation with his own ideas. She considers the legal, ethical, and technological aspects of self-disclosure in clinical social work from a feminist perspective. You can read Gibson's essay at the following link: http://link.springer.com/article/10.1007/s10615-012-0391-4#/page-1. Write an essay that frames Oreski's case through the lenses of her research. Do you think that some therapist self-disclosure is necessary? In what ways do Gibson's article and Oreski's case study complicate your own feelings on therapeutic self-disclosure? How do elements of the feminist theory that Gibson highlights relate to Oreski's ideas about the reconstruction of masculine identity? Use direct examples from each author in your answer, and most importantly, think self-reflexively about your own position on these issues.

2. Look at Oreski's reference list and locate some scholarly sources that could help you to think about your answer to the following questions: In what fundamental ways do humans help each other cope with traumatic experiences? How does that change when one person is a therapist and the other person is a client?

3. Briefly write up a case that you have become familiar with either through personal experience or in class. How might the case you have brought in breath new insights into Oreski's case? How did Oreski's case help you to rethink the experience you have shared?

References

Alaggia, R., & Kirshenbaum, S. (2005). Speaking the unspeakable: Examining the impact of family dynamics on child sexual abuse disclosures. *Families in Society: The Journal of Contemporary Social Services, 86*(2), 227–234.

Alaggia, R., & Millington, G. (2008). Male child sexual abuse: A phenomenology of betrayal. *Clinical Social Work Journal, 36*(3), 265–275.

Antoniou, A. S., & Blom, T. G. (2006). The five therapeutic relationships. *Clinical Case Studies, 5*(5), 437–451.

Audet, C. T. (2011). Client perspectives of therapist self-disclosure: Violating boundaries or removing barriers? *Counselling Psychology Quarterly, 24*(2), 85–100.

Baljon, M.C.L. (2011). Wounded masculinity: Transformation of aggression for male survivors of childhood abuse. *Person-Centered & Experiential Psychotherapies, 10*(3), 151–164.

Barrett, M. S., & Berman, J. S. (2001). Is psychotherapy more effective when therapists disclose information about themselves? *Journal of Consulting and Clinical Psychology, 69*(4), 597–603.

Bertrandoa, P. (2000). Text and context: Narrative, postmodernism and cybernetics. *Journal of Family Therapy, 22*(1), 83–103.

Besley, A. C. (2002). Foucault and the turn to narrative therapy. *British Journal of Guidance and Counselling, 30*(2), 125–143.

Beutler, L. E., & Hill, C. E. (1992). Process and outcome research in the treatment of adult victims of childhood sexual abuse: Methodological issues. *Journal of Consulting and Clinical Psychology, 60*(2), 204.

Bonovitz, C. (2006). The illusion of certainty in self-disclosure: Commentary on paper by Helen K. Gediman. *Psychoanalytic Dialogues, 16*(3), 293–304.

Briere, J., & Spinazzola, J. (2005). Phenomenology and psychological assessment of complex posttraumatic states. *Journal of Traumatic Stress, 18*(5), 401–412.

Cromer, L. D., & Goldsmith, R. E. (2010). Child sexual abuse myths: Attitudes, beliefs, and individual differences. *Journal of Child Sexual Abuse, 19*(6), 618–647.

Culbertson, R. (1995). Embodied memory, transcendence, and telling: Recounting trauma, re-establishing the self. *New Literary History, 26*(1), 169–195.

Cushman, P. (1990). Why the self is empty: Toward a historically situated psychology. *American Psychologist, 45*(5), 599.

Epstein, M. (2013, August 15). The trauma of everyday life: A guide to inner peace. *Penguin Group US: Kindle Edition.* Retrieved from Amazon.com

Freud, S. (1958). The dynamics of transference. In J. Strachey (Ed.), *The standard edition of the complete psychological works of Sigmund Freud* (Vol. 12, pp. 97–108). London: Hogarth Press.

Gibson, M. F. (2012). Opening up: Therapist self-disclosure in theory, research, and practice. *Clinical Social Work Journal, 40*(3), 287–296.

Gillon, E. (2008). Men, masculinity and person-centered therapy. *Person-Centered & Experiential Psychotherapies, 7,* 120–134.

Glass, L. L. (2003). The gray areas of boundary crossings and violations. *American Journal of Psychotherapy, 57*(4), 429–444.

Grossman, F. K., Sorsoli, L., & Kia Keating, M. (2006). A gale force wind: Meaning making by male survivors of childhood sexual abuse. *American Journal of Orthopsychiatry, 76*(4), 434–443.

Hanson, J. (2005). Should your lips be zipped? How therapist self-disclosure and non-disclosure affects clients. *Counselling and Psychotherapy Research, 5*(2), 96–104.

Hartman, S. (2006). Disclosure, dis-closure, diss/clothes/sure: Commentary on paper by Helen K. Gediman. *Psychoanalytic Dialogues, 16*(3), 273–292.

Herman, J. L. (1997). *Trauma and recovery.* New York: Basic Books.

Howard, G. S. (1991). Culture tales: A narrative approach to thinking, cross-cultural psychology, and psychotherapy. *American Psychologist, 46,* 187–197.

Hunter, M. E. (1990). *The sexually abused male, vol. 1: Prevalence, impact, and treatment.* Lexington, MA: Lexington Books.

Hunter, S. V. (2010). Evolving narratives about childhood sexual abuse: Challenging the dominance of the victim and survivor paradigm. *Australian and New Zealand Journal of Family Therapy, 31*(2), 176–190.

Jourard, S. M. (1971). Self-disclosure: An experimental analysis of the transparent self. Retrieved from http://psycnet.apa.org/psycinfo/1972-27107-000

Kia-Keating, M., Grossman, F. K., Sorsoli, L., & Epstein, M. (2005). Containing and resisting masculinity: Narratives of renegotiation among resilient male survivors of childhood sexual abuse. *Psychology of Men & Masculinity, 6*(3), 169–185.

Kia-Keating, M., Sorsoli, L., & Grossman, F. K. (2010). Relational challenges and recovery processes in male survivors of childhood sexual abuse. *Journal of Interpersonal Violence*, *25*(4), 666–683.

Knight, Z. G. (2009). Conceptual considerations regarding self-disclosure: A relational psychoanalytic perspective. *South African Journal of Psychology*, *39*(1), 75–85.

Koehn, C. V. (2007). Women's perceptions of power and control in sexual abuse counseling. *Journal of Child Sexual Abuse*, *16*(1), 37–60.

Lev-Wiesel, R. (1999). Feelings of adult survivors of child abuse toward their offender-parents. *Child and Adolescent Social Work Journal*, *16*(4), 291–304.

Lisak, D. (2005). *Male survivors of trauma*. San Francisco: Jossey-Bass.

Lisak, D., Hopper, J., & Song, P. (1996). Factors in the cycle of violence: Gender rigidity and emotional constriction. *Journal of Traumatic Stress*, *9*(4), 721–743.

Little, L., & Hamby, S. L. (1999). Gender differences in sexual abuse outcomes and recovery experiences: A survey of therapist-survivors. *Professional Psychology: Research and Practice*, *30*(4), 378.

Mandell, D. (2008). Power, care and vulnerability: Considering use of self in child welfare work. *Journal of Social Work Practice*, *22*(2), 235–248.

McAdams, D. P. (2011). Narrative identity. In *Handbook of identity theory and research* (pp. 99–115). New York: Springer Science & Business Media.

McAdams, D. P., & McLean, K. (2013). Narrative identity. *Current Directions in Psychological Science*, *22*(3), 233–238.

Middle, C., & Kennerley, H. (2001). A grounded theory analysis of the therapeutic relationship with clients sexually abused as children and non abused clients. *Clinical Psychology & Psychotherapy*, *8*(3), 198–205.

Pembecioglu, N. (2012). Building identities: Living in the hybrid society. *Scientific Journal of Humanistic Studies*, *4*(7), 46–59.

Penuel, W. R., & Wertsch, J. V. (1995). Vygotsky and identity formation: A sociocultural approach. *Educational Psychologist*, *30*(2), 83–92.

Platt, M., & Freyd, J. (2012). Trauma and negative underlying assumptions in feelings of shame: An exploratory study. *Trauma: Theory, Research, Practice, and Policy*, *4*(4), 370–378.

Prokopiou, A., Triliva, S., & Digridakis, M. (2008). Sustaining the dialogue by co-creating the sequence of meanings: A post-modern systemic approach developed within a Greek therapeutic context. *Journal of Family Psychotherapy*, *18*(4), 61–79.

Rogers, C. R. (1961). *On becoming a person: A therapist view of psychotherapy*. London: Constable.

Simon, V. A., Feiring, C., & McElroy, S. K. (2010). Making meaning of traumatic events: Youths' strategies for processing childhood sexual abuse are associated with psychosocial adjustment. *Child Maltreatment*, *15*(3), 229–241.

Sinclair, S. L., & Monk, G. (2005). Discursive empathy: A new foundation for therapeutic practice. *British Journal of Guidance & Counselling*, *33*(3), 333–349.

Sorsoli, L. (2010). "I remember," "I thought," "I know I didn't say": Silence and memory in trauma narratives. *Memory*, *18*(2), 129–141.

Sorsoli, L., Kia-Keating, M., & Grossman, F. K. (2008). "I keep that hush-hush": Male survivors of sexual abuse and the challenges of disclosure. *Journal of Counseling Psychology*, *55*(3), 333.

Tremblay, G., & Turcotte, P. (2005). Gender identity construction and sexual orientation in sexually abused males. *International Journal of Men's Health*, *4*(2), 131–147.

Tuval-Mashiach, R., Freedman, S., Bargai, N., Boker, R., Hadar, H., & Shalev, A. Y. (2004). Coping with trauma: Narrative and cognitive perspectives. *Psychiatry: Interpersonal and Biological Processes*, *67*(3), 280–293.

Van der Kolk, B. A., Roth, S., Pelcovitz, D., Sunday, S., & Spinazzola, J. (2005). Disorders of extreme stress: The empirical foundation of a complex adaptation to trauma. *Journal of Traumatic Stress, 18*(5), 389–399.

Vilenica, S., Shakespeare-Finch, J., & Obst, P. (2013). Exploring the process of meaning making in healing and growth after childhood sexual assault: A case study approach. *Counselling Psychology Quarterly, 26*(1), 39–54.

West, M. (2013). Trauma and the transference-countertransference: working with the bad object and the wounded self. *Journal of Analytical Psychology, 58*(1), 73–98.

5

REDEFINING RESILIENCE IN CHILDREN

A Story of Strength and Survival

Kim Stolow

Pre-reading Questions

1. How do you define resilience? Which factors have influenced your definition? What might lead you to characterize a client as resilient? Can you think of any ways that your definition or characterization might be controversial?
2. Describe how you would try to establish an environment of safety in which to treat someone who has been traumatized. What are your expectations going into a meeting with a client who has been traumatized? What techniques might you use to help a client who has been traumatized?
3. What do you know about dissociation as an effect of trauma? Some experts understand that dissociation is a coping mechanism for traumatized clients, but would you imagine dissociation as an act of resilience? Use an example to help make your point.

Tonyah and her five siblings were seated together on a small, worn couch, watching television in their apartment, an apartment that could barely accommodate the large family. Not far from where the children were sitting mesmerized by the glare of the television, Tonyah's parents were behind a closed, thin door. She didn't hear any yelling, thus a nervous reprieve from her nearly constant worry that her parents would choose to separate again. Yet, before long, the sound of her parents' yelling became her focal point as everything else disappeared into the background. Her heart began to race in anticipation of what would happen next. The sound of a slamming door startled Tonyah and her siblings as their parents moved the argument into the kitchen. Without conscious thought and without any true awareness, Tonyah lifted herself to the hallway near the front entrance of the home. All she could hear was the sound of her heart echoing her quick, shallow breaths. All other noise was miles away, and the space around her was in full spin. She fell into a fetal position, rocking back and forth into her frequently visited numb reality. The rocking and the numbness became Tonyah's only escape from pain. Without feeling in her legs, she made her way into the bathroom, as if someone or something else was controlling her body. There was no thought, just movement and pain, incalculable pain, and then an opportunity for relief; a razor slowly sliding across her scarred skin. Release. Calmness. Pervasive silence, save the echo of her heartbeat, and a warm sensation spread throughout her body. Tonyah fell to the floor, finally in control of her body again, finally feeling in control of her thoughts.

The local Regional Diagnostic and Treatment Center referred Tonyah to my private practice following a disclosure of sexual abuse by her maternal uncle. In my private practice, I specialize in working with trauma victims, specifically victims of child sexual abuse. Tonyah's abuse started when she was about five years old, and continued until she revealed her secret at the age of 12. When she was ready to disclose, she chose to tell her father, who ultimately left it up to Tonyah as to whether or not they would call the police. His only request was that Tonyah keep this a secret from her mother until a decision had been made. He feared how she would react, and the influence she would have on Tonyah's decision to tell her story of abuse to others. After a few days (and without speaking to her mother), Tonyah decided that she wanted to speak to the authorities. Tonyah's father escorted her to the police station, where she was interviewed and encouraged to divulge every humiliating, intimate detail of her abuse. Tonyah's uncle confessed, and for all the pain and trauma he caused, he was sentenced to 10 years in prison.

Common Beliefs About Resilience

"Children are resilient. They always bounce back, right?" is a question that I have heard over and over again in my clinical practice. This time, the question came from Tonyah's father, Richard, when he called to inquire about therapeutic services for his daughter. Richard needed to hear from me that his daughter was going to be all right; this sentiment echoed in every statement and question posed during our initial phone conversation and subsequent intake session. I acknowledged the trauma that Tonyah had endured, and validated his need to be reassured that his daughter would, in time, take steps toward healing. But I warned him that it would be a long process, with many ups and downs. Richard's questions regarding his expectations of Tonyah being able to bounce back, as well as my subsequent work with Tonyah, forced me to reconsider my own understanding and beliefs about resiliency. After a great deal of thought, reflection, and research, I came to my own conclusions. First, I saw how my beliefs (and those commonly held by society) not only impacted my clients' sense of self-worth and efficacy, but how these beliefs influenced the interventions that I utilized. The socially constructed view of resiliency also impacts how victims of trauma view their own traumatic response and coping mechanisms utilized to overcome the trauma. When working with victims of child sexual abuse, resiliency needs to be looked at differently. It cannot be measured by one's ability to bounce back, but rather the ability to adapt in order to meet the psychological demands of continuous trauma. In addition, the definition of resiliency also creates an interesting discussion of the mind/body connection. When seeking to understand resiliency, are we (researchers and clinicians) trying to understand the concept as part of the physical brain or the metaphysical mind? How we choose to understand resilience within these confines will also determine how and when we define someone as resilient. When working with survivors of sexual abuse, resiliency must be conceptualized as a function of both the mind and the brain, for both are directly impacted when exposed to trauma, and the clinical interventions that are utilized must follow accordingly.

Tonyah's story is not one that most would associate with the term "resilience." She crumbles in the face of conflict, dissociates when she is put in a position to feel something, mutilates her body when life becomes too unbearable, and covers herself completely as a means of protection. Tonyah survived horrific abuse by a man who was supposed to love and protect her. Her coping skills provided her with the emotional protection that she needed. Tonyah did not break, and when those coping skills no longer sufficed, she found the courage to expose her most intimate and shameful life experiences.

Many researchers have spent a considerable amount of time trying to define, concretize, and quantify the definition of resilience. Thomas Tredgold, an English engineer, introduced the term when describing how wood was able to accommodate sudden weight without breaking (McAslan, 2010). According to McAslan (2010), Mallet, another engineer, continued to develop this notion of resilience when discussing how certain materials were able to withstand poor conditions. Resilience soon became a term used not only in the world of engineering but in the social and behavioral science realm as well. Many definitions of resilience focus on the bouncing-back quality, as well as the use of adaptive functions. When the adaptive functions are considered, there is a focus on what many deem positive adaptations. But what constitutes a positive adaptation, and how do we measure the absence of symptoms? Many victims of trauma will not immediately show post-traumatic symptoms (Finkelhor & Berliner, 1995). While many would classify symptoms commonly displayed by Tonyah and other sexual abuse survivors, such as cutting, covering, and dissociation, as maladaptive, they are quite the opposite. These behaviors, while maladaptive at the time of therapy, were adaptive at the time of the abuse, and provided Tonyah with the ability to ultimately disclose and move toward taking some significant steps toward emotional healing.

The meaning of resiliency is not only a heavily researched topic; it has also become a socially constructed term that carries a great deal of meaning (Gray,

2011). Over and over again, in various forms, I have heard the phrase "children bounce back." This belief impacts not only how clinicians work with clients, but also how clients and their families view their post-trauma experience and therapeutic journey. Many victims of trauma have been exposed to, and adopt, this belief about resilience, and begin to look at themselves as dysfunctional or weak in nature. If society believes that children should bounce back after a traumatic event, surely those who do not bounce back will be looked upon as less than and weaker than those who do. Gray (2011), a social work researcher, asserts, "The most important interpretations create 'useful realities' that derive from client interpretations and meanings, stories and narratives" (p. 7). However, it is not just the interpretations of the client that impact the client's narrative of trauma and healing, but also those of the clinician. Clinicians who have little experience working with this population can fall prey, as I once did, to the socially accepted meaning of resilience. Dennis Saleebey, promoter of the strength-based model of social work, states, "Any approach to practice, in the end, is based on interpretation of the experiences of practitioners and clients and is composed of assumptions, rhetoric, ethics, and a set of methods" (Gray, 2011, p. 7). Clinicians are directly impacted by their own experiences and belief systems.

The moment I adopted a new way of defining resilience and adaptive coping skills, and introduced this idea to Tonyah, is the moment when true healing was able to come about. That moment is very clear in my mind, as it forever changed the way I worked with every client. On that particular day, about six months into treatment, Tonyah seemed very down and extremely frustrated. When I asked to explore her feelings of frustration, this is the dialogue that ensued:

Tonyah: I should be better by now.
Me: According to whom?
Tonyah: Everyone! My dad thinks I shouldn't have to go to therapy anymore. He thinks I'm using this as an excuse to be bad or whatever. He thinks I'm milking this. I don't even know what that means.
Me: Well, for now, let's focus on what you think. What does it mean to be better?
Tonyah: I don't know. I guess it means that I don't do stupid things, like cutting myself or sleeping with every guy who pays attention to me. I wish I could pay attention in school, and I wish I didn't hate myself so much. I wish I wasn't so angry. I thought kids were supposed to be strong. There are other kids in my school who were abused, and they don't have any of these problems.

Tonyah was beginning to exhibit a rare display of emotions. She often felt as though allowing herself to feel something and, worse yet, show it, would ultimately lead to a loss of control over herself. But there was no holding back at this moment. She knew exactly what her parents thought of her, and how society viewed her, and she spent a good deal of time wondering why she could not just get better like she was supposed to. Tonyah knew that everyone was giving up on her.

I could feel Tonyah's pain as she sat in the chair across from me. Rarely was I able to pick up on Tonyah's true emotions, but there was no mistaking how she felt in that moment. Tears flowed down her face uncontrollably, and she did nothing to stop them or wipe them away. At that point, it dawned on me that the way others viewed her reaction to years of sexual abuse was impacting her ability to heal. Was I also playing a part in her inability to understand why she engaged in these behaviors? I had spent so much time trying to get her to stop cutting and to be open to the experience of feelings. Was I inadvertently creating an image of failure? What if I helped Tonyah find a different way to understand her cutting, sexualized behaviors, and dissociation?

Me: Those are all good wishes. But what if there is a reason why you are doing all those things? What if doing those things helps you survive what happened with your uncle? What if you did exactly what your brain and body were supposed to do after so much trauma?

Tonyah: What do you mean?

Me: Your brain was impacted by the abuse. After people have been through a trauma, their brains actually change in order to survive. That is why you are having such a hard time concentrating in school, and why it is so difficult for you to manage when you feel such strong emotions.

Tonyah: So I didn't have a choice?

Me: Not really. Our bodies were created to adapt to our environment.

Tonyah: We learned about that in science class.

Me: Exactly. The problem is that your parents, your family, and everyone else out there who thinks you should be better don't really understand all of this. So they are going to say things to you that will make you feel like you should be better already, and that you shouldn't need to be in therapy. They are just saying that because they don't really get it. But we now know differently. Right?

Tonyah: It kinda makes sense. But he isn't abusing me anymore. So why am I still having all of these problems? When will it stop?

Me: Well, it took a while for you to adapt to the abuse. And now that it has stopped, it is going to take a while for you to adapt to a world where you aren't being abused. We have to help your brain learn that it is safe to change. It is going to take time. But the problems you are having now are not weakness. You are a very strong girl, and your very strong brain helped you survive something very bad.

Tonyah suddenly stopped crying and her whole demeanor changed. She rolled up her sleeves for the first time, displaying an arm's length of cuts. This was the first time I had ever seen any part of Tonyah's body besides the skin on her face.

Tonyah suddenly seemed lighter and less burdened, and for the first time I saw a glimmer of hope in her eyes. It took my own understanding of Tonyah's "maladaptive" behaviors, as well as my own reconceptualization of resilience, before I was able to provide her with a safe place to start the healing process.

It is my belief that human beings are inherently resilient. The appearance of this concept, however, is not always easily identified. Resilience is often masked under a cloak of what many would term dysfunction or maladaptive behaviors. To truly understand resilience, one must look back to a social worker's fundamental belief in the term "goodness of fit," a balance between a person and their environment (Miley et al., 2012). The social work profession conceptualizes individuals, and their subsequent problems, with an ecological lens. Heinz Hartmann, an ego psychologist, asserts that an ego can be seen as an "adaptive organ" (Germain, 1978, p. 539). Hartmann believes that through "autoplastic changes," the ego adapts in order to meet the demands of the environment. In this particular case, Tonyah had to find a way to adapt to years of sexual abuse that began at a young age. When her environment was no longer physically or emotionally safe, she used cutting, covering, and dissociation as means of creating an environment that met her needs at that time.

There is research and literature available that helps explain why children who have endured trauma will experience post-traumatic symptoms, and why this is not a reflection of resilience or lack thereof. Much of this research takes a child's development into consideration. According to Garbarino and Bruyere (2013),

> A traumatic experience that is cognitively and emotionally overwhelming may stimulate conditions in which the process required to "understand" these experiences itself has pathogenic side effects. That is, in coping with a traumatic event, the child may be forced into patterns of behavior, thought, and affect that are themselves "abnormal" when contrasted with patterns prior to the event as well as when compared with patterns characterized by the untraumatized child.
>
> *(p. 253)*

The mere experience of coping with trauma can, to the untrained therapist, appear pathogenic in nature, and can lead to a label of dysfunction. From a developmental perspective, Garbarino and Bruyere (2013) argue that trauma requires a child to make "developmental adjustments . . . [that] result from the inability of the child to assimilate traumatic experiences into existing schema (conceptual frameworks)" (p. 254). A child's experience of post-traumatic symptoms is an expected outcome when development is taken into consideration. Behaviors related to developmental trauma are unavoidable, and by nature cannot be related to the idea of resilience or lack thereof.

No one is immune to the effects of chronic trauma, and all children have a point where they will be impacted by a traumatic experience (Garbarino, 2014).

Garbarino defines children as "malleable rather than resilient" (p. 1367). He states that each "threat costs them something—and if the demands are too heavy, the child may experience a kind of psychological bankruptcy. What is more, in some environments, virtually all children demonstrate negative effects of highly stressful and threatening environments" (p. 1367). Garbarino makes the argument that every child who experiences trauma will experience some kind of trauma symptom, which is not always clear and measurable. For example, some children may be able to thrive in school and be functioning members of society, but have little ability to engage in healthy interpersonal relationships (Garbarino, 2014). One way that individuals of trauma may adapt is to play the part of a highly functioning individual. They do well in most measurable facets of social functioning, but suffer in silence. Many clients have come to my practice with no signs of trauma after disclosing years of abuse. Due to the high levels of secrecy inherent in sexual abuse, their adaptive coping mechanism was to pretend that everything was going well. They excelled in school and denied any deficits in their interpersonal relationships, and this façade continued well after they disclosed that abuse was occurring. These children would be labeled resilient, and often be discharged from counseling due to their ability to quickly bounce back. These children were often lauded for their ability to be so high functioning considering everything they had been through, and they were rewarded for not showing signs of trauma. This often makes it very difficult for the children when they do begin to experience distress. They often suffer in silence, or develop further feelings of shame when they can't continue to display a façade of normalcy. Child sexual abuse brings about a confusing array of dynamics that make the measurement of resilience so difficult. Typically, these children begin to show signs of distress within 18 months of disclosure (Finkelhor & Berliner, 1995). Garbarino and Bruyere (2013) argue that it is important not to measure torment from an outside perspective; traumatized individuals can "[fall] prey to existential despair later in life" (p. 259). The lack of post-traumatic symptoms immediately following a disclosure of abuse, as well as how we measure trauma symptoms, is yet another reason why defining and identifying resilience is no easy feat.

When determining whether a child who is a victim of child sexual abuse is resilient, it is vital that the clinician consider the particular dynamics involved in such a trauma. Child sexual abuse typically involves a normal child in an abnormal abusive relationship. When a healthy, normal child learns to "accommodate" for, or adapt to, the sexual abuse, his/her symptoms will be defined as abnormal but are actually "natural reactions of a healthy child to a profoundly unhealthy" environment (Summit, 1983, p. 180). Child sexual abuse typically occurs more than once. When a child has no way to stop the abuse, he or she must find psychological ways to cope with the repeated trauma. Ultimately, the child learns to accept and adapt. Often, in abusive situations, child victims begin to blame themselves for the abuse, because it is safer to think of themselves as "bad," rather than thinking badly of the trusted and loved family member who inflicts the abuse. Due to this splitting effect, children also develop a distorted sense of how they can be "good," and they often cooperate with the adult abuser's sexual requests. The perpetrator may give messages to reinforce this belief, offering that by cooperating they are saving their siblings from abuse, or other statements of that nature. Children may also come to genuinely believe that by disclosing the abuse they will cause their family harm. The accommodation also allows the child to step out of the role of the victim in order to achieve a sense of "power and control" (p. 184). However, by doing this, the child also takes on the responsibility for the abuse occurring, thus leading to feelings of shame and guilt. The benefits of staying quiet—protecting siblings, sparing parent(s) from pain, and preserving the family system—outweigh the harms of staying quiet.

During one particularly powerful session, Tonyah began to open up about how she managed to survive the abuse. Of course, Tonyah could not yet see this as means of survival and adaptation. That would not come for quite some time, and I noticed that Tonyah took a great deal of responsibility for the abuse occurring. To further assess this, I asked Tonyah to create a pie chart of responsibility related to the abuse, and to share it with me once she was finished. Tonyah quickly scribbled on the pie chart. It took her no more than a minute to fill it out, indicating that that this was either forefront on her mind or that she knew immediately who bore the most responsibility for the abuse. Tonyah turned the paper so I could see what she drew. She split the pie into two sections. She wrote 75% and 25% on her paper, with her uncle's name and her name written on the side.

Me: So your uncle is 75% responsible for sexually abusing you?

Tonyah: No! I am 75% responsible for my uncle sexually abusing me.

Me: What made you 75% responsible for the abuse?

Tonyah: I cried.

Me: How does crying make you responsible?

Tonyah: I cried in front of him. So he must have thought that I was weak, and that it was OK to do this to me.

Me: What else?

Tonyah: I wore a bathing suit in front of him.

Me: And how does that make you responsible?

Tonyah: My uncle must have thought that I was flirting with him, or that this was something I wanted to happen.

Me: Anything else?

Tonyah: I never told anyone. I never stopped him. I must have wanted it. I must have liked it or something. I never told him to stop. I just took it.

Tonyah believed that by crying in front of her uncle, she sent the message that she was weak and an easy target. So Tonyah stopped crying. In fact, Tonyah stopped feeling any emotion other than anger. She went through her life isolated from any feelings, even happiness or joy. Feelings became the ultimate threat, and any indication that the sensation of emotion was imminent caused dissociation and avoidance.

Tonyah refused to come to therapy for weeks at a time after a discussion related to the abuse caused her to feel emotion, which resulted in crying. Allowing herself to feel emotion became more dangerous than the abuse she endured. Tonyah's belief that by wearing a bathing suit she invited the abuse resulted in her completely covering her body, no matter the temperature. After all, she had to make sure not to send the same message to someone else. She protected herself in the only way she knew how, and took control in any way that she could. Throughout my work with Tonyah, I made sure to recognize the inherent strength and resilience in her ability to adapt in this way.

Through the current resiliency lens, the physiological impact of trauma is not always considered, and the label of dysfunctional, in my experience, often goes hand in hand with a prescription for psychotropic medication. The belief that children are inherently resilient, especially after traumatic experiences, seems to suggest that there is something about children that makes them immune to the effects of trauma and abuse. However, due to the significant brain development that occurs during early childhood, the truth is that children are even more vulnerable to the effect of trauma (Perry & Pollard, 1998). Bessell van der Kolk (1994), a psychiatrist who specializes in the research and treatment of trauma victims, points out that when a trauma victim is triggered, "the central nervous system (CNS) regions involved in integration of sensory input, motor output, attention, memory, memory consolidation, modulation of physiological arousal, and the ability to communicate with words" fail to operate properly (p. 34). In essence, victims of repeated trauma tend to exist in a constant state of survival, and this state of being interferes with all aspects of functioning. The brain is too busy surviving; it does not have time to tend to anything else.

Existing in a constant state of survival has emotional and biological implications. Van der Kolk (2006) finds that almost two-thirds of children who have endured trauma have symptoms reflective of this survival response, such as increased cardiac activity, high blood pressure, increased respiration, anxiety, and hypervigilance. These responses make it difficult for children to remain emotionally present and to regulate their own emotions and behaviors (Gaskill & Perry, 2002). In addition, when trauma is caused within the family system, the child is at greater risk for chronic affect dysregulation, destructive behavior against self and others, learning disabilities, dissociative problems, somatization, and distortions in concepts about self and others (Gaskill & Perry, 2002).

Tonyah was an adolescent who, through no fault of her own, experienced intense and often paralyzing post-traumatic symptoms. The extensive research done on trauma teaches us that her adaptive behaviors are expected and unavoidable, given the circumstances. As such, these behaviors should be recognized as acts of strength and resilience. In addition, it creates an interesting discussion about what the aim of trauma treatment should be—the brain or the mind, or perhaps a combination of the two.

Covering, Cutting, Sex, and Dissociation as Acts of Resilience

During my first meeting with Tonyah, I was a bit taken aback by her appearance. It was the middle of August on an incredibly hot and humid day, and Tonyah's body was completely covered. Her jeans fell way beyond her feet and draped heavily on the floor. She wore a long-sleeved shirt, with the sleeves too long for her arms pulled strategically beyond her fingertips. Tonyah wore a hat that was pulled down to partly cover her eyes. I had many clients who covered their bodies following a sexual assault, but this took covering to a different level. Typically, my clients covered so as not to send the wrong sexual message or to avoid being noticed. Tonyah's level of covering simultaneously screamed the words, "I am in danger" and "protection," providing me with insight into how Tonyah had adapted to her ongoing abuse. She was protecting herself not only from her uncle, but also from any other possible perpetrators. For Tonyah, the protection seemed to go beyond the physical. It was a protection against the vast, overpowering emotions that she kept locked for so long.

Clothing, or body covering, began as a form of physical protection. In fact, some primary purposes of clothing include protection, warmth, decoration, modesty, and symbolism (Gilman, 2002). Clothing first came about as a protective measure from the elements; shoes were protection for the feet and hats shielded the head. With clothing, we have the ability to adapt to changing or often harsh elements. Charlotte Gilman (2002), a feminist sociologist and writer, states, "Our clothing is as literally evolved to meet our needs as the scales of a fish or the feathers of a bird. It grows on us, socially, as theirs grow on them individually" (p. 4). Tonyah's need for adaptation was not only physical (protecting herself from further abuse), but psychological as well. It stands to reason that clothing could also provide a sense of psychological protection and barrier.

Me: I can't help but notice that you keep yourself completely covered from head to toe. Do you know why you do that?

Tonyah: It just feels better. It feels right. I feel more in control. I know that makes no sense. I don't know how to explain it.

Me: Actually it makes perfect sense. You get to decide how much of your body people get to see. Am I correct?

Tonyah: Kinda. I feel safe like this. I feel like I can disappear into the background, which is kinda funny because at the same time I totally stick out like this. I don't know. No one will think that I am coming onto them or anything like that. You know when it's cold out, and you put on your favorite pajamas, and you put your hair in a ponytail, and then you put on your favorite robe, even though the robe is kinda old and icky? But there's something about that robe that makes you feel so good and comfortable, and it doesn't matter how crazy you look? That's how I feel when I wear stuff like this. Otherwise, there's no way I could go to school. I feel like I would go crazy.

Clothing has become a form of nonverbal communication. We tell the world who we are by our choice of clothing. We communicate gender, class, and culture without saying a word. "Clothing and other personal artifacts nonverbally communicate information about individuals, the nature of their interpersonal relationships, and the overall context in which interpersonal interactions occur" (Reece, 1996, p. 36). According to Julie Seaman (2013), an author and lawyer, evolutionary theorists and sociologists have also linked one's state of dress with sexual selection. They assert that the clothing we pick is driven by "sexual attraction and mating behaviors" (p. 418). In many cultures, how a woman chooses to dress reflects her marital status. It is an outward sign to the community that this particular female is available. By this reasoning, Tonyah was not available, and her choice of dress clearly communicated this. Tonyah was not interested in mating behaviors. Her past experiences paired sex with violence, vulnerability, and abuse. Without using language, Tonyah let the world know that her body was closed, and not to be entered without her explicit permission.

Tonyah asserted her control by choosing not to decorate her body or to make her body visible to the opposite sex. Seaman (2013) suggests that clothing has become a way to control a female's sexuality, and that clothing choice is a societal norm passed down as a form of social control. Tonyah was rebelling against these societal norms. Interestingly, evolutionary scientists suggest that the "most constrained sex is the most decorated," a reflection of a power differential (Seaman, 2013, p. 418). Men assert their control over women by dictating how they will present their bodies when selecting a mate. In Western society, females are often expected to dress fancily, do their hair, and apply makeup in order to attract the opposite sex for mating. In her own way, and without consciously knowing it, Tonyah was stepping outside the control of men.

Clothing continues to evolve as a source of protection, but creates a sad commentary that woman exist in a world where such measures are necessary. It is important for the clinician to understand the role of clothing. Tonyah's decision to cover up allowed her the ability to be mobile in a society that no longer felt safe. It also allowed her the freedom to sit in my office and feel safe while we slowly peeled away the layer of hurt and betrayal. Not only was Tonyah's need to cover an indication of her pain, it was also, eventually, a sign of healing as she slowly allowed herself to experience emotions.

When Tonyah allowed the emotions, or when the emotions were forced to the surface, she had little means of managing them. As a way of adapting, Tonyah had learned how to shut off all feeling. She often described feeling numb, or a sensation of leaving her body, a type of dissociation. This was apparent from the beginning of my work with her.

Tonyah's first therapy session brought a wealth of information regarding how she managed to adapt to long-term abuse and trauma. I had already met Tonyah's father at the intake session, but this was my first time meeting her. She sat in her chair, eyes fixated on the floor. I noticed Tonyah playing with a string on her pants; she seemed nervous as she slightly rocked back and forth in the chair, a chair that she suddenly clung to as if it was her only protection from me. I softly introduced myself, and opted to refrain from trying to shake her hand, assuming that touching of any sort was not an option for Tonyah. I asked her if she would like to join me in my office, but also offered her the option of going for a walk or just sitting together in the waiting room. I wanted Tonyah to have some sense of control. I also knew that she was not coming to therapy voluntarily. Tonyah quietly stated that she was ready to come into my office. Without looking up from the floor, she stood and walked slowly behind me.

My office is fairly large, and strategically arranged to provide seating choices. My chair is placed in the middle of the room. Across from my chair is an over-sized couch, with another chair diagonal from mine that is much farther away than the couch, as well as a beanbag chair placed haphazardly near a small child's table. Tonyah chose the chair farthest from mine. She sat down and continued to play with the string on her pants. Tonyah's body language sent the message: "I am not safe here." She held everything so tightly inside, it was almost painful to watch. She held her hands tightly in her lap, her eyes were fixated on the floor, and her body appeared stiff. I tried to engage her in conversation regarding school and family life, but when I brought up the topic of the abuse, she quickly grew quiet and stared off into space, unable to easily ground herself in the present.

Me: OK. Are you comfortable standing up? I want to try something.

Tonyah: I guess so. What do you want me to do?

Me: I have this big rubber ball. I just want to throw it back and forth with you as we talk. Are you comfortable with that? You can remain exactly where you are.

Tonyah: Umm. OK. What's the point?

Me: Well I noticed that when you talk about things that make you sad, you go somewhere else. My guess is that your mind takes you somewhere else to keep you safe when you talk or think about unpleasant stuff. But I also want to give you a way to stay here if and when you want to. Make sense?

Tonyah: I guess so. But what if I am scared to stay here? What if I don't want to stay here?

Me: Well, my job is to create a place where you feel safe enough to stay and talk, and feel supported and comforted. You only have to stay in this space when you want to. I simply want to give you another option. For right now, we can just get used to throwing the ball and getting to know each other. Is that OK?

Tonyah nodded and continued to throw the ball back and forth with me as she gradually began to share some information about her life. The goal of throwing the ball back and forth was to keep Tonyah in the present. The simple motion of catching and throwing forced her brain to stay in the moment, to be more mindful. During this time, Tonyah shared that she lived with her mother, father, and two siblings. She also had three half siblings on her father's side; these siblings were conceived when Tonyah's parents were separated. During that separation, Tonyah lived with her maternal uncle for several years, and moved back in with her father about one year earlier. While living at her uncle's home, he sexually abused her. At this point in her story, Tonyah stopped throwing the ball. Her eyes glazed over and her body began to shake as she crushed the rubber ball in her right hand. I softly called her name, and Tonyah blinked as she regained some of her awareness. I gently told Tonyah that she could share her story at her own pace, whenever she was comfortable doing so.

The details of the abuse took some time for Tonyah to openly discuss. She spoke about it in small doses, then quickly withdrew or refused to come to counseling after she revealed a particularly hard detail. In time, Tonyah shared that the abuse included vaginal and anal penetration, as well as oral sex. She shared that the abuse started with innocent touching, and progressed as time went on. Tonyah was made to "practice" on other boys so that she was more "skilled" when she engaged in those activities with her uncle. As time went on, in order to spare her siblings from abuse, Tonyah would stay awake at night to make sure her uncle was not going into their rooms. If she suspected that her uncle was up, she would distract him by offering her body.

Tonyah continued to present with a blank stare that became even more distinct when my questions threatened this very purposeful fortress. Tonyah's dissociation began with the sexual abuse. Like many other sexual abuse survivors, Tonyah learned how to separate from her body during the abuse in a way that allowed her to disconnect from the emotional and physical anguish of the traumatic experience. Tonyah reported that she often created a fantasy-based environment to escape to, or saw herself floating over her body, while the abuse was occurring. Unfortunately, Tonyah's means of protection against the abuse became the way she handled any emotionally difficult experience. As explained earlier, due to constant reminders of the abuse, Tonyah was easily triggered and often experienced flashbacks. One of Tonyah's biggest triggers was watching her parents fight. Every time Tonyah's parents fought, she entered a state of panic, followed by a state of dissociation, self-injurious behaviors, and then relief and comfort. This was a typical pattern of behavior for Tonyah. She often described her general experience of living as numb, distracted, unfocused, and unclear.

Me: You seem like you are off in another world today.

Tonyah: I know (eyes cast down to the floor). I can't seem to keep myself here.

Me: What does that mean for you?

Tonyah: Like when I am in school . . . [long pause]. My grades are starting to drop. I can't seem to pay attention anymore. I just kind of go somewhere else.

Me: Where do you go?

Tonyah: That's the thing. I don't even know. It's not like I'm going to this awesome place in my mind that is fun and exciting. It is like I just stop being me. I don't know where I go. I mean, I know I am there. I don't have that split personality thingy everyone talks about. But it's like I am not there. And I try the stuff you taught me about, but it keeps happening.

Me: Does it happen any other time?

Tonyah: When I am having sex. But I do that on purpose. It is the only way I can get through it.

Me: Do you want to be more present? Or do you like going away?

Tonyah: I don't know. Sometimes I feel like it is a good thing. But sometimes I feel like I am missing out on stuff. I just wish I had more control over it. Like getting to pick when I go away. And I am worried about school. School is my way out of here, and I can't mess that up. But I don't think I will ever want to be in my body when it comes to sex.

The process of separating one's self during a traumatic event is not a new phenomenon in trauma victims. British psychiatrist Charles Samuel Myers (Van der Kolk, Van der Hart, & Marmar, 1996) first introduced the term "shell shock," referring to the process in which traumatic memories are kept separately from other memories. The term shell shock has been replaced by the term dissociation, which occurs on three levels: primary, secondary, and tertiary (Van der Hart, Van der Kolk, & Boon, 1998). Primary dissociation is the disintegration of traumatic memories that are commonly associated with one of the primary elements of post-traumatic stress disorder (PTSD), which causes the intrusive flashbacks. Secondary dissociation is the experience of a trauma victim leaving his/her body during the event and actually observing the trauma. According to Van der Kolk, Van der Hart, and Marmar (1996), "this dissociation allows the individuals to observe their traumatic experience as spectators, and to limit their pain or distress; they are protected from awareness of the full impact of the event" (p. 307). The successful use of dissociation after a traumatic event can lead an individual to overuse this adaptive mechanism as his/her first line of defense (Nash, Hulsey, Sexton, Harralson, & Lambert, 1993). This was especially true for Tonyah, who seemed to exist in a constant state of dissociation. Tonyah often felt that life in general was too overwhelming, and it was safer for her to remain in her own bubble of safety. She constantly fluctuated between feeling numb and feeling anger; any other sensation was overwhelming and unsafe. To continue to maintain her secret and her sanity, Tonyah learned to withdraw from the experience of emotional pain.

When it was impossible to withdraw from the world, or when the emotions became too powerful and overwhelming, Tonyah turned toward self-injurious behaviors. Her two methods of choice were sex and cutting. The choice to engage in sexual relationships following a history of sexual abuse often creates a lot of confusion for the client, his/her family, and even clinicians working with victims of sexual abuse. For Tonyah, sex was about control. For years, her uncle made all the decisions regarding her sexual experiences, including when they would occur, how often, the specific sexual acts that would be performed, and if any use of threat would be involved. At the age of 14, Tonyah now had a say as to with whom she would have sex, and under what terms and conditions. Tonyah is not alone in this means of coping. Briere and Elliott (1994) found that many victims of child sexual abuse use sex as a means of "closeness and intimacy" (p. 61). Indiscriminate sex may also

> provide distraction and avoidance of distress. . . . Sexual arousal and positive sexual attention can temporarily mask or dispel chronic abuse-related emotional pain by providing more pleasurable or distress-incompatible experiences. For such individuals, frequent sexual activity may represent a consciously or unconsciously chosen coping mechanism, invoked specifically to control painful internal experience.
>
> *(p. 61)*

For Tonyah, sex was also a very purposeful and immediate way to dissociate.

Me: I'm not going to beat around the bush here. I am confused. You tell me that you don't enjoy sex. You tell me that you go to another place in your head when you are having sex. Yet you continue to engage in this behavior. Can you help me to understand?

Tonyah: It's not that I don't like it. Actually, I don't know that I will ever like it. But it's not a big deal really. I don't even know it's happening when it's happening. It is just what I am used to. And I like the attention I get from him. This is just what I know. I don't know how to explain it.

Me: Does your boyfriend know what happened with your uncle?

Tonyah: No. What difference does it make?

Me: Perhaps there is a future for you where sex can be an enjoyable experience. And for that to happen, your partner will need to understand your emotional needs.

Tonyah: I don't think sex will ever be enjoyable for me, but I don't plan on not doing it either.

For Tonyah and other victims of sexual abuse, sex is often confused for love and affection. Tonyah used sex as her way of connecting and disconnecting in a manner that felt safe for her. Tonyah was able to gain control over her sexual experiences, and while it did not always make sense to me, it seemed to make complete sense to her.

Tonyah also engaged in a fair amount of cutting behaviors, which has also been linked with behaviors common to victims of child sexual abuse (Putnam, 1993). Tonyah truly gained a sense of relief, comfort, and balance after she cut herself. She felt no pain when she took the blade (or anything she could find) to her wrists, her thighs, her breasts, and her stomach. Euphoric is the only word that comes to mind when thinking back to how Tonyah looked when she explained to me how cutting helped her. Cutting allowed Tonyah to regain her composure when everything around her seemed to be falling apart. The only thing that made anything better was the physical sensation of a blade moving along her skin, and the warm flow of blood dripping from her veins. Tonyah could not tell me how she was feeling on a daily basis, but she could explain to me every sensation associated with cutting herself. Cutting afforded her a clarity that she was not used to, in a world that was "messed up" and "dirty." Cutting was her way of feeling alive when her own means of coping forced her into a world of dullness. By cutting herself, Tonyah was able to stop the chaos (dissociation), and at the same time, it helped her feel alive and present.

Cutting behaviors seem to have an adaptive function in victims of child sexual abuse. According to Putnam (1993), self-mutilating behavior "serves to temporarily reduce the psychic tension associated with extremely negative affect, guilt, intense depersonalization, feelings of helplessness, and/or painfully fragmented thought processes—states all too common among survivors of severe sexual abuse" (p. 61). Acts such as cutting should not be confused with suicidal behaviors, as the intent is quite different. Self-mutilation is often associated with dissociation, as individuals engaging in these behaviors often report a feeling of numbness, and deny feeling pain during these encounters (Van der Kolk, Perry, & Herman, 1991). While this was not always the case for Tonyah, individuals may use self-mutilating behaviors as a form of "antidissociation" (Klonsky & Muehlenkamp, 2007, p. 1050). Feelings of dissociation can be frightening, and self-mutilating behaviors can interrupt the sensation of feeling numb by introducing the feeling of pain. Cutting can also be used as a means of affect-regulation, an aspect of human functioning that is often severely impacted after prolonged exposure to trauma (Van der Kolk, 2001). Cutting behaviors are often followed by a sense of relief, and calm an individual's emotional state when they are unable to do that on their own.

Unfortunately for Tonyah, and for many of the child sexual abuse victims that I have worked with, she had little support in her life following her disclosure. She came from a chaotic family system, and her parents struggled to meet Tonyah's emotional needs even before the abuse occurred. This is common because the family often goes through a crisis of its own after a disclosure of sexual abuse, and is viewed as the secondary victim. Tonyah's mother, Alicia, stopped talking to her after she disclosed the abuse by her uncle. Alicia stopped functioning, and spent most of the day and night in her room alone, crying. Tonyah wanted to talk to her mom about the abuse, but was scared that it would send her "over the edge." She worried that her mother blamed her for the abuse, and refused to talk about it with her mom. While I had no concrete proof, I suspected that Alicia was also a victim of sexual abuse, which was something that Tonyah had also surmised, although it took years before Tonyah would admit that in therapy. In addition to her mother's emotional withdrawal from her life, Tonyah's father, who was once supportive of Tonyah and her healing process, grew tired of waiting for Tonyah to "bounce back." He felt that Tonyah should be back to her "normal self" by now, and could not understand why the process was taking so long. Tonyah's father now believed that Tonyah was using her victimization as an excuse to act out and get attention, and he wanted her to "snap out of it." Despite my own frustration with Tonyah's father, I was able to recognize that he needed Tonyah to "get better." In essence, Richard became a single father after the disclosure. He was forced to work two jobs in order to pay all the bills, and somehow had to find the time to be emotionally and physically present in order to meet the needs of all his children because his wife was no longer able to function as a wife or mother. She could not tend to her own emotional needs, or to the needs of her children. Due to Alicia's unwillingness to speak to Tonyah, or to work with me, and due to Richard's lack of engagement, Tonyah felt very alone after her disclosure. She could not count on her parents for emotional support, and knew that she had to do this on her own because most of her family (including her siblings) did not know of the abuse, and those who did know were not overly supportive. In fact, many family members continued to have a relationship with the uncle, and would frequently visit him in jail. Tonyah suffered in silence . . . again. Despite an unsupportive family environment that did not meet her emotional needs, despite the pain and discomfort of working through multiple traumas, and despite the fact that she was fighting this battle alone, Tonyah continues to come to therapy. This is yet another sign of Tonyah's resilience.

Therapeutic Intervention

How one chooses to define resilience will have a profound impact on how therapeutic interventions are utilized. It will create a very different experience not only for the client, but for the clinician as well. If the clinician believes that the client's behaviors of cutting, covering, or dissociating (or whatever adaptive mechanism the client has developed in response to the trauma) are dysfunctional and unhealthy, the clinician's interventions will often reflect that belief. Too often, I hear about a clinician's goal of stopping these "dysfunctional" behaviors, or replacing them with "less dysfunctional methods," rather than understanding their adaptive function. These clinicians often get frustrated when the behaviors do not stop within a short period of time, failing to realize that adaptation does not happen overnight. Tonyah's adaptive responses to abuse occurred over time as she recognized that her environment was not conducive to survival. Now that the abuse has ceased, Tonyah's adaptation to a healthier environment will take a good deal of time. When the clinician fails to respect the true nature of these behaviors, he/she runs the risk of sending a message to the client that they are, as one of my clients proclaimed, "bad at therapy," a message that has already been cultivated and ingrained into our general consciousness of what it means to be resilient. Think about how different the session will feel for both the client and the clinician if the adaptive behaviors are truly recognized as strength and resilience.

"I lost all my rights when I was five years old." This was a statement Tonyah made after approximately one year of therapy. It is a statement that still haunts me. Tonyah, still a child, learned at the age of 5 that she had no control over her body, and for that matter, her thoughts. She was forced to reimagine her reality in order to allow for her emotional survival. While the abuse was occurring, Tonyah lost her right to childhood ignorance and innocence. Once she disclosed, she gave up her right to anonymity, silence, and secrecy. This statement was a turning point for her. She became more comfortable, and subsequently began to open up in ways she never could in previous sessions. We worked on ways to help her transform her current coping skills into more adaptive methods. This was a slow process that needed to be handled with care, compassion, and a new understanding of resilience.

The therapy sessions began to afford Tonyah not only the opportunity to control her body and her thoughts, but they also taught her the skills needed to do so. In assessing Tonyah's capacity to manage and cope with her feelings, it became clear that she continued to have limited ways of managing her emotions and intrusive thoughts. Tonyah's traumatic experiences resulted in a persistent fear response, and a constant state of hyperarousal. She continued to be easily triggered by smells, sounds, and objects that reminded her of the abuse. One particular trigger was her uncle's home, where she was forced to go to visit her grandmother.

Trauma-focused cognitive behavioral therapy (TF-CBT) tends to be the model of choice when working with child victims of sexual abuse. As with cognitive behavioral therapy (CBT), TF-CBT is a concrete, theoretical approach that provides both child clients and their parents with structured and measurable techniques and outcomes. The TF-CBT model involves psycho-education; parent education; relaxation techniques; management of affect expression; understanding the connection between thoughts, feelings, and behavior; developing the trauma narrative; processing the traumatic experience; personal safety skills training; and coping with future trauma reminders (Deblinger, Cohen, & Mannarino, 2006). One main goal of the TF-CBT approach is to have the client create and then process their trauma narrative. Typically, trauma clients spend a great deal of time avoiding the thoughts and conversation of the actual trauma. The primary focus of this task is to allow the client to separate the trauma event from the negative cognitions and emotions that they have developed as a result of the trauma. This also serves as a way to desensitize the trauma, and to decrease avoidance and hyperarousal.

While TF-CBT is a popular model that is evidence based, it mostly focuses on higher level processing, which is often not being utilized due to the brain's response to trauma. It is important that "low brain regulation" be established before anything else can be effective (Gaskill & Perry, 2002, p. 40). Research suggests that "establishing a sense of safety and self-regulation (lower brain mediated) must supersede insightful reflection, trauma experience integration, relational engagement, or positive affect" (Gaskill & Perry, 2002, p. 40). Further, research shows that non-traditional methods that utilize a body-oriented approach prove to be quite useful as opposed to traditional talk therapy (Gaskill & Perry, 2002). One such method that has been helpful in the treatment of trauma victims is the use of yoga. Yoga provides clients with the skills to help regulate their arousal system, find comfort with their bodily sensations, and gain a sense of presence and mindfulness (Gaskill & Perry, 2002).

The most helpful intervention was the use of Tonyah's own body. A majority of the therapy sessions utilized yoga techniques (Van der Kolk, 2009), mindfulness, and essential oils, as well as other forms of movement, music, and breathing exercises. These tools helped Tonyah become more aware of and connected to her body, enabling her to gain more control over her ability to calm her body in times of stress. One of Tonyah's favorite interventions was the use of essential oils. Tonyah experimented with a variety of scents. She found that scents such as lavender helped her to calm her body, while scents such as lemon and pine helped her become more mindful. Movement was also very effective for Tonyah. There were times during our sessions when we would just walk around the room. I carefully adapted my own pace of walking and moving to mirror hers, and I was sure to keep a comfortable distance. Tonyah began feeling more comfortable in her own skin. She learned how to identify her emotional states by the sensations of her own body. And by identifying those sensations and emotional states, she ultimately learned how to regulate her own body. Of course this took time and a lot of practice on Tonyah's part.

Tonyah relearned how to experience and regulate her emotions. She had to learn how to keep her body calm and recognize actual signs of threat, rather than viewing the whole world as unsafe. I utilized a variety of tools to help Tonyah with this process. She was so disconnected from her body that most of the time she reported feeling "numb." To help Tonyah begin to process her own feelings, we began to utilize exercises that helped her first identify various feelings, and then connect those feelings with bodily states. Gradually, with a lot of work and patience, Tonyah was able to identify certain feelings that she was experiencing. Interestingly, as the other emotions surfaced, her anger began to dissipate. While Tonyah was able to identify the actual feeling, it still seemed as though she remained disconnected from that feeling. There seemed to be a disconnection between the cognitive thought and the actual bodily experience of the emotion. However, she was able to identify the thoughts, feelings, and bodily experiences, which was a step in the right direction.

Slowly we began to work on Tonyah's ability to contain some of the intense feelings she experienced, which ultimately led to her dissociation. Tonyah shared that the feelings that incapacitated her most were fear and shame. Her fear seemed to come about most while her parents were fighting, and shame seemed to permeate her life at all times. Tonyah walked around consistently believing that she single-handedly broke up her family, and that there was something about her that invited the abuse. She continued to cover most of her body with clothing after a year of therapy, although we made some improvement in this area. At this point in counseling, I asked Tonyah to draw a container for all the overwhelming thoughts and emotions that kept her from functioning in her everyday life. Before we began, Tonyah identified the following as thoughts and emotions that required a container: the sexual abuse by her uncle, her mother not speaking to her, her parents fighting, and feeling responsible for the abuse. We then discussed what her container would look like in fine detail. I asked her to consider how the container would be constructed, what material it would be built from, how sturdy it would be, how accessible, and where it would be located. I then asked Tonyah to draw her container so that she could have a concrete representation of it.

Me: Tell me what I am looking at.

Tonyah: You told me to draw a container for my thoughts (annoyance noted).

Me: Yes. Tell me in your own words about your container.

Tonyah: It's a chest. It is made out of steel. The kind you can't cut through. And the chest has a lot of locks on it.

Me: How many locks?

Tonyah: Would 1,000 seem silly?

Me: It's your container. It's anything you want and need it to be.

Tonyah: OK, 1,000 locks and there is no key. And it's trapped behind a jail cell that no one can ever get to. And the jail cell has a dozen more locks to make sure no one can get in.

As Tonyah began creating the container, not just physically, but in her mind, I saw a sense of calmness come over her, and she seemed more at ease. It was as if she could imagine herself having some control, even if just a little bit, over her feelings. She was sensing the possibility, and experiencing a sense of hope. As Tonyah gained mastery over her thoughts and feelings, she became much more comfortable discussing them, and spent less time running away from them. I noticed a marked difference in how often Tonyah would dissociate when discussing the abuse and all associated feelings. Tonyah began to use the container exercise when her parents were fighting, and when she had the urge to cut herself. When paired with other cognitive behavioral approaches and relaxation exercises, Tonyah saw a reduction in how often she needed to cut herself, and found herself able to walk away from the fighting rather than freezing in the moment.

At the age of 15, Tonyah expressed a desire to stop cutting herself. I purposely did not ask whether she cut that week because the behavior caused a great deal of shame. I allowed Tonyah to bring it up only when it was something that she wanted to discuss. This proved to be very useful, because Tonyah stopped seeing the behavior as something she needed to report on and be chastised for. To help reduce feelings of shame, I chose not to do a safety contract because I knew that Tonyah would cut again, and breaking the contract would only continue her feelings of emotional distress. I also chose not to have a countdown of how much time elapsed before she cut herself again. Instead, we spent a great deal of time understanding the behavior, the triggers, and the function of the self-injurious behaviors. We explored the idea that cutting provided relief, and she was feeding her emotional need. However, we also explored how this behavior was no longer helpful, and discussed the need to explore healthier ways of healing and managing her feelings. This technique successfully created a safe environment for Tonyah to explore and understand, without the fear of being judged and shamed. Eventually, through the help of yoga, breathing, and willpower, Tonyah found ways to comfort herself that did not include cutting. Primarily, she found her voice. She found a way to not only sit with her emotions, but to talk about and understand them. The ability to remain present through these untraditional methods, coupled with her ability to regulate her emotions, made cutting an unnecessary coping mechanism. Tonyah had relearned how to be in her own body, and her brain relearned how to function in an environment that no longer consisted of trauma.

Until there is a sense of safety within the therapeutic relationship, not much can be accomplished in therapy. The client must genuinely know that the clinician respects them and believes in their inherent ability to move forward and heal. Tonyah came to therapy seeing herself as damaged and incapable of healing, which played out over and over again in therapy as I approached each topic with the misguided belief that her post-traumatic symptoms were maladaptive. Once I developed a new way of conceptualizing resilience and adaptive behaviors, and changed my approach, Tonyah was able to truly begin her journey of growth and healing. Tonyah felt valued and understood. For the first time, she saw herself as a strong individual who was capable of protecting herself, and subsequently found healthier ways of coping in the absence of abuse and trauma.

Tonyah is not the only one who benefited from this new understanding of resilience and adaptation. Working primarily with victims of trauma can be daunting and exhausting. Therefore, it is easy to become weighed down by the stories of abuse, pain, and loss. As a clinician, viewing your clients as dysfunctional, weak, and hopeless will impact your emotional well-being, as well as your effectiveness with clients. My new understanding of resilience not only changed how Tonyah saw herself, but also how I viewed Tonyah's adaptive behaviors and the interventions that I chose to address these behaviors.

Conclusion: Far From Over

Tonyah's journey of healing is far from over. She slowly worked toward creating her narrative of the abuse. It was a very painful process, and one that Tonyah continues to struggle with. While Tonyah is able to talk about the details of the abuse, often without dissociation, her narrative is riddled with the theme of shame and guilt. While she knows, on some level, that the abuse was not her fault, she continues to blame herself. This is especially complicated by her relationship, or lack thereof, with her mother and her constant worry that her mother blames her. Tonyah's progress and emotional development has been awe-inspiring. She is now in a healthy relationship with a young man who treats her with respect. She has been able to discuss her abuse with her boyfriend, and he understands her need to abstain from sexual activities. Tonyah is starting to look into colleges, and has decided that she would like to major in criminal justice to pursue a career as a detective who works with abused children. Her family continues to be a source of stress and disappointment, but Tonyah is now able to separate their narrative from her own, and their voices no longer occupy much space in her mind.

Each time that Tonyah decided to come to therapy, to ignore her family's hurtful words, and to resist the urge to cut herself when life became unbearable, she demonstrated signs of resilience. Even more impressive was her ability to form a therapeutic relationship with me, despite her abusive past. While Tonyah has a long way to go and many battles to fight, she continues to do the hard work necessary to obtain emotional health.

Clinicians, and frankly, society, owe it to survivors of trauma to find a new way to understand resiliency and to be careful how that term is applied. The labeling of one as resilient or not resilient carries a tremendous weight. The label of resilience fails to take into consideration the biological impact of trauma, as well as the adaptive mechanisms inherent in human beings. It also forces the clinician to make a choice between the mind and the brain, rather than creating an intervention that acknowledges the individual as a whole.

Tonyah has forever changed my work with clients, and for that I owe her a debt of gratitude. Tonyah helped me to see strength in perceived weakness, and to appreciate the depths that an individual will go to in order to survive and thrive under the cruelest of circumstances. She not only provided me with an avenue to work with my clients more effectively, but she made the work more fulfilling and less of an emotional drain.

Resilience cannot be measured by the absence of symptoms, but rather by a child's ability to adapt in the face of an unsafe environment. The reconceptualization of resilience allows for an element of hope and a celebration of every client's inherent strength.

Close Reading Questions

1. Describe three ways that Tonyah tried to achieve "power and control" in order to step out of the role of victim. Was she successful? Did some of her attempts victimize her further? How might trauma-focused cognitive behavioral therapy help Tonyah to achieve "power and control"? Did you notice Tonyah's therapist attempting to use TF-CBT or other interventions?

2. Stolow writes, "The extensive research done on trauma teaches us that her adaptive behaviors are expected and unavoidable, given the circumstances. As such, these behaviors should be recognized as acts of strength and resilience." What is your reading of this statement? Can you zero in on two or three moments when Stolow exemplified this philosophy in her treatment plan? What did you learn from these moments? Is there something you would add to Stolow's interventions?

3. How have Garbarino and Bruyere's ideas about childhood trauma influenced and/or heightened your understanding of Tonyah's behaviors? Is there something you would add to or discount from their discussion? How does Stolow use Garbarino and Bruyere to help frame Tonyah's experience?

Prompts for Writing

1. Stolow asserts that Tonyah uses clothing as a form of non-verbal communication. Consider cultures in which women practice the covering of their bodies, and locate some textual evidence from which to summarize your understanding. For example, find Abu Lughod's essay, "Do Muslim Women Really Need Saving?" in connection with Stolow's insights. Discuss the relationship between Tonyah's practice of covering and some cultural practices of covering. What do these practices tell you about womanhood?

2. Read Stephen Oreski's case study, "Finding a Way Through the Darkness: Sexual Abuse, Self-Disclosure and the Therapeutic Alliance" (available in this series). Do you notice that Tonyah and Kevin exhibit similar expressions of resilience? Do you think that Tonyah's and Kevin's differences in gender affect their expressions of resilience? What other connections can you draw between these two cases?

3. What connections have you established between your own field work and Stolow's account of Tonyah's experience? Which social work concepts from Stolow's case study are applicable to your work in the field? Which social work concepts from Stolow's case study are most salient in your own practice and understanding in social work more generally?

References

Briere, J. N., & Elliott, D. M. (1994). Immediate and long-term impacts of child sexual abuse. *Future of Children*, 54–69.

Deblinger, E., Cohen, J., & Mannarino, A. (2006). *Treating trauma and traumatic grief in children and adolescents*. New York: Guilford Press.

Finkelhor, D., & Berliner, L. (1995). Research on the treatment of sexually abused children: A review and recommendations. *Journal of the American Academy of Child & Adolescent Psychiatry*, *34*(11), 1408–1423.

Garbarino, J. (2014). Ecological perspective on child well-being. In *Handbook of child wellbeing* (pp. 1365–1384). Dordrecht: Springer.

Garbarino, J., & Bruyere, E. (2013). Resilience in the lives of children of war. In *Handbook of resilience in children of war* (pp. 253–266). New York: Springer.

Gaskill, R., & Perry, B. (2002). Child sexual abuse, traumatic experiences, and their impact on the developing brain. In J. Myers, L. Berliner, J. Briere, C. Hendrix, C. Jenny, & T. Reid (Eds.), *The APSAC handbook on child maltreatment* (2nd ed., p. 55). Thousand Oaks, CA: Sage.

Germain, C. B. (1978). General-systems theory and ego psychology: An ecological perspective. *Social Service Review*, 535–550.

Gilman, C. P. (2002). *The dress of women: A critical introduction to the symbolism and sociology of clothing* (M. R. Hill & M. J. Deegan, Ed.). Westport, CT: Greenwood Press.

Gray, M. (2011). Back to basics: A critique of the strengths perspective in social work. *Families in Society: The Journal of Contemporary Social Services*, *92*(1), 5–11.

Klonsky, E. D., & Muehlenkamp, J. J. (2007). Self-injury: A research review for the practitioner. *Journal of Clinical Psychology*, *63*(11), 1045–1056.

Mannarino, A., Cohen, J., Smith, J., & Moore-Motily, S. (1991). Six and twelve month follow-up of sexually abused girls. *Journal of Interpersonal Violence*, *6*, 494–511.

McAslan, A. (2010). *The concept of resilience: Understanding its origins, meaning and utility*. Adelaide: Torrens Resilience Institute.

Miley, K. K., O'Melia, M., & Dubois, B. (2012). *Generalist social work practice: An empowering approach* (7th ed.). Boston: Pearson Education.

Nash, M. R., Hulsey, T. L., Sexton, M. C., Harralson, T. L., & Lambert, W. (1993). Long-term sequelae of childhood sexual abuse: Perceived family environment, psychopathology, and dissociation. *Journal of Consulting and Clinical Psychology*, *61*(2), 276.

Perry, B. D., & Hambrick, E. (2008). The neurosequential model of therapeutics. *Reclaiming Children and Youth*, *17*(3), 38–43.

Perry, B. D., & Pollard, R. (1998). Homeostasis, stress, trauma, and adaptation: A neurodevelopmental view of childhood trauma. *Child and Adolescent Psychiatric Clinics of North America*, *7*(1), 33–51.

Putnam, F. W. (1993). Dissociative phenomena. In D. Spiegel (Ed.), *Dissociative disorders: A clinical review* (pp. 1–16). Lutherville, MD: Sidran.

Putnam, F. W. (2003). Ten-year research update review: Child sexual abuse. *Journal of the American Academy of Child & Adolescent Psychiatry*, *42*(3), 269–278.

Reece, D. (1996). Covering and communication: The symbolism of dress among Muslim women. *Howard Journal of Communication*, *7*(35), 35–52.

Seaman, J. (2013). The empress's clothes. *Evolution's Empress: Darwinian Perspectives on the Nature of Women*, 406.

Steinberg, M. (1993). The spectrum of depersonalization: Assessment and treatment. In D. Spiegel (Ed.), *Dissociative disorders: A clinical review* (pp. 79–103). Lutherville, MD: Sidran.

Summit, R. C. (1983). The child sexual abuse accommodation syndrome. *Child Abuse & Neglect, 7,* 177–193.

Van der Hart, O., Van der Kolk, B. A., & Boon, S. (1998). Treatment of dissociative disorders. *Trauma, Memory, and Dissociation,* 253–283.

Van der Kolk, B. A. (1994). The body keeps the score: Memory and the evolving psychobiology of posttraumatic stress. *Harvard Review of Psychiatry, 1*(5), 253–265.

Van der Kolk, B. A. (2006). Clinical implications of neuroscience research in PTSD. *Annals of the New York Academy of Science, 1071*(4), 277–293.

Van der Kolk, B. A., Perry, J. C., & Herman, J. L. (1991). Childhood origins of self-destructive behavior. *American Journal of Psychiatry, 148*(12), 1665–1671.

Van der Kolk, B. A., Van der Hart, O., & Marmar, C. (1996). Dissociation and information processing in posttraumatic stress disorder. In B. van der Kolk, A. McFarlane, & L. Weisaeth (Eds.), *Traumatic stress: The effects of overwhelming experience on mind, body, and society.* New York: Guilford Press.

6

SOCIAL WORK AND SEX TRAFFICKING

Therapeutic Intervention in the Commercial Sexual Exploitation of Children

Kara Beckett

Pre-reading Questions

1. How would you define sex trafficking? How have you seen it covered in the media? Do you know of any policies in place to help victims of sex trafficking?
2. What barriers to typical therapeutic intervention might you face when working with a trafficking victim? How would you react to a client who returns to "the life" of sex trafficking while in treatment?
3. Do you think certain people or populations are more prone to being victims of sex trafficking?

Once thought of as a problem occurring "over there," across borders and oceans, the commercial sexual exploitation of children (CSEC) is ever-present in the United States.[1] Regarded as modern-day slavery, CSEC is a severe form of child sexual abuse, which encompasses a range of crimes and, in the broadest sense, involves a child who is utilized as an object in activities such as prostitution, stripping, pornography, and/or escorting in exchange for money, drugs, food, and/or shelter. In 2000, Congress established the legal definition of CSEC in the Trafficking Victims Protection Act (TVPA): "the recruitment, harboring, transportation, provision, or obtaining of a person for the purpose of a commercial sex act," including "severe forms of trafficking . . . in which a commercial sex act is induced by force, fraud, or coercion, or in which the person induced to perform such act has not attained 18 years of age" ("Human Trafficking Defined," 2016). It is important to note that "force" and other methods of compliance that seemingly take someone's choice away are not factors that pertain to persons under 18 years old; consent in these cases is irrelevant. It is also important to note that profits from human trafficking are estimated to be in the billions of dollars per year (Busch-Armendariz, Nsonwu, & Heffron, 2014), while the psychological costs to those who are trafficked are beyond calculation or comprehension.

Although the research literature and level of awareness is growing in reference to the overall issues concerning CSEC, significant gaps exist between theory and practice. A social worker without proper knowledge of CSEC victimization is unable to understand why a child may not want to be rescued from the clandestine world of sexual exploitation. The law enforcement officer who arrests children and consequently charges them with teen prostitution criminalizes their behavior. Members of society would wonder why some children would continuously place themselves in harm's way, and they view children as willing participants. The inability to grasp the demoralizing effects of the trauma bonds created to manipulate and gain power and control, thus leading a person to repeatedly run back to a pimp or away from those that seemingly care and want to assist with the healing process, challenges societal beliefs about the nature of sex work. "Juvenile prostitute" and "sex worker" are terms that have been used to identify minors who have been prostituted, but these words connote delinquent or offender status and reveal a lack of understanding of the effects of trauma.

Lost in between manualized treatments and the tensions of actual practice, social workers can feel powerless when there appears to be no progress in cases of CSEC. As a social worker who specializes in the treatment of children who have been trafficked, I present the case of Avani[2] to explore the phenomenological experience of social work practice in the field of CSEC, which is extremely difficult when the recidivism rate among children who have been trafficked is so high. If children, like Avani at age 15, so frequently return to "the life"—the lay term for involvement in child trafficking—how does this complicate treatment? Social workers must endeavor to examine each individual victim's experience and environment in order to provide effective treatment and to promote awareness of the complicated nature of sexual trauma.

> This time, Avani explained to me, it was different. The three days she had been gone had felt like an eternity. She recalled being taken into a strange house, then pushed into a closet from which she would only be released in order to engage in sex acts with numerous men. She had been sodomized and physically abused. Her wrists looked like they had been tightly bound, and there were burn marks from where her skin had been used to extinguish cigarettes. "I'm just tired, really tired . . . sore . . . I'm sore too." She had been forced to use drugs on a daily basis, a common tactic that pimps use to lessen their victims' fight, to make them more agreeable to customers, and to numb their pain. When Avani's adoptive mother, Karen,

received Avani's phone call after she had been missing, again, for days, she simply felt relief that her daughter had survived. She picked her up at a gas station, finding Avani disheveled and disoriented. Without being prompted, Avani said, "I don't want to talk about it. Just take me home."

We were at an impasse, 5 months into treatment. Although Avani's pattern of running away always led her back to situations full of striking similarities, this one sickened me. If traumatic experiences could be imagined on a scale, my sense was that this one could be considered the worst yet, the one that should create an illuminating moment, a change. It did not. When I arrived at Avani's home to help this time, I was confronted by Avani's lack of eye contact, slumped posture, and typical blasé attitude. The level of frustration and weariness was evident on Karen's face because this was an all too familiar scenario: the running away and the exploitation experience usually ended temporarily when Avani was picked up by the police, only for the cycle to begin again. One might think that a parent would display a certain level of emotionality, disappointment, or even anger in such circumstances; however, Karen's mild demeanor was consistent as she communicated in her usual soft-spoken voice, with little to no inflection. It was clear to me that Karen felt defeated. Moreover, circling thoughts of failure and doubt managed to creep inside my own otherwise healthy confidence in myself as a clinician. With the greatest intentions, combined with education, experience, and a passion to help, I felt paralyzed.

Avani had come out of her bedroom to see me, privately, after she had slept and showered. Akin to hibernation, a deep slumber was typical after she returned. It aided in Avani's recovery from days of minimal sleep and the copious amount of drugs and alcohol used for her to endure the daily trauma that was inflicted on her as a result of her body being used as a sexual object. This state of inertia would last, without interruption, until she awoke on her own.

Still, somehow, Avani's natural beauty never faded: she was tall and slender, with long, thick hair and prominent facial features that were accentuated by a tiny stud earring in her nose. I greeted her with a sympathetic smile and a side hug, and then I stated simply, "I'm glad you're safe. It's good to see you." Avani shrugged her shoulders and replied with her typical apathetic and detached response after returning home: "I'm fine." She was not crying; I was, only it went unnoticed as my tears flowed within.

Avani's Background

Avani was adopted from India and brought to the United States at age 9 by Karen, a single, middle-aged Caucasian woman. They lived together in an apartment in the suburbs of a southern metropolitan city. In India, Avani's life, at least according to records and reports, had been filled with suffering and trauma. The adoption agency divulged Avani's history of sexual abuse by her biological father,

her exposure to verbal, physical, and sexual abuse by both biological parents, and her subsequent abandonment by them on the streets of India. Prior victimization is a predictor for future exploitation; multiple studies have shown a correlation of environmental factors such as child neglect, physical and/or sexual abuse, and poverty contributing to an increased vulnerability and risk of being sexually exploited (Hom & Woods, 2013). According to Rachel Lloyd (2005), "Studies report that 70–80% of sexually exploited youth were sexually abused as children" (pp. 10–11). As a result of sexual abuse, children can develop a distorted perception of their self-worth, self-confidence, and self-esteem. There is also a propensity to self-blame for the abuse that occurred. The lines that determine healthy sexual boundaries are blurry, particularly when there is no treatment early on.

At the age of 6, Avani was taken to an orphanage after she was found walking by herself on the streets for an unknown amount of time. She endured physical abuse at the first of two orphanages in India. The whereabouts of her biological parents were unknown at the time of the adoption. Karen was told that Avani's biological mother may have died, but this has not been confirmed, and may never be. Avani's lack of impulse control, vulnerability, and extreme hyperarousal can be attributed to her disorganized attachment pattern (Hill, 2015).

During an extended visit to India, Karen met and bonded with Avani and believed that if she was provided with a loving, nurturing, and stable environment, Avani would thrive. Karen was not educated on the attachment issues that adopted children could face and falsely believed that love and permanence was all that was needed for Avani to thrive. In spite of this extensive traumatic history, Karen developed an attachment to Avani and continued with the extensive adoption process to bring her to the United States.

Karen doted on Avani and described their relationship as "loving" when she arrived in the United States. Aware of the significant assimilation and acculturation processes, including the language barrier that would occur once she arrived, Karen made every attempt to make the transition smooth for both of them. With full support of her parents, and other family members who lived nearby, Karen felt that she had prepared for the bumps that would occur along the road. However, she was not aware of how Avani's past trauma, coupled with her transition, would lead to future vulnerabilities.

Avani did not have a good educational foundation while in India, and her educational history before the age of 9 is unknown. When she began elementary school in the United States (3rd grade), many of Avani's peers made fun of her, and she suffered from low self-esteem as a result. This impeded her performance, and her grades were below average. Karen provided Avani with a tutor, and she even helped her at home, but the setbacks continued. Avani would frequently lose focus in class. She fidgeted and had a difficult time sitting still. Consequently, she was diagnosed with attention deficit hyperactivity disorder (ADHD) and was prescribed medication, but she did not take it as the doctor prescribed on a consistent basis. She would hold the medicine in her mouth and then spit it out. Karen became frustrated with the ongoing medication battle, and slowly but surely did not make her take it anymore.

Avani continued to pass through elementary and middle school, albeit with substantial difficulties. She began to interrupt the learning of other students by her incessant talking in class. She was failing most of her classes and had several referrals to the school social worker as a result. She would become frustrated at her inability to grasp most subject matter, especially English. Avani's trouble in school extended beyond her educational deficits as she continued to struggle behaviorally.

After Avani entered high school at age 15, there was a significant change in her behavior at home and in school. Her school attendance became sporadic at best, averaging about one to two days per week. Even when she did attend, she skipped several classes daily. She had more than 30 absences within the first 2 months of school. Karen confronted Avani about her questionable friendships, including the possibility of gang involvement, but Avani denied it, adamantly. At this point, Karen's gut instinct told her that it was a lie, as she had been caught in so many untruths already. In fact, Avani denied most of what she was confronted with, including her sexual activity. Karen was sure that she was sexually active due to the inappropriate messages that she found on her phone as well as encounters with teenage boys in her apartment when they were not supposed to be there. Frequent outbursts of anger, aggression, and violent behavior toward her adoptive mother and other authority figures escalated the more Karen questioned Avani's behaviors and attempted to implement disciplinary measures.

Avani left home regularly without permission, leaving for hours and even overnight, her whereabouts unknown. She became a chronic runaway who drank alcohol and smoked cigarettes and marijuana. Her emotions were erratic, fluctuating between sadness and anger. The excitement and joy that Karen felt about having a child of her own was overshadowed with hopelessness. She was slowly losing Avani.

Avani's Pathway to Entry

Various pathways can lead one into commercial sexual exploitation. While the average age of entry is between 12 and 14 years old, there are accounts of commercial sexual exploitation occurring in children as young as 8 years old (Smith, Snow, & Vardaman, 2009). No child is immune. With the prevalence of social media sites, where children and adolescents can 'friend' or 'follow' strangers and engage in conversations in chat rooms, the internet becomes a haven for recruitment. In a number of cases, fake profiles on various sites are created with a younger age, 'friendships' are formed, trust is established, ultimately leading to coercion for the child to leave home. Violence, kidnapping, seduction and coercion, responding to false advertising for dancing or modeling, and recruitment by peers are also techniques used to enlist children and adolescents (Kunze, 2009).

Typically skilled at targeting and recruiting juveniles, pimps seek out youth that are particularly vulnerable, primarily due to an unstable environment at their home of origin or home within a social service or judicial system. Fichtelman (2014) discusses the methodical approaches that pimps use as "they assess their targets needs and weaknesses and then use those factors to prey on unsuspecting children" at bus stops, schools, foster homes, shopping malls, teen clubs, homeless shelters, and group homes; the developmental stage, inexperience, and gullibility, combined with an unstable or traumatic background, makes it easier for a child "to submit to their own sexual exploitation" (p. 30).

A traumatic history beginning at home filled with turmoil and conflict can make a child more prone to running away, likely believing that a life outside of their home with the safety they desire to find is the lesser of two evils. Children who are runaways or throwaways are at an even greater risk of being lured into sexual exploitation. Research has shown a direct association of running away behavior with commercial sexual exploitation, as they become prime targets for pimps, offenders, and other predators (Estes & Weiner, 2001). Most are recruited within 48 hours of leaving home (Schapiro, 2010). Methods of survival become paramount, and runaways quickly find out that the need for food and shelter come with a high price.

Although many similarities exist that bind children and adolescents under the umbrella of CSEC, each person has an individual story. Avani was recruited shortly after she began high school by Mike, a 16-year-old male dropout who was a "runner"—a term used to describe runaways, but here used to describe someone aiding a pimp—that recruited female adolescents for a pimp. Avani was 14 years old at the time. Mike came to Avani's school almost daily and was able to develop a relationship with her. He garnered her trust and made her feel special, something that Avani was seeking. This process, otherwise known as "grooming," was the result of a subtle, gradual, and purposeful way of establishing trust with Avani. She was manipulated into thinking that she gained an alliance with someone trustworthy, seemingly appearing to care about her. Avani finally felt valued.

Already feeling ostracized in school due to her lack of friendships and poor academic skills, all contributing to her low self-esteem, Avani was vulnerable and reveled in the attention. After several brief visits for shallow conversation, Avani was subsequently coerced into leaving school under the guise of smoking marijuana. Immediately after they arrived to the home, Avani was forced into a bedroom by another man known as James and brutally raped. After he finished, he told her that he was her pimp. Prior to being allowed to leave the home, James threatened to kill Avani and her family if she told anyone or did not comply with what she was ordered to do: "Violence is used because it convinces the victim that the perpetrator is omnipotent and that resistance is futile, even dangerous" (Palmer, 2010, p. 50). The following day after this traumatic ordeal, Avani was picked up from school on a daily basis, with her body used as a sex object, bought by countless johns. Avani realized that her body was not her own anymore, and her mind followed shortly thereafter. She was a mere commodity. Avani's will was broken, and the power and control dynamic was established.

Treatment for Avani

The Referral

The most important advancement affecting the provision of services to child victims of CSEC has been the coordination between law enforcement, school personnel, hospital personnel, and social workers in which the social worker serves as the single point of contact; this model differs from the case management model because social workers are given access to confidential information usually guarded by law enforcement operations and other policy measures (Busch-Armendariz, Nsonwu, & Heffron, 2014). Whereas child "sex workers" are often picked up by police, charged with prostitution, and often incarcerated (which temporarily, at least, keeps them safe from "the life"), new trust building surrounding the issue of CSEC among police and social workers led a local detective to be my referral source in Avani's case. This detective had heard Avani's name mentioned in a different case as he was trying to infiltrate a crime ring, and he figured she might, at least, be at risk. Thus, she would receive counseling services to address the issues that were impacting her at home and in school.

As a contractual provider for the community-based agency serving severely emotionally disturbed (SED) children and adolescents, I was used to working with children and adolescents who presented with serious behaviors. Although there were various mental health services offered, such as individual and family therapy, and therapeutic groups, I primarily provided intensive services under the Intensive Family Intervention (IFI) Program. These services are largely provided in the home, school, detention facilities, and hospitals. Collaboration in cases like Avani's was the norm because those children who were referred, especially to IFI, came from other agencies such as the Department of Family and Children Services, Department of Juvenile Justice, and school settings.

IFI services provide the highest level of care offered in a community-based setting, which gives social workers insight into the living conditions of their clients. IFI provides a wide range of services for the family, including individual and family therapy, behavior management, crisis intervention, case management, treatment planning, and reassessment. These services are provided on a short-term basis at least three times per week, and during crises the hours increase. Intensive services are utilized to stabilize disruptive behaviors and to allow the child to remain in her natural environment. If this goal is not accomplished, the next level of care is an out-of-home placement, such as a psychiatric residential treatment facility (PRTF), which Avani attended at one point during her treatment. IFI services not only help the child, but it also helps the family cope with significant stressors as a result of the severe disruption of family functioning. IFI service delivery is accomplished by a team approach that keeps everyone involved in contact for a minimum of 90 days.

Acting out in school and home, defiance toward authority figures, anger, skipping school, and running away, Avani's referral form was representative of many adolescents I see in community-based services. Avani's tumultuous relationship with her adoptive mother also led to threats and episodes of violence in the home. I remember thinking about how much it read like the typical presentation of behaviors I would see on a referral form, only I knew better.

The Assessment

Discussing 'safe topics' such as Avani's favorite hobbies and foods in an effort to find similarities between the two of us seemed to relieve some of the thick resistance that Avani initially displayed. The use of open-ended questions also helped with furthering the dialogue. As she felt more relaxed with me, her true self started to slowly emerge. Avani became lively when speaking of topics of interest, like her favorite television shows, with smiles and even bouts of laughter here and there. The exchange on superficial matters opened the door to a more focused conversation of why I was there. Avani seemed to feel more at ease with the understanding that I was there to help and did not serve as a parental figure. Further, she knew that I would continue working with her either individually or with a team under the IFI program, even after the assessment.

Avani was less comfortable with open-ended questions of substance, and she had a difficult time elaborating without being prompted. She shared that she experienced "sad feelings" occurring at least 5 out of 7 days per week. She identified that these "sad feelings" had escalated in the past 3 months. When I asked Avani to describe the sad feelings she was experiencing, she stated, "I don't know . . . I'm just not happy." However, when asked to identify if she cries or isolates, she immediately responded, "Yes!" The inflection in her voice varied depending on what was discussed.

Avani was open when she discussed her inability to control her anger, which resulted in frequent anger outbursts, occurring at least three to four times a week. Her anger was typically projected toward her adoptive mother by cursing, throwing objects, and yelling. Why wouldn't Avani direct anger toward the men controlling her? She had been brainwashed and threatened that her family would be killed if she disobeyed, so perhaps her outrage at Karen was actually a way of protecting her. After her anger outbursts, she became restless and experienced difficulty falling and remaining asleep. During times of agitation and anger, Avani had suicidal thoughts. She made statements such as "I want to die . . . I want to be with my mother in heaven." However, there was no clear plan for follow through.

As the assessment questions became move invasive, Avani's discomfort grew more evident. Questions surrounding her past history of trauma were met with brief moments of silence and full on dissociation. Avani disclosed that she was raped 3 months prior, but would not discuss the details of what happened or who the alleged perpetrator was. What she did offer was a glimpse of the effects, such as isolating herself and not wanting to speak to anyone, including her adoptive mother. Avani also experienced a loss of interest in activities she used to enjoy, such as dancing. She stated, "I don't care about anything really." She was unable to identify one item or person that she cared about. It was clear that she experienced feelings of worthlessness in statements such as "no one likes me . . . I don't have any friends."

In assessing her past and present drug use, Avani admitted to smoking marijuana since the early summer, after starting high school. Although she was not completely clear as to why and how it began, I attributed her disclosure of the rape that same summer as a factor. Avani "occasionally" drank alcohol to the point of intoxication while smoking marijuana. She admitted that she was influenced by other peers in school to try it, and it developed into a "habit" as a result. She began leaving home without permission. Initially, it began as her sitting outside after an anger outburst, which later evolved to leaving without letting her adoptive mother know. However, this behavior increased in severity; she typically left in the middle of the night and would not return. On each of these occasions, she was found by police officers and returned home.

While it is relevant to gather quantifiable data in order to determine a starting point to gauge her symptoms and whether or not they decrease or increase over time with treatment, it is also vital to listen to Avani's lived experience and listen for what was not verbalized. Her personal account provides some context into her life and a better understanding of the behaviors that follow. As clinicians, it is important listen to the story, while recognizing that the label resulting from the assessment is not necessarily an integral component in the actual treatment and does not equate to a successful treatment.

The Treatment Plan

Avani began IFI services with a team of three mental health professionals: two clinicians and a behavioral specialist. The IFI team was also able to work with the school social worker and teachers in order to provide an intensive level of care to keep her stable in the community. As one of the treating clinicians, it was my desire for her to remain stable in her community setting; however, after our first visit, it was doubtful that this would happen.

Avani was not home for the first scheduled session with the IFI team. In fact, she had not returned home from school that day. Karen, frustrated but still calm, described the daily accounts of Avani, her behavior, and her increasing state of unwillingness to comply with her mother or any other adult figure: "She just keeps getting worse, I don't know what to do anymore." She started out with a system of rewards and consequences where Karen attempted to take her cell phone and television privileges. When Avani went to locate her belongings and could not find them, she acted as if she did not need or want them. Nothing Karen tried worked. We discussed other behavior modification plans with Karen but, in crisis mode, we established a plan given the likelihood that Avani might not return home.

Avani did return home later that night and was not responsive to Karen when questioned regarding her whereabouts. Karen became increasingly concerned about her escalating behaviors and her safety. When Karen came home early from work the following day, during school hours, she saw Avani walking with another male. After Avani arrived home, and Karen expressed her anger about her conduct, Avani lashed out, "Fuck this, I do what I want to do . . . just leave me alone!" Filled with frustration, Karen yelled at her. Avani left the home, again, just before the team was due to come and make another attempt at meeting her.

Karen knew her options, especially if Avani did not return home. She did not want to call the police, and she was reluctant to file an unruly charge in juvenile court against Avani, because she feared that Avani would "never" return home and feared that she could be taken away from her. It was clear that more proactive measures were needed because Karen was no longer in control, even with the addition of intensive services.

It is the goal of the clinician to decrease suffering, discover underlying issues that create turmoil, and ultimately help the client to develop new ways of coping. This occurs through the psychotherapeutic process. However, Avani's absence during the team's multiple trips to her home meant that Avani was unable to be an active participant in her own treatment. The level of frustration was growing within the IFI team. Avani's non-appearance would impact whether or not her case would remain open. "Anger directed against the self or others is always a central problem in the life of people who have been violated" (Van der Kolk, 1989, p. 392). This can also lead to aggressive behaviors during treatment. Engagement is difficult in treatment due to their mistrust of others. According to Herman (1992):

> Traumatic events call into question basic human relationships . . . breach the attachments of family, love, and community . . . shatter the construction of the self that is formed and sustained in relation to others . . . undermine the belief systems that give meaning to human experience.
>
> *(p. 51)*

Trauma can "damage the patient's ability to enter into a trusting relationship" (Herman, 1998, p. S145), therefore impacting the helping relationship. Running away abruptly halts services in residential or community-based treatment, which is why building a trusting therapeutic relationship/connection and remaining consistent as a provider is paramount.

A sense of relief overcame me when I was finally able to lay eyes on her since the assessment and make attempts at building a rapport.

"I need help with my anger . . . I just can't take it!" Avani exclaimed with her arms crossed.

"I can see you're upset. What happened?"

"I can't take it! She always tries to control me. I should be able to do what I want." Avani's tone grew louder and louder.

"That's why I'm here Avani. The whole team is here for you and for your mother. Where do you want to start Avani?" I responded in a low and calm tone hoping to counteract her rising voice.

Short quick breaths were followed by silence that filled the room for what seemed longer than it actually was. I waited, knowing that it was important for Avani to know that I was still present and comfortable in her silence, even though it was deafening. Avani's irritation was a result of being confronted by Karen after she did not return home from school. Karen responded by yelling at her, which did not resonate well. Avani lashed out by cursing, yelling, and making threatening gestures in response. This call and response had become the normal interaction, and Karen would back down, frightened by Avani's vitriol.

After my individual session with Avani, the IFI team was only able to see her one time altogether as opposed to the three sessions that were scheduled the following week. Her pattern of behavior continued by coming home late after school. Avani pushed Karen's boundaries right to the edge, as she was aware that her mother had threatened to file an unruly charge if her behavior continued.

What was most important at this point was to establish a plan for safety due to Avani's worsening behaviors. During this family session with the team, a safety plan was developed and reviewed due to Avani's escalating behaviors. It was important for Avani's feelings to be validated and for her to be a part of the process. Avani helped to determine what the consequences of her actions would be. We left with a plan, albeit with the knowledge that the plan would probably crumble.

Avani ran again, a couple days after the visit. Even after being rescued, several times, Avani always found a way back into the life. It proved to be quite difficult for her to separate and accept the assistance she so needed in order to recover from her trauma. Sexually exploited children often display symptoms of trauma bonding, also known as Stockholm syndrome. "Just as victims of domestic and family violence stay with their abuser, victims competed into prostitution are often caught in the same dangerous cycle" (Fichtelman, 2014, p. 30). It was challenging to work with Avani, as I had to constantly tell myself that this was her world, one that was grim to enter. I had to accept that she was the sum of her individual and collective experiences. This time, she was already gone for over 24 hours. Another argument between Karen and Avani was the catalyst for her departure, or so it seemed. Karen's version includes verbal threats as a result of giving Avani a consequence of taking her phone privileges. "She exploded . . . yelling, cursing, called me names. I didn't know what she was going to do." Avani went to her bedroom to take her self-timeout and listen to her radio, a coping skill she identified that would help her calm down. The radio was loud, providing enough noise so Karen would not hear her pull the window up and climb out, unsuspectingly. Karen went to check on her after about 20 minutes, but she was gone. Karen followed through with her part of calling the police and filed a missing person's report. As a team, we developed a plan for if and when Avani returned that included crisis stabilization, and we followed up with Karen for status checks.

Although there was already speculation in reference to whether Avani was being sexually exploited, it was at least evident that she was high-risk based on her telling behaviors and previous victimization. Detective Louis met with Karen regarding Avani's disappearance to keep her updated and provide some sort of ease by letting her know that he was actively looking for her. Just as I suspected, involvement with a pimp was confirmed when she was found almost two weeks later.

Due to the time lapse of services with Avani running away, and mandated guidelines, Avani's IFI case was closed. However, a tentative plan was already developed for her and would be implemented once she returned. Providing a continuum of care, and the stability that she needed of a familiar face, I arranged and accompanied Avani and her mother to the hospital for a full medical exam. At this specialized facility within the hospital setting for children, young girls like Avani could come without fear of being shunned or judged.

While waiting to be called, Avani's moods swung like a pendulum, never slowing down enough to remain in one spot for long, before picking up speed and swaying to the other side. I noticed how Karen tried to console Avani by putting her hand on her shoulder; Avani quickly moved away. Karen made several attempts to speak to Avani, mostly small talk in an effort to pass the time. Initially, Avani seemed pleasant and cordial toward Karen, but this was quickly replaced with providing curt one-word answers, to finally not responding to Karen at all.

Observing her in the waiting room, I saw a scared 15-year-old girl for the first time. She was curled up in the chair, with her head on her knees, waiting to be called. Silence ensued. I thought about how easy it could be to forget when faced with the insurmountable issues and troubling behaviors, with the inability to slow down and process her developmental age compared to her life experiences.

The fast pace of this crisis oriented case also hindered the opportunity to truly self-reflect. Avani is a child.

As a standard hospital practice for this type of visit, Avani took a cupful of pills and a couple of needle sticks as a preventative against pregnancy and any sexually transmitted infections she could have been exposed to while on runaway status. A complete rape kit, medical exam, and a forensic interview by clinical social workers on staff trained to work with children and adolescents who have been sexually exploited completed Avani's hospital visit. Remarkably, Avani was open enough during her forensic interview confirming what was already suspected and providing key information in order for a more thorough investigation and possible arrest of her pimp and other people involved.

Avani's Continued Fights and Flights

Even though Avani was forthcoming when it came to providing the police with information about her pimp, her exit from "the life" was far from over. Having worked this case and others like it, I learned that child victims of CSEC were too mired in their shame and pain to stay put at home. Avani continued to run. And she continued to return. She was caught in a cycle like fight and flight, and her own personal sense of initiative seemed to have been lost. As Jayagupta (2009) reported, trafficking victims are not easily reintegrated into society. Traditional trauma treatment approaches often serve to retraumatize victims, leading them right back to the streets because they think that have nowhere else that they truly belong. I tried to focus on affect stability, behavior modification, healthy environments, and a sense of safety rather than to push toward the roots of Avani's trauma. I felt that if I ever guided Avani to her memories, I might trigger her to run again. I did educate Avani on how trafficking works to exploit vulnerable people, but even the slightest body language suggesting judgment—or anything other than unconditional acceptance—might cause her to dissociate. Therefore, I have found that the most I can do in Avani's case is to just be present when she can tolerate the modicum of comfort my alliance with her could provide. I wish I could share more resources and techniques, but just the retelling of this case leaves me feeling like I just do not have the answers I need to be who Avani needs me to be.

The insufficient understanding regarding the severity of this violent crime against children and adolescents, and the severe impact on their psychological health, can prevent even the most seasoned professional from being able to successfully engage, let alone treat victims of CSEC. Until there is a greater comprehension of the phenomenology of CSEC, the tensions that exist, and the magnitude of the mental, physical, psychological, and emotional impact it has on a person, it will remain difficult to address the 'how-to' in reference to the engagement and effective treatment of victims.

Close Reading Questions

1. What do you make of Avani's mother's experience and reaction to her daughter's victimization?
2. Describe what you found interesting about Beckett's intervention. How would you have handled the situations that Beckett faced?
3. Why does Beckett say that Stockholm syndrome is typical of trafficking victims? Do you agree that Avani did, in fact, experience Stockholm syndrome?

Questions for Writing

1. Draw upon Healy's chapter to discuss the complicated dynamics of "victim" and "offender" as they apply to Avani and Charles. How are these cases connected by these terms and the clients' experiences of social work intervention?
2. Why do you think Avani blames her mother for the anger issues that lead her to leave the house?
3. Beckett discusses the emotions she experienced when working with Avani. Design a self-care regimen for a social worker who specializes in the treatment of clients involved in sex trafficking. Are there any elements specific to sex-trafficking work that your self-care plan addresses?

Notes

1. Domestic minor sex trafficking (DMST) is another name for CSEC in the United States.
2. All names and identifying information have been changed to respect client confidentiality.

References

Busch-Armendariz, N., Nsonwu, M. B., & Heffron, L. C. (2014). A kaleidoscope: The role of the social work practitioner and the strength of social work theories and practice in meeting the complex needs of people trafficked and the professionals that work with them. *International Social Work, 57*(1), 7–18.

Estes, R. J., & Weiner, N. A. (2001). *The commercial sexual exploitation of children in the US, Canada and Mexico*. Philadelphia: University of Pennsylvania, School of Social Work, Center for the Study of Youth Policy.

Fichtelman, E. B. (2014). The double entendre of juvenile prostitution: Victim versus delinquent and the necessity of state uniformity. *Juvenile and Family Court Journal, 65*(3–4), 27–46.

Herman, J. L. (1997). *Trauma and recovery*. London: Pandora Google Scholar.

Herman, J. L. (1998). Recovery from psychological trauma. *Psychiatry and Clinical Neurosciences, 52*(S1), S98–S103.

Hill, D. (2015). Attachment regulation and the attachment relationship. In *Affect regulation theory: A clinical model: Manuscript in preparation for publication*. New York: W. W. Norton.

Hom, K. A., & Woods, S. J. (2013). Trauma and its aftermath for commercially sexually exploited women as told by front-line service providers. *Issues in Mental Health Nursing, 34*(2), 75–81.

Human Trafficking Defined. (2016). Retrieved from https://www.state.gov/j/tip/rls/tiprpt/2016/259066.htm

Jayagupta, R. (2009). The Thai government's repatriation and reintegration programmes: Responding to trafficked female commercial sex workers from the Greater Mekong Subregion. *International Migration, 47*(2), 227–253.

Kunze, E. I. (2009). Sex trafficking via the internet: How international agreements address the problem and fail to go far enough. *Journal of High Technology Law, 10*, 241.

Lloyd, R. (2005). Acceptable victims? Sexually exploited youth in the U.S. *Encounter: Education for Meaning and Social Justice, 18*(3), 7–15.

Palmer, N. (2010). The essential role of social work in addressing victims and survivors of trafficking. *ILSA Journal of International & Comparative Law, 17*, 43.

Schapiro Group, T. (2010). *Adolescent girls in Georgia's sex trade: Tracking study results.* Atlanta, GA: Schapiro Group.

Smith, L., Snow, M., & Vardaman, S. (2009). *The National Report on Domestic Minor Sex Trafficking: America's Prostituted Children.* [PDF file] Washington, DC. Retrieved from https://sharedhope.org/wp-content/uploads/2012/09/SHI_National_Report_on_DMST_2009.pdf

Van der Kolk, B. A. (1989). The compulsion to repeat the trauma. *Psychiatric Clinics of North America, 12*(2), 389–411.

7

SOCIAL WORK WITH AN ADOLESCENT FEMALE SEX OFFENDER

Jesselly De La Cruz

Pre-reading Questions

1. Describe what comes to mind when you think of a "sex offender." What are your personal feelings about people who commit sex offenses? In what ways may you encounter a sex offender in clinical practice?
2. What are the common myths about sex offenders as per the Center for Sex Offender Management (CSOM)? How does gender socialization (male vs. female) and age (adult vs. juvenile) contribute to public perception of who commits sex offenses?
3. How would you define sexism? Rape culture? And do you believe that women from different races and ethnicity have distinct challenges when it comes to sexism and rape culture?

Female adolescent sex offenders (FASO) are a complex clinical population because of the sociocultural dynamics that influence the disclosure of and system responses to female-perpetrated sexual abuse, the prevalent duality of FASOs as offenders and victims of sexual abuse, and the gender-specific considerations of the sexual, emotional, and relational development unique to the life cycle of women (Center for Sex Offender Management, 2007). Contributing to the mystery surrounding FASOs, girls represent only about 7% of juvenile arrests for sex offenses (Office of Juvenile Justice and Delinquency Prevention, 2009b), creating obstacles for quantitative studies to determine effective treatment approaches. In addition, there is little literature with clinical case studies illustrating a person-in-environment perspective of female adolescents in sex offender–specific treatment. In the court-mandated sex offender–specific outpatient treatment of a teenage girl who committed a violent sexual assault on a 9-year-old girl, traditional sex offender treatment approaches were challenged to meet her therapeutic needs. A case study approach encourages providers to reflect upon their therapeutic flexibility to meet the needs of the client as the central vehicle for treating sexually abusive behavior. This case study aims to examine the complexity of restorative justice approaches when working with FASOs. Furthermore, providers working with FASOs are challenged to consider the implications for treatment when viewing trauma from a larger cultural framework as it applies to urban youth, specifically the impact of rape culture upon young girls of color.

Sarah

Looking at the picture on my phone of a young, teenage girl wearing a cap and gown, a formal black dress, and the small purse I had given her as a gift for her elementary school graduation, stirred up conflicting feelings of pride and anguish as her therapist. "Hey, but I have a question, what happened to your knee? You are wearing a Band-Aid? Did you hurt yourself?" I asked. "I fell and scraped my knee on my way to school. What happened was that there was a shootout when me, my momma, and my baby were going to the graduation," she said casually. My heart sank as I realized that it was June; when the summer heat sets in, the gun violence in her neighborhood rises faster than the temperature. When I inquired about her safety, she replied, "I'm fine. My momma was crying a lot because she fell, too, and she was carrying my baby." The heartbreaking images of my client with her 8-month-old son and mother lying on the street pavement ducking gunshots flooded my head. "Did anyone else get hurt?" I asked. "No. It was just some boys. The cops came." I had been working with Sarah for about a year in an intensive outpatient program for juvenile sex offenders, and the complex layers of Sarah's life as a young girl growing up in an environment that was inundated with violence and chaos often felt insurmountable to her recovery. However, Sarah was surviving her circumstances, and I learned that her secret of survival was the matter-of-fact stance she had toward her experiences. Sarah made it seem as if being caught in a shootout was just another day. As her therapist, there were many moments, like this one, when I tried to visualize how I would have survived the circumstances of Sarah's world, such as being caught in random gunfire on my way to my elementary school graduation.

While there is a vast distance between my world and Sarah's world, I realize that violence was a stark and tragic reality in the lives of many youth, like Sarah, with national studies indicating that approximately "sixty percent of children in the United States are exposed to violence in their daily lives" (Office of Juvenile Justice and Delinquency Prevention, 2009a). Complex trauma develops from the repeated exposure to multiple traumatic events, and in children and adolescents, results in impaired functioning among seven domains including "attachment, biology, affect regulation, dissociation, behavioral regulation, cognition, and self-concept" (National Center for Child Traumatic Stress, 2003). In the graduation photo, Sarah showed me yet another instance in her life where she experienced a traumatic event, and just kept going without a second thought—she was caught in a shootout, went to her graduation, took a celebratory picture, and continued with her day—all the while adapting like humans do. Unfortunately, Sarah's exposure to violence was so embedded in her daily life that it prevented her from having an opportunity to pause, and process the trauma, the threats to her and her family's lives, and, for Sarah, there never was a pause from the chaos—except when she came to therapy.

Sarah's emotional disconnect from her traumatic experiences is the clinical phenomenon of dissociation, an underlying theme throughout her treatment. Dissociation can occur on a continuum; it is not automatically the result of trauma, and, to some degree on the lower end of the continuum, considered normative in children and adolescents (ISSD, 2004). However, dissociation is most often encountered in clinical practice within the symptomatology associated with complex trauma (National Center for Child Traumatic Stress, 2003). According to the International Society for the Study of Dissociation (2004), dissociation is characterized by the "developmental disruption in the integration of adaptive memory, sense of identity, and the self-regulation of emotion" (ISSD, 2004, p. 123). Ultimately, dissociation is a survival instinct to protect oneself from the awareness of violence and other life-threatening events (Hornstein & Putnam, 1992). In Sarah's case, the juxtaposition of her dissociation unfolded in treatment as a coping strategy that she used to disconnect herself, and to manage the fears she developed from the overwhelming violence and chaos she encountered regularly (Hornstein & Putnam, 1992). The same adaptive dissociation also facilitated her sexual offense. When I listened to Sarah's disclosure of her sexual assault, I learned that she committed her sexual offense in a fugue state—a state of mind to which she was so accustomed that she described it like just another mode of being for her. As a result, integrating trauma-focused interventions into Sarah's sex offender–specific treatment became integral to her recovery.

Given the devastating impact of sexual abuse upon victims, families, and communities, offender rehabilitation is a multifaceted effort that cuts across the legal, social, and psychological disciplines (Gannon, Dixon, & Craig, 2013). Therefore, a transdisciplinary approach is a key aspect of the assessment, management, and treatment of sex offenders, particularly in addressing the complex needs of FASOs. Social policy is presented with the complex task of restorative justice, a community response aimed at repairing the harm caused by sexual offending by empowering the victim, and asserting that the offender assume full responsibility for the abuse (Tsui, 2014). Despite juvenile justice efforts to rehabilitate youth offenders, public interest in protecting children from sexual exploitation and violent crimes has led to more punitive legal responses to juvenile sex offending, such as the implementation of the Sex Offender Registration and Notification Act (SORNA) under the Adam Walsh Child Protection and Safety Act of 2006 (McAlinde, 2008). However, there has been insufficient evidence that SORNA reduces the risk of sexual reoffense, and, equally important, has a negative long-term impact upon adolescents whom, as research also indicates, are not likely to reoffend (Caldwell & Dickinson, 2009). The concept of restorative justice as applied to FASOs is even further complicated by the ambiguous line between offender and victim, as is often the case of female offenders. Specifically, in Sarah's case, Sarah was at both ends of the law—as an offender when one of the stipulations of her adjudication was that she was mandated to register as a sex offender indefinitely, and as a victim when she became pregnant from a statutory rape with a boyfriend who was several years older.

Ultimately, developing a therapeutic relationship with Sarah required more than just a psychological understanding of complex trauma; it required a broader perspective of the way in which historical, legal, and sociological structures shape women, and how adapting to a culture that exploits women can lead a young girl to identify with her aggressor. The painful state of Sarah's sexual trauma is weaved into a historical, cultural, and sociological discourse on the detrimental impact of the negative images and narratives that Sarah and other young girls receive from rape culture about what it means to be a girl. Herman (1984) defines rape culture as a shared belief system where violence against women is tolerated, even promoted, because of the sexual objectification and gender role socialization of women. Moreover, Spelman (1988) highlights the oppression uniquely experienced by women of color, noting that, phenomeno-logically, the experiences of racism and sexism were much infused in the experience of Black women. In Sarah's case, she related to the Black women she saw in music videos and movies that frequently fused glorified images of sex and violence. Richardson (2013) also describes the way in which young, Black girls are "harassed, pressured, or seduced into becoming sex objects" (Richardson, 2013, p. 338). More than normalization and denial, Sarah's choice to violently sexually abuse another little girl suggested that Sarah had actually internalized the messages of rape culture. Internalized sexism is a concept describing "when women enact learned sexist behaviors upon themselves and other women" (Bearman, Korobov, & Thorne, 2009, p. 10). The crux of the influences of the fused images of sex and violence on Sarah's psyche led Sarah to normalize her rape, deny the experience as an act of violence against her, and in essence fuel her motivation to gain power by sexually abusing her victim.

A Clinical Picture of Female Adolescent Sex Offenders

The scarcity of literature on FASOs is palpable. Research on FASOs continues to be in its infancy, and the low incidence of sexual offending by female adolescents contributes to the limitations in our understanding. However, the lack of knowledge is also reflective of the marginalization of FASOs, and the perplex-ing problem of working with them. In an exploratory study by Hendriks and Bijleveld (2006), the lack of literature on FASOs contributes to the underreport-ing of sex offenses by adolescents in general, and to an "under-estimation" of FASOs' problems (Hendriks & Bijleveld, 2006, p. 33). In addition to Hendriks and Bijleveld (2006), many other scholars also refer to the cultural implications affecting the underidentification of sexual abuse perpetrated by female ado-lescents (Fehrenbach & Monestersky, 1988; Higgs, Canavan, & Meyer, 1992; Turner & Turner, 1994; Wijkman, Bijleveld, & Hendriks, 2014). Specifically, FASOs are a clinical population that complicates two major cultural phenomena about gender roles and socialization in society, and the perpetuation of sexual abuse. First, the dynamics of FASOs complicates the cultural concept of girls as victims. Feminist theory highlights the way in which beliefs about gender, sex, and power that dominate our culture can impact how society views women and girls, as well as how they view themselves. Sexism is also identified as a precur-sor to the perpetuation of gender-based sexual violence (Herman, 1984). With sexual violence being more about power than sex, FASOs challenge the power dynamic in the cultural narratives of girls as being primarily victims of sexual abuse. Second, the fallacy that "girls do not sexually offend" contributes to the stigma that discourages victims from disclosing female-perpetrated sexual abuse. This fallacy originates from a reductionist cultural narrative about the expression of female sexuality, and the expectations of women and girls as safe caretakers and nurturers.

Further complicating the cultural misconceptions of women and girls, explor-atory studies on FASOs demonstrate the frequency with which young girls are indeed victims of sexual abuse, as well as the regularity with which girls are placed in the position of a babysitter or caretaker for younger children. Exist-ing research highlights the prevalence of past sexual and physical victimization among FASOs and, paradoxically, that being in the role of caretaker and nurturer for younger children often facilitated FASO's abusive behavior (Fehrenbach & Monestersky, 1988). While FASOs are described as heterogeneous, the prevail-ing theme that connects existing literature is the assertion that FASOs experience pervasive trauma, more so than adolescent males who sexually offend (Van-diver & Teske, 2006; Van der Put et al., 2014). In addition to the chronic histories of childhood abuse, FASOs are also more likely to experience chronic familial instability and to have a predisposition to psychiatric disorders (Hendriks & Bij-leveld, 2006). Any combination of these dynamics is commonly identified as the key factors that fueled sexually abusive behavior. In comparison, gender role expectations for men and boys creates an environment that often makes men and boys less likely to disclose personal histories of sexual abuse and more likely that their acting out behavior be labeled as antisocial tendencies (Easton, 2014, p. 245). The same expectations simultaneously contribute to a larger, unspoken cultural concept of men and boys as dangerous and criminal. As a result of the increased likelihood of reported history of trauma among women and girls as opposed to men and boys, FASOs are often more likely to be diverted from the legal system to social service and mental health programs, despite having committed serious and often violent sexual offenses (Hendriks & Bijleveld, 2006).

Yet the majority of existing research is primarily descriptive in nature with few publications focusing on treatment, resulting in inadequate resources for mental health programs to be effective in clinical practice with FASOs. Female adolescents complicate sex offender–specific treatment because they undermine our understanding of gender roles, sex, power, and abuse. Moreover, our current insights from research on working with sexually abusive youth are male dominated. Despite the dearth of publication on the treatment of FASOs, there are two distinct yet connected themes that emerge from the available literature, and that are valuable for practitioners. First, there is enough evidence to suggest that FASOs have salient qualities that require gender-specific approaches. Discussions on working with women and girls involved in the justice system draw from the relational model of women's psychology (Miller, 1976; Gilligan, 1982; Covington, 2007). Specifically, Miller (1976) says that women develop their identity within relationships; as opposed to disconnecting from others and becoming independent, women and girls' sense of connection with others is tied to their psychological health, and interdependence is a sign of strength. Furthermore, Robinson (2011) stated that even committing "sexual abuse is a way to either connect to or disconnect from a relationship" (Robinson, 2011, p. 7). The second theme that ties together the existing literature is the importance of integrating the treatment of dissociation and complex trauma into the sex offender–specific treatment. The clinical picture currently describing FASOs provides sufficient evidence for practitioners to implement trauma-focused interventions. While the two themes are distinct, gender-informed treatment and the treatment of dissociation are akin in that the approaches have the mutual therapeutic goal of developing a healthy sense of connection with self and others (Miller, 1976; ISSD, 2004; Covington, 2007).

Yet, there is contention between addressing FASOs' complex trauma as the imminent treatment priority, and the standard sex offender–specific treatment goals such as accepting of responsibility for the sexual offense, increasing victim empathy, relapse prevention, and the host of other targets analogous to offender rehabilitation. Indeed, the complexity of sex offender treatment lies in the delicate balance of focusing on the offending behavior, while addressing the offender's underlying clinical needs. Balancing the seemingly competing goals is particularly difficult when working with FASOs who are mandated to treatment for their sexual offense and not necessarily for their victimization. The "righting reflex," as Miller and Rollnick (2013) assert, is "the desire to fix what seems wrong with people" (Miller & Rollnick, 2013, p. 5). Faced with the ethical responsibility of protecting the community from sexual violence, practitioners providing sex offender treatment are often torn by the righting reflex to "fix" the sexual offending behavior, resulting at times in a punitive stance toward treatment. However, Turner and Turner (1994) and Robinson (2011) both note that addressing the relationship between victimization and perpetration is the core psychological conflict facing FASOs in treatment. Turner and Turner (1994) go on to further describe that sexually abusive behavior in female adolescents is often the result of the relationship between victimization and perpetration, and the young girl's identification with the aggressor. In response to the righting reflex in sex offender treatment, Turner and Turner (1994) suggest that in order for treatment to effectively mitigate the risk of future sexual offending behavior, the ethical responsibility for practitioners working with FASOs is to focus on treating the victim inside the offender.

Sarah's Story

She read like a monster on paper—a teenage girl who was arrested for multiple charges including kidnapping, aggravated sexual assault, terroristic threats, criminal restraint, and possession of a weapon for unlawful purposes for her use of a large metal rod to hit her 9-year-old female victim during an assault that lasted about four hours. Specifically, Sarah verbally threatened, physically assaulted, and retained the little girl against her will for several hours, during which she forced her to remove her clothing and engage in oral sex. Apparently, Sarah and her friend, a girl from her class, decided that they wanted to attack the 9-year-old girl, who was on her way home from school on this day. Their motivation appeared to be boredom and a desire to inflict brutal violence. Their target was a random child who Sarah and her friend had not met before this day. The reports also said that there were some school-age boys nearby that saw Sarah, her friend (the co-defendant), and the victim. The boys reported to the police that they knew Sarah, but referred to her street name: "Shay." According to the police, the boys were initially apprehensive to share what they saw because they knew "Shay" as someone not to mess with—a bully, a thug. However, the boys eventually told the police that "Shay" had offered to sell the victim to them for $20, so that the little girl could perform oral sex on them. The boys told police that they said no to "Shay," got scared, and that one of the boys later told his parents, who then called in to report Sarah and the name of the street where the boys last saw her.

In addition to the severity of her offense and her street reputation, Sarah's case continued to shock officials when she was arrested and detained. Medical evaluations and interviews with the social worker at the detention center revealed that Sarah was unknowingly 6 months pregnant at the time of her arrest. She had just turned 13. Two weeks after she was detained, the judge showed leniency with Sarah because she did not have a prior juvenile court record, despite her reputation as a thug. She was released from the detention center to the care of her single mother, under the condition that she be placed on electronic monitoring for community supervision. A few months passed, and, after a long court review process, the judge sentenced Sarah with the maximum term for juvenile probation and mandated sex offender–specific intensive outpatient treatment. While her charges were downgraded to one count of sexual assault, her adjudication still required that she comply with the Sex Offender Registration and Notification Act (SORNA), where she would have to register as a sex offender with local police every year for a minimum of 15 years, at which point she would be eligible to appeal.

The intensive outpatient treatment program for sexually abusive youth where I work, and where Sarah was mandated to attend, was located out of a community mental health center. The community mental health center provided a combination of services for adults and children from predominantly low-income and working poor, Hispanic, and African American families. In hopes of reducing the risk of recidivism for juvenile delinquency, the program was contracted by the juvenile justice system to work in collaboration with the local juvenile delinquency court and to provide risk evaluations and outpatient treatment for low-risk sexually abusive youth living in the surrounding urban community. Sarah arrived at the mental health center for her initial appointment with me and was accompanied by her newborn son and mother. With a quick glance, Sarah could have easily been disregarded as just another teenager on the street. However, as I took a closer look at her, the alarming contrast between Sarah's physical features and her attire symbolized the juxtaposition of her adolescent development. Sarah's hot pink, Hello Kitty T-shirt and blue jeans hugged her mature, womanly curves. The headband that was holding back her long, dark-colored curls from her face had a matching pink bow. Surprised and conflicted by the stark visual contrast, I quickly scrambled to shift my frame of mind from the violent, abusive, and evil adolescent that I had anticipated meeting to the babyish, sweet smiling, brown-skinned face in front of me. However, the horrific images that I had created in my imagination from the victim statements flashed through my mind just as I put out my hand to greet Sarah and her mother.

Reflexivity in Working With FASOs

The disturbing experience of reading Sarah's case files found its place in my senses, as a cold sweat dampened my hands, my heart raced, breaths shortened, and the intrusive images of Sarah's sexual offense flowed in and out of my consciousness. Practitioners working with violent offenders often adopt a bravado defense as a form of self-preservation (Bond, 2006). However, having an inflated sense of confidence that one is not vulnerable to physical and psychological injury by a client, and romanticizing an offender's sexually deviant behavior, is an illusion. While the semblance of safety allows the practitioner to engage in a therapeutic relationship with a violent offender, "bearing witness" to the disclosures of sexual perpetuation by offenders can result in vicarious trauma (Hernandez-Wolfe, Killian, Engstrom, & Gangsei, 2015, p. 157). My physiological response had confirmed that, despite their omnipresence in sex offender treatment, deplorable acts of aggression that embody the darkest corners of human nature rarely lose their disquieting impact. As we entered the privacy of my office, Sarah's gaze quickly traveled the walls and corners of the room as she sat down in the chair, angling herself away from me. Once she had taken in the room, she zoned in on the gray metal door of a storage cabinet next to her chair. She began rearranging the word magnets that I had strategically placed in arm's reach of clients on the cabinet. As she intensely avoided looking at me, the room remained quiet, with the exception of Sarah's shifting around of the magnets. We both felt the uncertainty of the unspoken process that was happening between us. Sarah's silence revealed an intense emotionality and frailty. While Sarah likely feared being judged by me for her offense, I worried about whether I would be able to tread lightly enough through the conversation with her and succeed in gaining access to the internal world behind her offending behavior.

While scoping out Sarah's demeanor for signs of retreat, I gently led the conversation to her sexual offense.

> Sarah, I know you have shared your story many times with police and lawyers. And, I am going to ask you if you could share it one more time with me. Can you tell me, in your own words, what you did?

Sarah's shame enveloped my office. She crossed her arms and held herself tightly. As her gaze drifted away, and the tone of her voice dropped to a soft whisper, Sarah blurted out the details of her offense in one long, arduous breath. Her shoulders dropped as she released herself from her tight grip, signaling her recovery from the event of telling her story. While Sarah returned to the room, I remained still, hoping that my silence would conceal my trepidation. Jolted by Sarah's scripted disclosure, I looked down at the scattered reports on my desk from Sarah's case file, dumbfounded. The accuracy with which Sarah's story mirrored the statements by the victim and witnesses was remarkable. But, more importantly, was I watching Sarah's literal reenactment of why she did what she did? Was Sarah telling me that she lost conscious thought and movement as she had just done in my room while committing her offense? I remain in shock of how she had the literalness of memory and simultaneously disappeared from the room. Struggling to believe it, my mind continued to race with questions. Sarah's disassociation had left me feeling disconnected from what I had just seen.

Person-in-Environment Implications in Working With Sarah

When Sarah froze and clammed up in conversation with me, I recognized that she was not quite ready to talk. Her difficulty was not surprising, as the complexity of her trauma had been unfolding week after week in therapy. Sarah's mother shared the many ways in which the vibrations of complex trauma existed throughout Sarah's family. She revealed that while she was shocked about Sarah's sexual offense, she was not surprised about Sarah's pregnancy, regression, and disassociation. Sarah's mother even related to Sarah's sexual trauma as she frankly told me: "Yea, it happened to me, too. I was fourteen. I didn't notice until my great-aunt told me I was showing. Sarah's father was 25." Even more so, the traumatic and chaotic disruption in the relationships with mothers, fathers, brothers, sisters, and cousins was fused in almost every story Sarah and her mother shared about their family. Substance abuse, gangs, violence, death, and incarceration had historically made separation from self and others a common occurrence in Sarah's family. Compartmentalizing the roadblock that existed between Sarah and talking to me in sessions, complex trauma has been proven to negatively affect areas of the brain associated with verbal communication, thoughts, and memory (Green & Myrick, 2014). The expectation of Sarah to express herself verbally in therapy was unreasonable, as the "complex trauma" that had weaved into the fabric of Sarah's life had short-circuited her cognitive processes.

Sarah spent the first 6 months of treatment playing in my office. Week after week in sessions, she eagerly engaged in imaginative play like she was 5 years old. Her main characters were the "little people," comprising all the baby figurines and an older, brown-skinned woman figurine. She introduced the "little people" narrative the day that she noticed my sandbox. As she gently relaxed her hands in the coolness of the sand's fine, grainy textures, Sarah placed the babies in the sand, as if they were in one room, with the older woman above them. The safety of the figurines had always been very important to Sarah. She would protect them with a guard dog and a miniature stop sign placed outside of the fences that enclosed their space. Very different from the storyline that led her to therapy, Sarah never engaged them in sexual play, and the harm to the figurines was always from outside of the sandbox. Fink (1976) "considers the phenomenology of the play environment as the realm of reality to which the child may be adapting" (p. 896). He addresses the transference of the play environment onto cognitive development and integration, and the tragic intersectionality between racism, sexism, poverty, and violence as themes surrounding Sarah's "little people." The hostility from the outside world came to life one day when she placed the figurines in some shaving cream, and the family lost each other in a terrible snowstorm. When they made it out alive, after much suspense, watching Sarah's happy ending was a tragic, dramatic irony.

In spite of her continued environmental stressors throughout her duration in treatment, Sarah's sense of connection with herself and toward me grew stronger enough to talk more about her disassociation, after several months of imaginative play in weekly sessions. One day, I took out the crayons, markers, and multicolored paper, and asked Sarah if she would draw a picture of herself. As I connected my phone to a small speaker, and played her choice of the Keyshia Cole radio station on the Pandora application on my phone, Sarah looked at the supply of tools to express herself laid out on the small table in front of her. Sarah drew "Shay," a girl with long, curly hair, a purple glitter shirt, and a frowning face. Sarah said, "Shay had to be bad," and "isn't going to be scared of anybody." As she described her familiarity with violence, death, and incarceration, Sarah shared how she needed to become "Shay" to protect herself by having others fear her. She said, "Shay knows how to get around in the streets. Nobody messes with her." She said that while she needed "Shay" in her everyday life, she was working on not becoming "Shay" anymore because she did not really like her and she "always gets in trouble." She drew "Sarah." "Sarah" was wearing a shirt with a mix of pink and purple glitter, and her expression was calm. When I asked Sarah to tell me about herself, she said that she was a girl who loved and cared for her son, wanted to be a good mother, was a "good girl" with hopes and dreams of doing positive things in her life, and enjoyed being playful, as she had in therapy sessions. While she said she preferred to be Sarah, she admitted that she did not know how to have others "respect" and acknowledge her without "Shay."

Conclusion

In her anthropological studies, Margaret Mead stated, "human nature is potentially aggressive and destructive and potentially orderly and constructive." While this case study explored the disheartening truths of Sarah's survival, the intended purpose of examining Sarah's case was to generate an awareness among practitioners as to the theoretical, ethical, and practice implications to understanding the life experiences of urban, minority youth offenders like Sarah. Trapped in an environment where gangs, community violence, and drugs permeated life, ultimately the potential for Sarah to become a young girl who used sex to feel powerful was tremendous. When Sarah referred to "Shay," her street persona, as someone who had power over others, as opposed to being disempowered, as she was in her life. The intersections between racism and sexism that played out culturally and historically in Sarah's first world experience were also part of the fundamental complexities of Sarah's disempowerment, and the brutal reality of her sexual offending behavior. Even more so, the insurmountability of the community violence that Sarah faced also complicated the task of social and cultural institutions that were intended to safeguard Sarah from committing her sexual offense. Despite the increased understanding of the marginalization of communities like where Sarah lives, a culturally sensitive integration of the historical, sociological, and economic issues into current social policy continues to fall short in meeting Sarah's rehabilitative needs.

If practitioners wished to shift perspectives of female sexuality with a girl like Sarah, the discussion on the traumatic impact of the sociocultural denigration of women cannot be silent. However, what are the words for the particular experiences of young girls of color witnessing a rape culture, where women and girls, who look like them, are disempowered, and, ultimately, were systemically victims of rape in America's history of slavery. If we consider the contextual trauma of young girls of color, what maladaptive responses might they experience as they develop their sexual self and their relationships with others? How might they seek out power in relationships, and in their sexuality, and how might these concepts contribute to sexual offending? If not victim, what alternatives do adolescent girls like Sarah, who are raised with distinct cultural messages about sex and violence, ultimately have but become a perpetrator? Finally, who are the available victims in a culture where women are traditionally the targets of violence? The case of Sarah denotes the importance of a person-in-environment perspective when working with FASOs. There would be very little hope for a practitioner to impact change in treatment with Sarah using a reductionist concept of trauma. Reducing sexual trauma to personal histories of sexual victimization or familial instability minimizes the detrimental impact of a rape culture within urban youth, the potential for internalized sexism among young girls of color, and the intersectionality of poverty and racism in urban communities that makes recovery for girls like Sarah obstinate. Integrating a transdisciplinary understanding of Sarah's internal and external world, as well as other youth like her, increases the effectiveness of addressing the recidivism of the youth offender, as well as the safety and protection of victims, existing and potential, in the community.

Close Reading Questions

1. What is the prevalence of female adolescent sexual offending? What are some of the contributing risk factors that precipitated sexual offending for female adolescents? How are female adolescent sex offenders different from male adolescent sex offenders?
2. Discuss the clinical considerations for working with women and girls in the criminal justice system. What is the focus of treatment when working with female adolescent sex offenders in particular?
3. Reflect upon the therapist's experience in working with Sarah. How would you describe the therapist's countertransference toward Sarah?

Prompts for Writing

1. Discuss the way in which this case study challenged your perception of sex offenders. Identify the implications of the person-in-environment perspective in conceptualizing the case of Sarah.
2. What is rape culture? Internalized sexism? Discuss the intersections of race, ethnicity, and gender. Discuss your reactions to the TED Talk video and the music video clip. How would you implement these sociocultural ideas in clinical practice with violence against women and children?

Media Resources for Class Instruction

1. De La Cruz, J. (2014). Rape culture and media. Rutgers University. https://drive.google.com/a/scarletmail.rutgers.edu/file/d/0B1OtTm09yKLDSn JMXzJQZl85QWc/vjiew
2. TED TalkWomen. (2010). Tony Porter: A call to men. www.ted.com/talks/tony_porter_a_call_to_men?language=en

References

Bearman, S., Korobov, N., & Thorne, A. (2009). The fabric of internalized sexism. *Journal of Integrated Social Sciences, 1*(1), 10–47.

Bond, K. (2006). Clinician's descriptions of their experiences as sex offender therapists. Unpublished manuscript, Oklahoma State University, Stillwater.

Caldwell, M., & Dickinson, C. (2009). Sex offender registration and recidivism risk in juvenile sexual offenders. *Behavioral Sciences and the Law, 27*(6), 941–956.

Center for Sex Offender Management. (2007). *Female sex offenders.* Maryland: Giguere, R. & Bumby, K.

Covington, S. (2007). The relational theory of women's psychological development: Implications for the criminal justice system. In R. Zaplin (Ed.), *Female offenders: Critical perspectives and effective interventions* (2nd ed., pp. 113–131). Gaithersburg, MD: Aspen.

Easton, S. (2014). Masculine norms, disclosure, and childhood adversities predict long-term mental distress among men with histories of child sexual abuse. *Child Abuse & Neglect, 38*(2), 243–251.

Fehrenbach, P., & Monestersky, C. (1988). Characteristics of female adolescent sexual offenders. *American Orthopsychiatric Association, 58*(1), 148–151.

Fink, R. (1976). Role of imaginative play in cognitive development. *Psychological Reports, 39*(1), 895–706.

Gannon, T., Dixon, L., & Craig, L. (2013). *What works in offender rehabilitation: An evidence-based approach to assessment and treatment.* Hoboken, NJ: Wiley.

Gilligan, C. (1982). *In a different voice: Psychological theory and women's development.* Cambridge, MA: Harvard University Press.

Green, E., & Myrick, A. (2014). Treating complex trauma in adolescents: A phase-based, integrative approach for play therapists. *International Journal of Play Therapy, 23*(3), 131–145.

Hendriks, J., & Bijleveld, C.C.J.H. (2006). Female adolescent sex offenders: An exploratory study. *Journal of Sexual Aggression, 12*(1), 31–41.

Herman, D. (1984). The rape culture. In J. Freeman (Ed.), *Women: A feminist perspective* (pp. 45–53). Mountain View, CA: Mayfield.

Hernandez-Wolfe, P., Killian, K., Engstrom, D., & Gangsei, D. (2014). Vicarious resilience, vicarious trauma, and awareness of equity in trauma work. *Journal of Humanistic Psychology, 55*(2), 153–172.

Higgs, D., Canavan, M., & Meyer, W. (1992). Clinical notes: Moving from defense to offense: The development of an adolescent female sex offender. *Journal of Sex Research, 29*(1), 131–139.

Hornstein, N., & Putnam, F. (1992). Clinical phenomenology of child and adolescent dissociative disorders. *Journal of the American Academy of Child & Adolescent Psychiatry, 31*(6), 1077–1085.

International Society for the Study of Dissociation (ISSD). (2004). Guidelines for the evaluation and treatment of dissociative symptoms in children and adolescents. *Journal of Trauma & Dissociation, 5*(3), 119–150.

McAlinde, A. (2008). Restorative justice as a response to sexual offending: Addressing the failings of current punitive approaches. *Sex Offender Treatment, 3*(1).

Miller, J. B. (1976). *Toward a new psychology of women.* Boston: Beacon Press.

Miller, W., & Rollnick, S. (2013). *Motivational interviewing: Helping people change.* New York: Guilford Press.

National Center for Child Traumatic Stress. (2003). *Complex trauma in children and adolescents.* Los Angeles: Cook, A., Spinazzola, J., Ford, J. et al.

Office of Juvenile Justice and Delinquency Prevention. (2009a). *Children's exposure to violence: A comprehensive national survey.* Washington, DC: Finkelhor, D., Turner, H., Ormrod, R., Hamby, S., & Kracke, K.

Office of Juvenile Justice and Delinquency Prevention. (2009b). *Juveniles who commit sex offenses against minors.* Washington, DC: Finkelhor, D., Ormrod, R., & Chaffin, M.

Richardson, E. (2013). Developing critical hip hop feminist literacies: Centrality and subversion of sexuality in the lives of Black girls. *Equity & Excellence in Education, 46*(3), 327–341.

Robinson, S. (2011). *Growing beyond treatment manual: A guide for professionals working with teenage girls with sexually abusive behavior.* Holyoke, MA: NEARI Press.

Spelman, E. (1988). *Inessential woman: Problems of exclusion in feminist thought.* Boston, MA: Beacon Press.

Tsui, J. (2014). Breaking free of the prison paradigm: Integrating restorative justice techniques into Chicago's juvenile justice system. *Journal of Criminal Law & Criminology, 104*(3), 635–666.

Turner, M. T., & Turner, T. N. (1994). *Female adolescent sexual abusers: An exploratory study of mother-daughter dynamics with implications for treatment.* Brandon, VT: Safer Society Press.

Van der Put, C. et al. (2014). Psychosocial and developmental characteristics of female adolescents who have committed sexual offenses. *Sexual Abuse: A Journal of Research and Treatment, 26*(4), 330–342.

Vandiver, D. M., & Teske, R., Jr. (2006). Juvenile male and female sex offenders: A comparison of offender, victim, and judicial processing characteristics. *International Journal of Offender Therapy and Comparative Criminology, 50*(2), 148–165.

Wijkman, M., Bijleveld, C., & Hendriks, J. (2014). Juvenile female sex offenders: Offender and offence characteristics. *European Journal of Criminology, 11*(1), 23–28.

8

IN-HOME TREATMENT FOR IN-HOME SEXUAL TRAUMA

The Case of Becky

Ruthie Norman

Pre-reading Questions

1. What do you know about using countertransference to conduct therapy in an in-home setting? What is the difference between countertransference and vicarious trauma? How might you protect yourself from the vicarious trauma that you may experience if reading this case study of incest?
2. How would you feel working with a child victim of sexual abuse in her home to gather evidence for her removal, knowing that, likely, the perpetrator is present in the home?
3. Have you any experience with a system of protection that fails? How do you feel when protective systems fail?

I beeped my keys three times to make sure that my car was locked, and I shot a look of primal fear through the car window as I walked on weary legs, worried that the empty child seat in the back might expose my vulnerabilities. I scanned the façade of my client's residence. Metal poles, like the kind you would find in a jail cell, secured the windows. My mind raced through its usual checklist of trepidations. Could someone run my license plate to find out where I live? How fast could I get back to my car, just in case? With each step toward the door, I double-checked my cell phone, wondering if anyone from my agency knew where I would be today. A child screamed. A woman cursed. The stench of marijuana could not mask the distinct scent of urine that permeated the air. I found the door to my destination, pocked with bullet holes, and knocked. It was another day at the office for me in my job as an in-home therapist. I can't seem to get used to it, but I suppose that this is my normal.

"Who?" That's what the man yelled from inside. I stated my name and credentials with any resolve I had inside me cracking. All of my instincts told me to turn around. But just then, Becky, the 12-year-old girl I was there to help, opened the door, and I smiled warmly, feigning indifference to the dirt caking the floor, the sour smell oozing from the kitchen, and the cockroaches crawling on the wall. I acknowledged, with a pause, the man yelling in the background: "I told you we don't need a shrink coming up in here, knowing our business and telling us what to do!" I kept myself from flinching visibly as a way to respect Becky's experience of what is considered normal in her world.

Becky waved me inside and directed me to sit on a flea-infested couch. As she double-padlocked the door and began to piece together a puzzle of gold-colored security chains, I tried to distract myself from the fact that I was now locked inside with her. I reviewed what I knew from Becky's file in my head. I was here because Becky had been exhibiting oversexualized behavior in school. Her parents—presumably the people who could not stop arguing about my presence in their home—had no transportation and were unable to bring Becky to the office. I was truly meeting my client where she was: stuck in a low-income housing project replete with gang violence, drug activity, 11 registered sexual offenders, and no easy way out. I felt that if I could hide my discomfort, then maybe we could both keep pretending that we would engage in normal therapy.

But who was I kidding? In-home therapy is not normal therapy. When the forebears of social work conducted their friendly visits, I imagine that they faced very difficult but very different circumstances. Now that visiting has evolved, in many cases, into a state-sponsored initiative in the 21st century, I know that as an in-home therapist I will be viewed not as a therapist but as a snitch, an intruder, a spy sent in to sniff out illegal behaviors, someone who comes to take a child away from a family. Without any control over the way I am perceived or the environments in which I work, I almost always feel that I am in danger. Conducting therapy in unsafe situations, however, is often part of clinical social work. In-home therapists play a vital role in making treatment possible when clients and their families lack transportation, lack childcare, and lack the understanding of why therapy is needed. In-home therapy makes it possible for the government to make services convenient in situations where the client cannot handle any more struggle. Although it seems counterintuitive to place a social worker in danger for a matter of convenience, there is often no other viable way to reach some of the most desperate clients. It is not usually possible or preferable to remove clients, who feel dignity with autonomy, from their unsafe situations.

I write to bring awareness to the importance of in-home therapy, especially in cases of sexual trauma that takes place within the home. Moreover, I aim to help clinicians to understand the potential risks and benefits of ensuring safety while managing countertransference and establishing a working alliance. In-home therapy clinicians need to consider personal safety, as well as client safety, during application of clinical treatment. We need to balance the risks and rewards of in-home therapy. I offer Becky's case, a victim of sexual abuse, and my experience working with her, to make this point.

In-Home Therapy, Safety, and Countertransference

In-home therapists put themselves in harm's way each day in an effort to help our clients in their most vulnerable states. Not only do in-home therapists work with vulnerable, at-risk populations, but for many families, therapy services are court ordered, thus resulting in anger-provoking situations. Therapists often enter these situations alone and with little or no safety training, expected to enter the lives of families when they are at their worst, solve seemingly intractable problems, and help clients with life-threatening challenges (Kelly, 2010). Many of the skills required to assure safety and implement safety guidelines are learned with field experience. But in-home social work is a dangerous profession that has increased with assaults and deaths of clinicians.

The NASW (2013) proposes that clinicians should assess and take appropriate steps prior to conducting a home visit, such as completing a risk assessment prior to each visit. A risk assessment includes a review of the following: environmental factors, client's living space, proposed work activities, increased risk due to client's condition, worker vulnerability, condition of emergency, and mutual safety discussion planning with the client. Despite these recommendations, it is important that therapists accept the reality that violence is inevitable, and it occurs in social work practice (Ringstad, 2005). Many guidelines of the risk assessment seem nearly impossible to adhere to. The NASW (2013) risk assessment asks: "Have any events occurred in the neighborhood within the last 48 hours that might increase risk (for example, homicides, abductions, robberies, drug raids)?" Hence, social workers work in high-crime areas where events increasing risk occur every day. The NASW asserts,

> While even the most comprehensive and detailed safety policies cannot assure safety at all times for all parties, the conscientious use of safety policies underscores the importance of safety to staff, clients, administration, and governing boards. Raising awareness about safety can create a level of preparedness that helps build an agency climate of safety.
>
> *(2013)*

When providing in-home therapy services for child maltreatment cases, the most important factor is assessing the living environment. Traumatic events that occur in childhood can be psychologically overwhelming and threatening to a child's sense of security and safety, potentially leading to subjective feelings of fear, shame, helplessness, anger, and worthlessness (Cohen, Mannarino, & Deblinger, 2012). The "Child Physical and Sexual Abuse: Guidelines for Treatment" (Saunders et al., 2004) report says that "Since many abused children continue to live with the caregivers or siblings who have hurt them . . . this focus on safety is a priority"; an evaluation of risk during the initial assessment helps to identify what contextual treatment interventions are necessary, so "therefore, understanding the level of risk for harm in the child's environment and subsequent safety planning are the first steps in assessment in abuse cases" (p. 24). Therapy can be counterproductive when children exhibit posttraumatic stress disorder (PTSD) symptoms while still living in fear producing environments and situations. According to the guidelines for treatment, recommendations include that

> Treatment of fear and anxiety symptoms likely will be fruitless or even harmful because it would be appropriate for a child to continue to be afraid and vigilant in such a situation. If treatment continues, children may be desensitized to real danger cues, placing them at greater risk in the future.
>
> *(p. 24)*

Ellen and Turner (1997) argue that "As children get older, living in a neighborhood where crime is commonplace may lead them to believe that it is acceptable, or even 'normal' " (p. 841). Consequently, workers' safety can be compromised given their clients acceptance of their unsafe environment.

Unlike the home environments therapists go into, traditional office and agency environments often actively promote safe practices. Common practices include working environments that allow clinicians to easily exit in an unsafe situation, access to an alarm system, restricted access to potential objects that may be used in a harmful way (e.g., scissors, stapler, office decor) secured entrances, presence of a supervisor or additional staff when meeting with a client with safety concerns, well-lit hallways and space, and secured telephone lines in case of an emergency. However, in-home therapy does not offer a predictable setting like most traditional in-clinic office spaces. Therapy in the home can occur in the bedroom, bathroom, kitchen, living room, attic, porch, backyard, car, driveway, nearby park, school, library, or local coffee shop. Simply identifying an appropriate treatment area can be challenging; the clinician must keep in mind if the identified space is safe, appropriate, healthy for the relationship, productive, and ethical. Consequently, assessing whether a space is considered appropriate or safe without being judgmental, disrespectful, or discriminatory, is difficult.

Ensuring safety is complicated with in-home therapy without an established working alliance or the ability to manage feelings and countertransference reactions when faced with problem-saturated clients, families, and communities. Every day, clinicians face the ongoing difficulties of managing countertransference and the barriers to forming alliances in the context of in-home treatment. Establishing a working alliance is challenging when countertransference is complicated by safety, race, class, and poverty. Worker safety is partly produced by the effectiveness and degree of the working alliance. In the absence of a working alliance it is hard to imagine clinician safety, yet it is also impossible to imagine that an alliance is possible when intense emotions are experienced in the presence of child sexual abuse. Reynolds–Mejia and Levitan (1990) state,

> Therapists no less than other human beings tend often to impose upon the family their own expectations regarding how the family should react, feel, and process their trauma. In a therapeutic setting, however, the expectations may subvert the healing process.
>
> *(p. 59)*

The problem of countertransference, worker safety, and establishment of a working alliance, is intensified in the in-home setting.

The working alliance, a construct that characterizes the therapeutic relationship (Lambert & Barley, 2002), has been more broadly defined as collaboration between the therapeutic participants to facilitate healing (Bachelor & Horvath, 1999). Without a working alliance, safety seems impossible. Yet in an effort to minimize a family's defensive outlook on treatment, developing a working alliance is crucial. Effective communication, in part, is grounded in the skills of listening and responding and vital to the working alliance. Hence, recognizing and respecting differences in client race, values, culture, gender, and social attributes also fosters communication.

While the working alliance enhances safety for in-home therapists, countertransference can affect the formation of this alliance, creating additional barriers with ensuring safety. Freud's term, countertransference, refers to the analyst's unconscious and defensive reactions to the patient's transference. Subsequently, broader definitions of countertransference developed to include all emotional responses of the therapist to the client, rather than merely those pathological distortions by the therapist resulting from his or her own unresolved historical issues (Reynolds–Mejia & Levitan, 1990). In the treatment of child sexual abuse, it is almost impossible to not feel strong emotions. In particular, in the in-home setting, these intense feelings can destroy any prospect of achieving a therapeutic process and countertransference issues play a prominent role (Reynolds–Mejia & Levitan, 1990). Reynolds–Mejia & Levitan write, "The governing theme of these reflections is that countertransference reactions will always weave a spell upon therapists' emotions, and thus always present a danger of superseding the professional's therapeutic agenda" (p. 61).

Clinicians who do not feel safe potentially place themselves at risk for experiencing negative emotional reactions or vicarious trauma as part of a countertransference experience. Reynolds–Mejia and Levitan (1990) find that a clinician's capacity for empathic tolerance is challenged by in home treatment, and "the risk of spontaneous acting out of countertransference is proportionally increased by the additional immediate stimuli, the lack of familiar and protective surroundings, and increased opportunities for the family to test the therapist's boundaries and adaptive resources" (p. 57). As Reynolds-Mejia & Levitan suggest, "The in-home setting poses greater threats to the therapist's sense of control, competence, and personal and professional adequacy, thereby compounding the therapist's anxiety" (p. 57). Despite these threats, in the case of a sexually abused child, therapists must process their feelings and reactions while simultaneously acting as healing agents.

The Case of Becky

(Warning: This case material contains a disclosure that may be difficult to read.)

Becky's case, a referral from her middle school counselor, reported Becky exhibiting sexualized behaviors in the school environment, as well as a long history of allegations that she has been maltreated by her parents. The counselor reported Becky sought attention from her peers, as well as her teachers, through use of sexual language, drawing and writing sexual explicit pictures and stories, and frequently exposing her body inappropriately. Her counselor reported that on two occasions, rumors were spread about Becky being caught in the boys' bathroom performing oral sex. Becky denied these allegations. Another report involved Becky writing a story about a sexual fantasy with her male gym teacher. The counselor reported numerous attempts to meet with Becky's parents about her sexualized behaviors, with no contact ever being made.

Becky had a long history of trauma. At age 7, Becky was placed in foster care and separated from her sibling, following her parents' 6-month incarceration for drug charges. After 15 months, Becky was reunited with her mother, father, and 10-year-old sister Julisa. From the age of birth, Becky was exposed to ongoing domestic disputes between her parents, gang retaliations, substance abuse, and multiple exposures to crime in her neighborhood. Despite Becky's trauma history, Becky had no prior history of receiving mental health services.

"As you can see, I don't live in a safe neighborhood." Becky pointed to a wall filled with R.I.P. memorial picture frames. "Yesterday, another cousin—Macho—was shot down. Police blocked off my street, and people weren't allowed to leave their houses. Macho's mom screamed the entire time. They made her stand behind the yellow tape. It was sad, but my dad said that whoever did this is going to regret it. I wonder who will be next." Becky's high risk, unsafe, violent, police involved neighborhood was her normal. Her descriptions of normal went against everything I was ever taught, thought, or experienced.

Becky's father, Luis, had been diagnosed with bipolar disorder and PTSD. He had been in and out of jail since he was 14 and had a long history of trauma. Both his brother and his father had been brutally murdered right in front of him. Luis was placed in foster care, but his real family had always been his gang. He was an alcoholic and daily street drug user, and during home visits, his behavior was erratic. Luis had teardrops tattooed near his eyes and "FUCK YOU" inked into his knuckles. During more than one treatment session, he was incoherent, but Becky and I continued therapy through his moans, grunts, and random screams. Usually, he paced around the home, frequently entering the room, and walking right back out without saying a word. It felt like surveillance, and I couldn't imagine how Becky could ever feel any sort of safety with him around. I certainly felt at risk. I tried to work out a plan with Becky's mother so that she could call me to cancel if Luis was unstable, but it was clear early on in treatment that she was helpless. Becky's mom had a history of sexual abuse. As a result, she turned to drugs and prostitution at 14 years old. That's when she had met Becky's father, who was 10 years older and a well-respected gang member. She told me, "Luis took me in. He offered to take care of me." I blinked at her in disbelief, but she did not flinch, not even as gun shots rattled in the near distance.

Many factors challenged Becky's safety, as well as my own safety, especially my inability to develop a working alliance in Becky's home. Language barriers presented safety concerns and challenges with establishing a working alliance. As a native English speaker, I could mostly understand but not respond in Spanish, which was the language in which the family was fluent. My concern was intense during one session when I was not able to understand what was being said, creating discomfort and unpredictability. Becky's mother and father began to speak in Spanish. Their tone of voice increased, and Becky's father was becoming visibly angry. [In Spanish:] "If this lady don't leave my house she's gonna wish she did, this gun is loaded and I'm not scared to use it." Becky informed me: "Dad says he thinks you should leave now, because he doesn't agree with you and is getting angry." Becky later informed me in a session what her dad had really said the day I was asked to leave. She reported that her mother was trying to calm him down, but it doesn't always work.

These types of home visits also present many complexities with confidentiality. It is common that neighborhoods and communities look out for one another. Often, while walking to Becky's house, I was approached by neighbors inquiring about my presence at the house. In an effort to protect the family's confidentiality, I am ethically obligated not to identify the family whom I am working with. Because of this obligation, I often felt threatened by the inability to explain my presence to a group of gang members who are protecting their turf. Ignoring or informing the group that it is confidential information can lead to retaliation. Becky's father viewed his neighborhood as part of his family because everyone in his gang looked out for each other. With no working alliance established with Becky's father, it was hard to imagine protection from the angry community members who saw me as a threat. I never felt safe either in Becky's home or the surrounding neighborhood.

Frequently, confidentiality and safety issues occurred when sessions were interrupted by Becky's friends, extended family members, or neighbors. Becky's family had minimal boundaries, and they were unable to recognize the inappropriateness of neighbors or family members intrusively entering into our therapy session. I could not always predict or control who may be part of the therapy sessions. It was not an option to consider Becky's family members safe just because she did. Thus, my mind was usually preoccupied with how to manage my safety. When Becky wanted to sit outside for privacy, I feared crossfire. When we were inside and she locked the door—mostly because neighbors and family members often entered our therapy sessions—I worried about how I could exit quickly in an emergency. Becky wanted us to meet in her attic, and I felt guilty telling her that her "safe space" was scary to me. We ended up meeting in the bathroom.

"My dad told me to keep my mouth shut or there would be big problems for me and you, and you know how my dad is." Twelve-year-old Becky had the inclination to protect me. "I'm going to tell you anyways." Her hands were shaking, and the fear in her eyes made my stomach turn. I couldn't deny her. Suddenly I heard her father come home. "That lady is here again? If she doesn't leave my house she's gonna wish she did." Despite the yelling beyond the door, Becky and I hunkered down in the sweltering room. Unable to speak, I handed her a pen and a pad, and Becky sobbed as she began to write the horrific details of the night before.

> Last night, I tried to run away. My uncle and father did those really bad things to me again. But this time, it happened to my younger sister, too. I screamed as loud as I could, but no one helped me. First, my father told me to go downstairs in the basement because he needed to talk to me. My uncle is always the first one to come down. I watched in fear as my uncle opened the door. I knew exactly what was going to happen. He told me to take off my clothes and sit on the couch. He always tells me that if I don't do exactly what he tells me, then when my father comes, I will pay. My uncle covers my mouth when I scream, but only when he has sex the normal way with me. When he's going to have sex with me in my butt, he puts a long sock in my mouth because it really hurts, and I scream loud. Last night I had to pay for being disobedient. I told mom, but she told me there was nothing she could do. I hate when my dad urinates on my face. I don't know what is worse, the sex or pee. Mom makes me clean up the pee after, and dad and my uncle laugh about it.

I immediately began safety planning with Becky. I informed her that I was going to leave her house, go to my car, and call child welfare services. I wanted to take Becky with me. I informed her that I would come right back in and stay with her. Becky made me promise I was not leaving her. I told Becky not to say anything to her parents. I told her to pretend everything was fine and that she did not need to tell them that she disclosed the situation to me.

Walking down Becky's attic stairs is a memory I cannot forget: the fear and anxiety as I smiled at the uncle and father and said, "I'll be right back, I have to get something in my car." I felt trapped. Internally, I froze; externally, I wanted to scream and cry and tell the adults what I was really thinking about them. Somehow, I stayed professional. I called child welfare services, and an emergency response team was soon on their way. Once child welfare workers arrived, I walked back in the house with them. I had made a promise to Becky.

I was not prepared for what happened next. As I went back upstairs to the attic, Becky informed me that she told her mom that she told me what had happened. Becky told me that her mother was very angry and told her that everyone was going to go to jail because of her. Becky cried as she pleaded for me not to tell anyone what she disclosed. I felt angry. How could a mother react this way? I wanted Becky's mother to be supportive, to be angry at the adults who hurt Becky, and to protect her daughters. And then, when the child welfare workers questioned Becky, Becky refused to speak. She told the workers nothing had happened. Becky's mom reported to the workers that Becky had attempted to run away the night before, and this lie was her way of trying to get removed from the home. She insisted that Becky was making up lies and stories. Becky's dad told the workers how much he loved and cared about Becky.

The response team looked at me and said, "There's nothing we can do. Becky says nothing happened, and she's not talking." Strong countertransference feelings were aroused—I needed to rescue Becky, I had to defend her, and she wanted this, too. Furiously, I pleaded my case. I begged for child welfare services to remove the children. I requested that I be present for support to empower Becky to at a minimum disclose sexual abuse via her father and uncle. I began by telling Becky she was strong, I was here to support her, and she was going to be kept safe. Once feeling safe, Becky disclosed the abuse. I informed the workers that the local police needed to be called to be present during the removal process. After all, I knew Becky's family history, the risk factors, and the potential safety risks that could occur during the removal process.

As the police arrived at the home, the adults in the home become angry and threatening. Becky's father began making verbal threats and aggressive gestures. He shouted to the police that I was a baby snatcher, full of lies, and that I was going to pay for this. As the children were removed, Becky's father began destroying the home property. I ducked and shielded myself as objects were thrown. While the police attempted to calm him down, Becky's uncle ran from the home and has been missing since. Becky was successfully removed from the home, temporarily, pending an investigation.

One week later, I received a threatening voicemail on my office phone. The voice was disguised: "You will pay for this. I am coming after you. Watch out!" Flooded with emotions, I immediately assumed it was Becky's father. Indeed, he knew the vehicle I drove, the agency where I worked, and most concerning, that we lived in the same community. The fear I once held, feeling unsafe while working in the home or environment of a client, now progressed into my personal life. Feeling unsafe became, for a time, "my normal." The constant stress associated with personal safety affected my mind, body, emotions, and behaviors.

I struggled to maintain my outer mask, my societal face, that is acceptable to the clients I am serving while in their environment. My outer mask attempted to react "normally" to the high-risk environment required by my work, regardless of how I was feeling internally.

Discussion

Clinical services provided in Becky's home and community setting had become increasingly unsafe and unpredictable; safety limitations contributed to difficulties with managing countertransference. Pretending to feel comfortable or safe was difficult, more so because Becky's family was sensitive to the vibes I conveyed. On one occasion, Becky's mother asked me, suspiciously, if I was worried about my vehicle parked outside. As I shook my head, pretending not to judge her neighborhood, I questioned myself as I watched the three male teenagers surround my vehicle pointing at my expensive wheels. Still, because social workers are taught to respect our clients' homes—or, as Boyd-Franklin and Bry (2000) recommend—to "go with the flow" when conducting therapy in the home, I tried to avoid the inclination to impose rules or my own sense of order (p. 39). In an effort not to hinder the therapeutic relationship, many times I refrained from voicing my own disbelief of how this family could engage in therapy with any expectation of progress in such a chaotic environment. During treatment, Becky's father often went to his room and turned up his music to display his anger. The vibration went through my body and I could not concentrate, respond, or listen effectively, or hide my anger. I informed Becky I could not engage in therapy during these circumstances, and not recognizing countertransference, added that nor should she. Becky replied, "You'll get used to it." Becky was desperate for our relationship to blossom and nothing was going to get in the way.

Addressing safety concerns with a family before establishing a therapeutic relationship can hinder continued treatment if as a result the client now feels threatened, insulted, or disrespected. Setting safety preventives, boundaries, and rules for therapy services when delivery is conducted in a client's home is challenging to say the least. During home-based sessions, it is not unlikely for the family to be guarded and uncomfortable as their home environment offers added insight to their lives. Becky's father Luis was certainly distrustful of me, affecting the working alliance. While I recognized that Becky's father's statements could stem from "healthy cultural suspicion," (Boyd-Franklin & Bry, 2000), I was cognizant to not be dismissive of my own countertransference. We both recognized each other's power held in our positions. He was fearful of me, as I was seen as a threat to him and his family, a mandated reporter, a snitch, and an untrusted intruder. Likewise, I was fearful of him, as I saw him as powerful, untrustworthy, dangerous, and a risk to my safety.

Much literature on treating trauma and sexually abused children emphasizes being fully present in the moment with the client, which helps to create a safe environment. As a practicing clinician, I know that for therapy to be as successful as possible, it is crucial that the clients feel they are safe. However, just as it is important for the client to feel safe in therapy, I argue that it is just as important for the therapist to feel mentally and physically safe. Becky's case illustrates the many safety concerns that left me as the therapist feeling foremost, unsafe, insecure, and uncomfortable, which, therefore, compromised treatment. Still, during my sessions with Becky, I felt that the burden of safety lay within me, as the therapist. I was to make sure Becky was safe in order for progress to be made. Developing a sense of safety is intuitively necessary; we not only need to feel safe, but like to, and seek this feeling of safety. Of course, Becky's disclosure of sexual abuse made me feel unsafe and manifested itself in the form of anxiety, which disturbed my ability to concentrate and think effectively. I was no longer attuned to my client. My ability to be attuned during this intense moment in therapy while feeling unsafe hindered my reactions, and even more so, my interventions with my client. As my emotions became overwhelming, I felt my internal world spiraling out of control. Reynolds–Mejia and Levitan (1990) assert that "The timely and regular sharing of countertransference material, at a therapeutic level, is the most powerful force for change the therapist can offer" (p. 61), but without a working alliance or feeling safe, sharing my countertransference material was unimaginable.

My treatment with Becky continued 16 months after her sexual abuse disclosure. I met with Becky weekly at her foster care placement. During this time, Becky had weekly supervised visits with her parents. Much of our therapy consisted of safety planning, mainly because I was aware the plan was for her to return home. Throughout our treatment together, Becky constantly worried about returning home. She cried and begged for me to not send her back home. She wrote me letters begging for me to adopt her, pleading she would be the best daughter ever. Becky's cries for help, kept me awake at night. Becky was reunited with her parents. Her father was found not guilty, and both parents completed the required parenting classes necessary to regain custody. Becky asked why I was not going to be her therapist anymore when we said our final goodbyes. Telling the truth seemed impossible. Since my final session with Becky, I have never been the same. I feel as if I failed to keep her safe. I lost my confidence in the system that was supposed to protect her, but still, I continue my work.

Close Reading Questions

1. Pick three quotes from Norman's chapter that you can read into as a way to describe in-home therapy with victims of in-home sexual trauma from a phenomenological perspective. In other words, describe, through the interpretation of Norman's words, the experience being a clinician in the case of Becky.

2. Why does Norman say that a working alliance promotes clinician safety? Was there any way that Norman could have established a working alliance in this case?

3. Why does Norman bring up Boyd-Franklin and Bry's idea of "healthy cultural suspicion"? How does that phrase apply in this case and in other cases that you've encountered?

Prompts for Writing

1. What countertransference or vicarious trauma did you experience while reading this chapter? Be sure to define "countertransference" and "vicarious trauma" in your answer, even though Norman does not give exhaustive definitions of these terms. What do these terms mean to you? And what is the relationship between these terms?

2. Which problem associated with in-home therapy sticks out to you as most important to solve? Why? And how would you solve it?

3. What can a therapist learn from thoroughly knowing a client's environment? Find connections between Norman's case study and several other case studies to make your argument. For example, would it be possible for Busfield to treat her client without a thorough understanding of social media? Would it be possible for Lado to treat her client without an immersion in military culture?

References

Bachelor, A., & Horvath, A. (1999). The therapeutic relationship. In M. A. Hubble, B. L. Duncan, & S. D. Miller (Eds.), *The heart and soul of change: What works in therapy* (pp. 133–178). Washington, DC: American Psychological Association.

Boyd-Franklin, N., & Bry, B. H. (2000). *Reaching out in family therapy: Home-based, school, and community interventions.* New York: Guilford Press.

Boyd-Franklin, N., Cleek, E., Wofsy, M., & Mundy, B. (2013). *Therapy in the real world: Effective treatments for challenging problems.* New York: Guilford Press.

Cohen, J. A., Mannarino, A. P., & Deblinger, E. (Eds.). (2012). *Trauma-focused CBT for children and adolescents: Treatment applications.* New York: Guilford Press.

Ellen, I., & Turner, M. (1997). Does neighborhood matter? Assessing recent evidence. *Fannie Mae Foundation, 8*(4), 833–866. Retrieved January 10, 2015, from www.centerforurbanstudies.com/documents/electronic_library/neighborhoods/does_neighborhood_matter.pdf

Kelly, J. (2010). The urgency of social worker safety. *NASW News.* Retrieved July 4, 2015, from www.socialworkers.org/pubs/news/2010/10/social-worker-safety.asp

Lambert, M. J., & Barley, D. E. (2002). Research summary on the therapeutic relationship and psychotherapy outcome. In J. C. Norcross (Ed.), *Psychotherapy relationships that work: Therapist contributions and responsiveness to patients* (pp. 17–32). Oxford: Oxford University Press.

National Association of Social Workers. (2013). Guidelines for social worker safety. Retrieved January 15, 2015, from www.socialworkers.org/practice/naswstandards/safetystandards2013.pdf

Reynolds-Mejia, P., & Levitan, S. (1990). Countertransference issues in the in-home treatment of child sexual abuse. *Child Welfare*, *69*(1), 53–61.

Ringstad, R. (2005). Conflict in the workplace: Social workers as victims and perpetrators. *Social Work*, *50*, 305–313.

Saunders, B. E., Berliner, L. & Hanson, R. F. (Eds.). (2004). *Child physical and sexual abuse: Guidelines for treatment* (Revised Report: April 26, 2004). Charleston, SC: National Crime Victims Research and Treatment Center.

9

THE SILENT WAR WITHIN

Military Sexual Trauma

Marisol Lado

Pre-reading Questions

1. What do you think about when you envision military sexual trauma? Based on your clinical knowledge or experiences, what barriers do victims of military sexual trauma face?
2. What might make the experience of military sexual trauma different from sexual trauma experienced in the general population? What makes it similar?

The art of war, both professionally and creatively, requires much thought, consideration, and exquisite execution. Over centuries, countless individuals have mastered plans of warfare, military skills, unit cohesion, and tactics of survival. Through art, countless individuals have attempted to recreate the horrors, beauty, and internal and external conflicts of being in war. One theme that remains consistent throughout war and military history is that of sexual power and rape. While there are numerous ancient paintings depicting rape in various cultures, one chapter of Roman history specifically stands out and has been recreated by many artists, including Pablo Picasso, and sculptors throughout time—*The Rape of the Sabine Women* (O'Hara, 2015). Nicolas Poussin's famous 1633 recreation of this scene depicts the legendary story of rape in which an army of Roman men, led by Romulus, abducts (which, in context, truly means to rape) Sabine women and takes them as their wives against their will, sending the Sabine men away, unable to save their women (Costello, 1947). This art of war, the art of its history and its victims, the story of its power and dominance, remains relevant still as we fast forward to our current day and current issues within the military culture.

Contemporary military sexual trauma has not drifted far from its ancestral beginnings and has not evolved in regard to managing the stigmatization that keeps victims silent, to putting an end to the military culture that is conducive for sexual violence, and to reducing the number of incidents and victims. Instead the trend we see in research, statistics, and social media is that the incidence of military sexual trauma is increasing in numbers (Valente & Wight, 2007). In fact, it seems like research and the media are regularly calling to attention new and troubling evidence regarding military sexual trauma and its influence on mental health outcomes. When considering the fact that military sexual trauma seems to be a pervasive and structural issue, we must ask ourselves, is there something unique about military sexual trauma as opposed to sexual trauma in general society?

Although one might argue that sexual assault is no different whether it is committed in the context of the military or in the general population, one is hard-pressed to negate the fact that there seems to be something particular and unique about military sexual assault. In exploring the nature of military sexual trauma (MST) through a frame that poses ontological questions, we are challenged to consider what is unique about the experience of MST as opposed to sexual trauma experienced in general society. Allowing ourselves to explore the complexities of MST enables us to consider myriad influences and keeps us close to the lived experience of victims. In particular, the influences we explore include an acute understanding of the betrayal experienced by victims of MST. They are betrayed by an individual whom they have come to trust as well as an organization to which they have surrendered their entire lives. What emerges is a conceptualization of MST that is as unique as each individual we encounter, and that honors the complexity of addressing sexual trauma within military culture and amid pain and suffering.

A History of Military Sexual Trauma

There is no doubt that the concept of military sexual trauma has evolved since its beginnings, which can be linked to the Tailhook Scandal. In 1991, at the Navy Fliers' 35th Annual Tailhook Association Convention in Las Vegas, it was reported that 83 women and 7 men had had been victims of sexual assault and harassment while at the conference (Winerep, 2013). Victims shared that, during the convention, unsuspecting women were surrounded by male Navy Aviators and passed down a gauntlet of men who grabbed at their bodies, attempted to undress them, and ripped off their clothes as they were taunted and catcalled (Valente & Wight, 2007). The ensuing scandal led to a congressional hearing on June 30, 1992, in which section 1720D of Chapter 17 of Title 38 ("veterans benefits") of the US Code was passed, offering treatment to veterans who are the victims of sexual trauma (US Code Title 38, Part II, Chapter 17, Subchapter II 1720D). Additionally, an amendment was made to the Veterans Health Care Act of 1992 titled Title I Women Veterans Health Programs that made explicit provisions for the counseling of female victims of sexual assault or trauma. Ultimately, Tailhook served as a symbolic beginning to victims opening up about the reality of sexual trauma in the military.

However, Tailhook did not elevate awareness of MST to an adequate level of concern. In reality, MST was not recognized as permanent, pervasive problem. Rather, MST was considered a temporary issue for which a temporary solution was provided. The Veterans Administration (VA) was authorized to provide counseling to women veterans only until December 25, 1995. To add more insult to injury, the female veterans who sought out the temporary counseling could only attempt to do so within 2 years of discharge and treatment was limited to only 1 year. It was not until 1994 that military leadership began to recognize that MST was not declining in numbers, despite the mandated education of clinical staff and outreach to veterans. Instead there was more of a need, and treatment did not meet need. In reality, authorization was only extended until December 31, 1998. Due to demand, treatment was finally extended to men, there were no more limits placed on length of treatment, and requirements that limited the period during which veterans were permitted to seek treatment were lifted.

Additionally, in 1995, the Veterans Health Administration released a directive authorizing all MST-related services to be made free of charge. From there on it seems that the Veterans Administration began to make appropriate changes by recognizing MST as "important" in the computer systems, the implementation of a new MST software application, and the extension of care until 2001, then again to 2004, and finally to permanent status in 2004. Additionally, veterans had no minimum length of service requirements to apply for benefits and did not need to file a claim to receive services for MST. An MST coordinator was also implemented as the liaison to all services, extending outreach and education out to the community, sometimes to accommodate the veteran for requests for a therapist/provider of a given gender.

As MST continues to evolve, so does the definition of sexual trauma and the proposed interventions. The Veterans Health Administration has also implemented a mandatory screening tool to all veterans that enter the VA system. The MST screen tool consists of a two-item screening measure asking (a) "When you were in the military, did you ever receive uninvited or unwanted sexual attention?"; and (b) "When you were in the military, did anyone ever use force or threat of force to have sex against your will?" (Rowe, Gradus, Pineles, Batten, & Davison, 2009).

Although the screening tool and MST services are now open to both men and women, the research implies that comparably more women than men fall victim to MST (Hall, Sedlacek, Berenbach, & Dieckmann, 2007). Compounding this fact is the added consideration of increased women participating in the military. For the first time in American history, women serving in the conflicts of OIF (Operation Iraqi Freedom) and OEF (Operation Enduring

Freedom—Afghanistan) are finally recognized, in essence, as serving in combat (Katz, Bloor, Cojucar, & Draper, 2007). Given the large numbers of servicemen and women who have been deployed during our extended wars in the Middle East and in Afghanistan, the number of MST victims, specifically women, is increasing.

Despite developments in service provision, screening, and availability, barriers to treatment and services still remain prevalent for MST victims. Although the screening tool has allowed for the collection of data, there is still "subject aversion" and stigma attached to sexual trauma and seeking treatment (Hall, Sedlacek, Berenbach, & Dieckmann, 2007). Additionally, Hall, Sedlacek, Berenbach, and Dieckmann (2007) find that even within the Veteran Health Administration there exists a lack of knowledge of services and a lack of organizational support for the providers working with MST victims. These issues create a potential for secondary trauma for veterans who disclose their sexual trauma, as they run the risk of receiving an inappropriate intervention—or none at all. Particularly for women veterans, the disparities in those seeking services have also been noted in "service utilization, access points, diagnostic categories, and compensation claims" (Hall, Sedlacek, Berenbach, & Dieckmann, 2007). The absence of an organizational map of services and internal education and training for providers regarding MST continues to create barriers for treatment. Rather than working diligently to change the culture of sexual trauma that persists in the military, the VA inadvertently furthers the stigma associated with sexual trauma and alienates victims, leaving them revictimized and potentially retraumatized.

The military culture extends beyond the perpetrators and often influences the way victims of sexual trauma react to treatment options. Research shows that even when veterans *do* disclose their traumas, be it on their own or with the help of the two question screening tool, victims often deny services for many reasons such as "wanting to tough it out," wanting to prove to friends and family that they are "fine," fear of being labeled as "weak," or fear of having a record or documentation of some mental health disorder (Katz, Bloor, Cojucar, & Draper, 2007). These stigmas, although relevant to when veterans seek treatment in the VA, is mostly born from their military service and training.

Ultimately, when a service member has become a victim of military sexual trauma, she must confront the outcomes of disclosure. These outcomes vary depending on the timing and nature of the disclosure. If the service member chooses to not disclose while remaining in the military, the service member will have to deal with her internal suffering alone, and she often must rely on her own ability to obtain treatment. If the victim discloses the MST while still in the service, more often than not she is attacked and/or harassed by members of her own unit and usually of higher rank. Additionally, the service member might be forced to be around the perpetrator and work in close proximity on a day-to-day basis, leaving the victim to feel helpless and putting her at continued risk for more assaults and harassment. Furthermore, disclosing MST while on active duty can cause major disruptions in one's military career, as high-ranking officers who write evaluations and make recommendations for advancement are most often men and are part of the very system that enables the continued perpetration of sexual assault. As such, even if justice is sought after and obtained, which is often not the case, victims are left with the burden of disclosure, which leads to further victimization within the military complex by the culture that breeds sexual assault in the first place (Litz & Orsillo, 2004).

As common as MST is in today's military culture, victims are still encouraged, implicitly and explicitly, to suffer in silence. Even in the initial beginnings of the Department of Defense's SAPRO Program (Sexual Assault Prevention and Response Office), administrators educated the military via video by informing the potential victims, who were only played by women, not to dress provocatively, never to walk alone, and not to call attention to oneself. Although the video was in response to the current wars in Iraq and Afghanistan and the increasing number of MST reports, the video reflected dated and misogynistic attitudes about sexual assault that protects the perpetrator and places the majority of the blame on the victim. Examples like this indicated that the Department of Defense and the Veterans Health Administration are behind in approaching MST in an appropriate, treatment-focused way, that works to change military culture.

I just want to die.

—Lexi, US Army

Lexi is young woman that joined the army right after high school with dreams of a military career that would help her take advantage of the educational opportunities that she would not be able to attain on her own or with her family. Lexi enlisted for the typical 4-year military commitment. She served during peacetime—right before the 9/11 attacks, Operation Iraqi Freedom (Iraq), and Operation Enduring Freedom (Afghanistan) began. She shared how being a soldier gave her identity and family. She loved being in uniform and was proud to be where she was in her military career. Lexi was never written up and was deemed a good soldier by her superiors. She had 2 months left in her military contract, and she was deciding whether to re-enlist or to go to school full time on a benefit provided by the VA, when everything changed.

Instead of planning her future, Lexi was discharged from the army with an "Other than Honorable Discharge." The army, responding to Lexi's suicide attempt and psychiatric treatment that resulted in her inability to perform her duties, decided to let Lexi go. What was not known at the time was what had changed for Lexi to have such a drastic emotional shift. Instead of exploring what had happened to cause a significant change in Lexi's well-being and performance, as she described, she was treated badly by her superiors, and her symptoms were downplayed or disregarded. She ultimately felt ashamed and guilty for taking up space and time in the military hospital. Rather than being cared for like a family member, Lexi felt alienated and alone. All the while, Lexi was sitting with the pain of her secret—the fact that she was the victim of a violent rape at the hands of another soldier who was a military police (MP) officer on base.

Lexi shared that she attended a movie night for enlisted service members on base, something not unordinary and considered safe, being that it is planned and provided by the base and military. After the movie, as Lexi was going to her car in the parking lot, she was attacked by two male soldiers. One held her down while the other, the military police officer, raped her. After the rape, she was left in the parking lot—in shock and alone. Lexi shared that she grew up with police officers in her family and was taught at a young age not to go against police because one will never win against them and their power. At that moment, Lexi silently surrendered and never reported the rape for fear of retaliation. But the violations did not end. The MP also guarded the gate of the base, and Lexi spoke of how he would abuse his power. She recalled how, any time she entered the base, he would torment her by pulling her over unnecessarily and having her car fully inspected just because he could.

Lexi attempted to make a complaint about the excessive searches but instead was categorized as "bitch." Soon after, she shut down emotionally and attempted suicide for the first time in her life. When asked how she was feeling at that moment, Lexi shared, "I just want to die." As Lexi's emotions and symptoms unfolded, Lexi was discharged by the US Army. To further wound Lexi, this all (including the discharge) occurred 2 months shy of completing her contract, and she was informed that she was deemed to have non-veteran status (also called incomplete tour of duty) because she did not complete the minimum number of days in the service that would entitle her to any benefits and/or ability to file a claim.

For 10 years, Lexi was hospitalized repeatedly for psychiatric symptoms, she attempted suicide four times, and she was cutting regularly. Lexi experienced long bouts of panic attacks, depression, anger, anxiety, and a powerful desire to be isolated. Lexi recognized that her rape had changed her and that she needed help, but she was unable to seek or afford the treatment as she had no insurance. It was not until a fellow female soldier, who was also a military sexual trauma survivor, explained to her that her time in service is irrelevant if she was a victim of MST and informed her that the first step was to file a claim with the VA. Soon after, Lexi's fellow soldier put her contact with a veteran service officer (VSO—a person that assists veterans with the paperwork to file a claim) to assist her in filing a claim. The VSO referred Lexi to the Vet Center for treatment, and she immediately began individual therapy at no cost.

However, as doors began to open, other very important ones remained shut and barricaded. Therapists at the Vet Center are informed that service members who experience MST are entitled to all benefits and services related to their trauma and that no barriers should exist, even while the official claim is pending. With this knowledge, Lexi was referred to the inpatient MST program at a local veterans hospital. The referral was made over the phone and the appropriate paperwork was sent in. Lexi received a verbal approval, a confirmed bed assignment, and a start date. On the day that Lexi was to begin her 6-week inpatient program, she was turned away at the door due to her non-veteran status in the system (she was flagged in the computer to not receive benefits or treatment). Lexi was devastated and felt betrayed again—second-guessing that the VA really wanted to help her. Ultimately, some individuals at the Vet Center were able to help her change her status in the computer, and she was able to start treatment at the inpatient facility the following day. From that moment on, the staff at the local veterans hospital, her therapist, and her VSO advocated and fought endlessly for Lexi to receive what she was entitled to according to the VA directive on MST survivors.

It took 2 years for Lexi's claim to be fully processed. Although Lexi was granted 100% service connection, she has only been granted full coverage temporarily and will be reassessed in the near future. Furthermore, despite being granted 100% service connection, Lexi continued to encounter barriers, such as trouble obtaining the education benefit provided by the VA to go back to school. Lexi experienced resistance when engaging with the VA regarding her education benefits because the VA made a correlation between her symptomatology and a possible inability to focus on and/or complete tasks in school. Therefore, the VA initially denied her the education benefit. The temporary status of her service connection still looms as yet another hurdle to not only validate her MST, but what to allow her to continue to get treatment.

For many veterans, obtaining VA disability benefits is a complicated, long, and daunting process. However, according to Schingle (2009), and experienced by Lexi, there is an additional, grueling "evidentiary burden" (pg. 156) that is unique to female veterans seeking disability compensation for post-traumatic stress disorder (PTSD) from MST, as compared to their male counterparts. It is acknowledged that, for both men and women, MST is linked to an increase in mental health disorders/diagnoses, specifically PTSD (Maguen et al., 2012). According to the research by Maguen et al. (2012),

> female veterans with a history of MST were five to eight times more likely to have current PTSD, three times more likely to be diagnosed with depressive disorders, and two times more likely to be diagnosed with alcohol use disorders, compared with female veterans without MST.
>
> *(p. 62)*

Female veterans have the added burden of proving that MST has occurred and that their PTSD symptoms are a result of the sexual trauma. This challenge, partnered with the misogynist nature of military culture, results in a daunting task that female victims of MST must face, reliving their trauma in an attempt to validate their experiences.

When filing a claim for PTSD through the VA, in theory, every veteran has to provide proof of illness in order to receive compensation for and entitlements to the service connection. However, when considering PTSD proof for combat trauma versus military sexual trauma one cannot deny the inherent disparities with regards to the burden of proof and the cultural acceptance of and value placed on each type of trauma. Currently, for any veteran to receive service connection for PTSD related to combat exposure they must "(1) have a medical diagnosis of PTSD, (2) have credible supporting evidence that the stressor/situation actually occurred, and (3) medical evidence linking the current symptoms and claimed stressor/situation" (Schingle, 2009, p. 165). In simpler form, the veteran only needs to prove that he or she was with a unit that was attacked or threatened. The military arranges proof for combat veterans, as there is an agreed-upon understanding of the dangerous nature of combat, along with an easily identifiable aggressor/perpetrator. However, in reference to proving PTSD as the result of MST, the burden of proof is magnified and made especially difficult to receive services and compensation. Inherent in the male-dominated culture of the military is a devaluation of the gendered experiences of women, including their vulnerability to sexual assault and violence. Additionally, there are often no witnesses, and when there are, witnesses might be reluctant to come forward for fear of the repercussions involved. Furthermore, accepting that MST has caused PTSD would require that the military at least discipline and at most dismiss and prosecute the perpetrators who are not as easily vilified (for military leadership) as the "other" encountered in combat violence. As such, the experience of providing "proof" for MST is far more nebulous and fraught with the potential for victim-blaming and rejection.

> They told me, "Man up."
>
> —*Sam, US Marine Corps*

Sam is a quiet African American man who has struggled with drugs and alcohol addiction for the past 30 years of his life. He has also spent various periods of time in and out of jail. Sam joined the US Marine Corps (USMC) in the early 1980s. When he joined, it was considered peacetime. However, his enlistment was completed amid the backdrop of the demonstrations and demands being made by Vietnam War veterans to be recognized along with getting treatment for what would eventually be understood as PTSD. Sam wanted a military career. He had enlisted after high school and looked forward to retirement after 20 or more years in the military. He wanted nothing more than to be a Marine.

Sam had what he would call a "normal time" in service. He survived boot camp, he woke early for PT (physical training), he had duty (work assignments), he learned to follow orders, he respected the chain of command (the military hierarchy of rank that determines who you should go to when there is trouble or a complaint), and he trusted the military—his (new) family. After initial training and time in the States, Sam received orders to be stationed in Okinawa, Japan, in 1985. Although he was married, Sam went overseas with the intention of maintaining a long distance relationship with his wife. Sam would recall how he was always complimented for his good looks and his kind heart, but he never spoke of stepping out of his marriage or entertaining any outside attention.

Sometime in early 1985 on in his tour of duty in Japan, Sam was playing football with other Marines in his unit on the weekend. His roommate, John, a white male of the same rank, played as well while his girlfriend, also a young white enlisted Marine, looked on and took photographs. Sam recalled this day in a haze, not truly remembering the details. Sam noted that he "just experienced it as any other day" when they had down time. It was not until days later that his roommate, John, developed the pictures his girlfriend took that changed Sam's life as he knew it.

When John went to pick up the developed photos from his girlfriend's camera, he discovered that majority of the pictures taken during the football game were of Sam. Sam was completely unaware that this was the case and had no concern over it. He never mentioned any inappropriate relationships or interactions with his roommate's girlfriend at any point. However, the photos enraged John, and he, along with four other Marines, took Sam in the middle of the night to an unknown location and beat Sam endlessly. At some point during the beating, Sam was stripped from the waist down and was sodomized/raped repeatedly with a beer bottle. Sam did not recall how long the violence lasted, but remembered being yelled at, being belittled, and being called every racist and derogatory name in the book. Sam remembered that, at one point, John said to him, "you want to fuck a white woman . . . we'll show you."

Once he was able, Sam went to his military command to make a report of the incident. To his shock and disbelief, he said, "they told me to man-up." Sam reported that he felt helpless. Within days he became despondent, depressed, and began to isolate. Sam's wife, who was back in the States, was writing to him and trying to contact him to no avail. As she worried due to his lack of response, she contacted his unit. Sam was then forced (as he put it) to respond to his wife and to inform her that he was doing well. However, Sam shared that she knew something was going on with him because he no longer sounded like the man she knew—he was no longer the man he was once, nor would he ever be again.

Within weeks his wife was granted permission to go to Japan and be stationed with Sam along with her two children. Sam shared that upon her arrival he already knew his marriage was over. He was unable to trust, unable to be intimate, and unable to love. During this time, word of his sexual assault got around the base and spread quickly among other service members in his unit. The story was out and he was made the mockery of the base. Other service members began to make comments heckling him and, as Sam states, he was "treated like everyone's bitch."

Sam was soon after discharged as Other Than Honorable (a not so highly regarded discharge/exit from the military) due to "dereliction of duty." In essence, this meant that he was unable to fulfill his military obligations. According to Sam, he was "pushed out"—betrayed for the betterment or cohesiveness of the unit. Sam was devastated by his trauma and again by his discharge. At his discharge, when he was preparing to return back to the States, he and his wife also ended their marriage, and she decided to stay in Japan. She had a job she enjoyed and had begun a relationship with another Marine. Sam felt nothing and shared that when he went home he went back to nothing.

It was not too long after being home that Sam turned to alcohol and then drugs to cope with his trauma. Sam reported that prior to his discharge he never experimented with drugs or drank excessively, but within a short time he became addicted to heroin and constantly sought out the high to avoid feeling the pain of his trauma and betrayal. Sam attempted to go to school and work, but was never able to be fully present and/or complete tasks. He spent the past 30 years of his life in and out of jail, drug and alcohol treatment programs, and temporary jobs. He attempted suicide four times.

Sam went to the Vet Center for treatment under the recommendation of another veteran friend that was attending a male MST group. Initially, a male therapist saw Sam and his session visits were minimal until he went to a PTSD and addictions inpatient program for 6 months. It was there, for the first time since he attempted to tell his command about his attack, that he opened up about his trauma. Sam struggled verbalizing his sexual assault, but with the help of his therapist in the program he was able to write his story. At the end of his treatment he was referred back to the Vet Center, but instead of returning to his prior male therapist he requested a female, as he discovered he would never be able to trust or share his trauma with another male. Sam eventually got the courage to file a claim with the Veterans Administration for MST and PTSD secondary to his sexual assault. Unfortunately, to date his claim remains pending due to lack of evidence.

Although there is very little research specific to male military sexual trauma and the numbers in research and statistics state that the occurrences are higher in females than males, we must not dismiss its existence and not assume that lower reported MST by males implies that it is not a problem. Male veterans are more prone to have PTSD as a result of combat exposure; however, they have a higher chance of developing PTSD from MST due to stigma and silencing culture linked to the sexual trauma (Schingle, 2009). This correlation is so significant that research conducted on this topic has stated that men have a 65% chance of developing PTSD linked to MST in comparison to the 39% chance of PTSD from combat experience (Schingle, 2009). Considering the dominant, male paradigm of the military, it is not surprising that MST has devastating effects on its male victims.

The extended denial of benefits translates to an institutional collusion in refusing to validate the service member's experience of military sexual trauma in order to avoid taking responsibility for the logical conclusion—altering military culture toward one that does not prop up male sexual aggression. Instead, victims are expected to deal with their pain in secret in order to be considered good soldiers, to further their military careers, and to remain a member of their military family that has so violently and profoundly betrayed them. Working with MST victims requires a fine attunement to the initial betrayal being done by the perpetrator as well as the secondary betrayal at the hands of the military leadership to silence and deny the survivor's experience.

Yes, military sexual trauma can be linked to the experience of incest in the civilian world. But it is an internal betrayal at the hands of the authority figures in the military, along with identification with their aggressor, that makes the outcome so perplexing to negotiate and results in the levels of traumatic response seen in both Lexi and Sam. Service members are trained and taught from day one at boot camp/basic training (the physical, mental, and emotional indoctrination individuals must successfully complete to become part of the selected military branch) that the military is one—one unit, one team, one group, one family. Individuals become programmed to trust each other and count on one another for support because the ultimate goal is to always complete the mission. "No man left behind." "An army of one." "Semper fi" (always faithful). But what happens when one of your own, a person you should trust with your life, has become your perpetrator? Here is where the triad of betrayal unfolds and where healing becomes uniquely challenging for victims.

Conclusion

The Department of Defense and the Veterans Administration do not seem to collaborate on the issues related to MST. Instead they pawn the case back and forth on what is deemed in the moment a concern for either federal agency. Meanwhile, the victim remains unattended, helpless, and his or her experience is minimized to being just a burden of paperwork. Oftentimes, once a service member has been violated, or when he or she has decided and/or is ready to file a claim with the Veterans Administration, the case remains in the very initial phases due to having to prove oneself and/or to see if the case fits the description/definition of MST according to the interpreter.

The Department of Defense and the Department of Veterans Affairs need to correct the disadvantages faced MST survivors so that the current trend of triple betrayal is ultimately eliminated and replaced with the appropriate treatment of services and benefits. However, this may be a grander task that the military needs to address. Maybe the direction we need to go to is beyond the military, as similar situations happen in other groups—like families and incest; universities where students are raped and dismissed and promiscuous; and in religious institutions like the Catholic church, where it took years for priests to be held accountable in any sort of way for sexually abusing children. Do we as a larger community, as a society, need to start elsewhere? Maybe there is a way that incestuous groups can heal themselves. Perhaps, rather than focusing on the victims, we have to focus on the toxic misogyny that perpetuates rape culture and enables perpetrators to walk free.

Close Reading Questions

1. How does the betrayal experienced by both victims extend beyond the immediate betrayal of the victim/perpetrator dyad? How is it more complicated and more difficult to treat?
2. What do you think about the idea that military sexual trauma is an institutional problem that needs to be faced by the military? How does Lado link the influence of misogyny to the prevalence of MST?

Prompts for Writing

1. How does Lado's discussion of what makes MST unique from sexual trauma in the general population challenge dominant narratives regarding trauma and trauma treatment? How does Lado provide an understanding of trauma that extends beyond a traditional PTSD diagnosis?
2. What does it mean for sexual assault to be "institutionalized"?

References

(n.d.). Retrieved January 12, 2016, from https://en.wikipedia.org/wiki/The_Rape_of_the_Sabine_Women

Costello, J. (1947). The rape of the Sabine women by Nicolas Poussin. Retrieved January 12, 2016, from www.metmuseum.org/pubs/bulletins/1/pdf/3257295.pdf.bannered.pdf

Hall, M., Sedlacek, A., Berenbach, J., & Dieckmann, N. (2007). Military sexual trauma services for women veterans in the Veterans Health Administration: The patient-care practice environment and perceived organizational support. *Psychological Services*, 4(4), 229–238.

Katz, L., Bloor, L., Cojucar, G., & Draper, T. (2007). Women who served in Iraq seeking mental health services: Relationships between military sexual trauma, symptoms, and readjustment. *Psychological Services*, 4(4), 239–249.

Kimerling, R., Gima, K., Smith, M., Street, A., & Frayne, S. (2008). The Veterans Health Administration and military sexual trauma. *American Journal of Public Health*, 59(6), 2160–2166.

Litz, B., & Orsillo, S. M. (2004). Ill. *The returning veteran of the Iraq War: Background issues and assessment guidelines.* Iraq War clinician guide.

Maguen, S., Cohen, B., Ren, L., Bosch, J., Kimerling, R., & Seal, K. (2012). Gender differences in military sexual trauma and mental health diagnoses among Iraq and Afghanistan veterans with posttraumatic stress disorder. *Women's Health Issues*, 22(1), e61–e66.

O'Hara, F. (2015). *Jackson Pollock*. Pickle Partners Publishing.

Primer on Military Sexual Trauma for Mental Health Clinicians. (2011, March 1). Retrieved January 12, 2016, from www.mirecc.va.gov/cih-visn2/Documents/Provider_Education_Handouts/MST-A_Primer_on_MST_for_Mental_Health_Clinicians.pdf

The Rape of the Sabine Women. (2015, February 2). Retrieved January 12, 2016, from www.ancient-origins.net/news-history/rape-sabine-women-002636

Rowe, E., Gradus, J., Pineles, S., Batten, S., & Davison, E. (2009). Military sexual trauma in treatment-seeking women veterans. *Military Psychology, 21*, 387–395.

Schingle, J. (2009). A disparate impact on female veterans: The unintended consequences of VA regulations governing the burdens of proof for post-traumatic stress disorder due to combat and military sexual trauma. *SSRN Electronic Journal, 16*(1), 155–189.

Silver, R., Boon, C., & Stones, M. (1983). Searching for meaning in misfortune: Making sense of incest. *Journal of Social Issues, 39*(2), 81–101.

Valente, S., & Wight, C. (2007). Military sexual trauma: Violence and sexual abuse. *Military Medicine, 172*(3), 259–265.

Winerep, M. (2013, May 13). Revisiting the military's Tailhook scandal. Retrieved January 12, 2016, from www.nytimes.com/2013/05/13/booming/revisiting-the-militarys-tailhook-scandal-video.html

10

SOCIAL WORK, SEX ADDICTION, AND PSYCHODYNAMIC TREATMENT

Alan Oxman

Pre-reading Questions

1. What is an addict? Is addiction about how often you do something or about how often you think about something? Can and should these two forms of compulsion be separated, at least in our theoretical thinking about addiction?
2. What is a sex addict? Many conceptualizations of the sex addict would place someone who committed rape once or molested a child once, under the same heading as someone who spends 6 hours a day watching internet porn. Does it make sense to lump these two groups together?
3. Are sexual crimes necessarily indicators of mental health issues? Is someone who commits rape or pedophilia necessarily suffering from a mental health problem? Can one be a criminal yet not suffer from a mental health issue?

There are many theories of compulsion and addiction with wildly contradictory conceptual frameworks and recommended interventions. This chapter will outline a treatment with a self-identified addict, Drew, wherein a non-judgmental witnessing of his story served as the intervention of choice, in a way that did not necessarily obviate the need for other treatments, but might serve as a model for an adjunctive psychodynamic treatment for addicts also engaged in other treatment models (primarily the 12-step model, which is the prevailing interpretive model in today's addiction environment).

The 12-step conceptualization of addiction has become the dominant mode of understanding certain compulsions in our society—one where the addict has a defect and the only hope of containing this pathology is abstinence and constant vigilance through 12-step attendance. But what I keep seeing in my patients who self-identify as addicts and have attended 12-step meetings is that despite the feeling of social connection, acceptance, and brotherhood that they feel at meetings, they bristle at the notion of being an abject label that can never be cured, that is defective, and that must follow an abstinence-only regimen for the rest of their living days. They're left with a delimiting sense of being a category, with all the pathology residing inside themselves, yet with no acknowledgment that maybe the compulsive behavior is a symptom, a response to trauma, and that if the trauma were processed, acknowledged, and worked through, they might not necessarily have to be identify themselves as damaged goods for the rest of their lives.

Ultimately, I'm not saying that the 12 steps or a neuroessentialized (medicalized and brain-centered) view is wrong, but that each individual is unique and does not fit into a simple label, so deeply exploring each individual's particular lived experience, which can be therapeutic and transformative in and of itself, may be the wisest path when working with someone who has sexually compulsive thoughts.

Drew

My first session with Drew began on a crisp, cool October afternoon. As he entered my office, I saw that my new patient had the sweet, pointy face of a Keebler elf. Even though I knew from his intake that he was 41 years old, he had a manner and bearing that reminded me of a little boy. After sitting down in the chair opposite mine, he looked up at me, smiling sheepishly. I gently smiled back and asked, "What brings you here?" Without pausing, Drew leaned forward and said, "I'm a sex and love addict." My head began to swirl. How could this slight, short, sweet-faced man be a sex addict? What was a sex addict? What was a love addict? I wanted to know what these labels meant. As he described his life, Drew made it clear that for him it was a compulsion to think about sexually charged scenarios. He spent hours each day watching porn and couldn't get to work, fall asleep, or even get through a difficult day without turning to porn, Craigslist, Backpage, peep rooms, or some other sexually charged location. Sometimes, just crossing the threshold out of his apartment was so terrifying that he had to play porn on his phone while he walked out the door, or he couldn't leave. Other times, after a stressful meeting at work, he would hide in a bathroom stall, or even leave the building, and walk to a local diner, where he scanned through prostitutes on the Backpage app, never calling, but calmed just by looking and fantasizing. So much of what he dreamed about was meeting a woman who would act out his sexual fantasies. When he scanned Backpage, he wasn't masturbating, just looking, and the frisson seemed to lie in the potential for meeting, which pointed to a desire for human connection as the source of the compulsion. Perhaps Drew had become dislodged or cut off from an integral part of himself, a deeply needy part starving for connection, and through some primal internal calculus, porn, prostitution, and intimacy through dating sites became the only outlet for this need.

Sex Addiction

I'd worked with many self-identified alcoholics and drug abusers, but before meeting Drew I had never before met a self-identified sex addict. After I began researching the term, I found a dizzying tapestry of theories and academic squabbles as to whether the category even existed, who fit the category, and what the best treatment was for someone who fit the category (if you believed the category or pathology even existed). One thing for certain is that the term has taken on a life of its own, and that the notion of a "sex addict" has become firmly ingrained in our popular consciousness. Over the last 40 years, the term has grown at a dizzying rate. Just looking at the *New York Times*, there were zero references to "sex addict" in the 1960s, then one in the 1970s, 15 in the 1980s, 51 in the 1990s, and 61 between 2001 and 2007 (Reay, Attwood, & Gooder, 2013, p. 5). What caused this explosion? Could it be the combustible mix of the internet and the 24-hour news cycle injected into the lives of the rich and powerful? Maybe, due to the speed and lack of privacy in our internet age, there are more celebrities, politicians, and business leaders caught in sex scandals, scandals that invariably bring more attention to the issue of sex and sexuality. Crushed under the weight of cultural scrutiny and judgment, those caught in sex scandals can jettison responsibility for engaging in societally prohibited sexual practices by accepting the disease of "sex addiction," a disease that can be treated medically at a rehabilitation facility, where the "addict" leaves not only treated for their medical problem, but with the taint of immorality and criminality reduced.

Could the growth in the category of "sex addiction" also be a reaction against the convulsive effects of the internet on our collective sexuality? With the birth of the web and other modern technologies, we're in the midst of a new mindspace and digitalized intersubjective matrix of human sexuality that allows for almost endless exploratory avenues. Maybe society's "superego" is reacting against this opening up with a backlash and then pathologizing individuals who overindulge in this brave new world. One of the largest beneficiaries of this pathologizing of sexual thoughts and behaviors is the world of addiction entrepreneurs and highly profitable sex addiction rehab businesses. There's also been a huge growth in 12-step groups that specifically target "sex addicts," including Sex Addicts Anonymous, Sexual Recovery Anonymous, Sexaholics Anonymous, Sexual Compulsives Anonymous, and Sex and Love Addicts Anonymous. The 12-step movement, like almost any evolving movement, always needs new members in order to thrive and flourish, and it has quickly set up shop in this attractive new market.

The word addict originally meant "slave," or to be a slave to something. What a great target for the rehab industry and the 12-step movement: the person who is a slave to their sexual thoughts. Who among us isn't a slave to their sexuality, their sexual thoughts, and their sexual self-image? There's a commonly disseminated meme, based on questionable interpretations of Masters and Johnson's groundbreaking work on human sexuality, that the average boy thinks about sex every 7 seconds. Obviously, this is an urban myth, but an actual study done in 2012 by researchers at Ohio State found that men participating in their study had sexualized thoughts, on average, 19 times a day (Fisher, Moore, & Pittenger, 2012). If the deeply intertwined sex rehab and 12-step groups (most of the rehab businesses employ some aspects of the 12-step methodology) can successfully pathologize repeated and intrusive thoughts about sex, then they are surely creating a huge new market for their services.

There's no question, however, that there are people, including Drew, who suffer terribly from their obsessive thoughts and behaviors around sex. What is unclear is to what extent these are symptoms of deeper issues and problems, which if they were not manifesting as sexually compulsive thoughts and activities might come out in other compulsions or self-harming behaviors. Depending on whom you read, these underlying mechanisms are problems in attachment, shame, impulse control disorders, obsessive-compulsive disorders, and neurobiological disorders. I suspect each person is unique and the underlying causes of one's "sex addiction" varies greatly from person to person, which would call for a singularly tailored approach for each individual. I hoped to find out, directly from Drew, by listening as closely and openly as possible to his story, how he viewed and experienced himself as a unique person first and foremost, and then, second, as a set of symptoms, and labels.

During our second session, Drew described, in detail, a horrible childhood at the mercy of his intrusive and torturing father, who couldn't keep his hands off of Drew, and his distant mother, who was too scared to ever stand up to his father. If the family were riding in the car, Drew's father would squeeze Drew's leg until it hurt; if they were watching television, his father would scratch Drew's head until it bled. Each morning, in a cramped bathroom, Drew was forced to watch his naked father shave and shower. With moist eyes, Drew described his father's "naked balls right near my face." Even though Drew was undersized for his age, his father would force Drew to have pose-offs in the mirror, humiliating Drew for his tiny calves. During one of their long bike trips, when Drew was about 11 years old, his father soaped him all over his body, including his genitals, at a public YMCA shower. With a hard edge to his voice, Drew described the other men in the shower as doing nothing. As our work together unfolded, this became a recurring theme: other adult men not helping Drew and even revictimizing him. I felt inspired to offer Drew a different experience—if he would let me.

Psychoanalyst Jessica Benjamin writes of her emotions working with a severely traumatized patient: "I also found myself telling her spontaneously that no matter what she did, she would always have a place in my heart, that she could not break our attachment or destroy my loving feelings" (2004, p. 36). After hearing what Drew had been through, I had a strong urge to share similar feelings with him, from which I abstained because I sensed that he would feel impinged upon by such a strong and personal communication so early in our relationship. In a sense, I was following my own abstinence model, abstaining from an overly close emotional connection with Drew, because these feelings seemed dangerous, capable of overwhelming him, or possibly even the both of us. My plan, in order to protect Drew, was to communicate these feelings non-verbally, by gaining his trust slowly, over a long period of time.

Later in the session, Drew described his sex addiction in more detail.

Drew: I'll spend hours looking at my computer. I have multiple screens up, and I watch porn as well as Myspace and Craigslist and OkCupid. I watch movies and TV shows, but I always have to have at least one small screen with porn going. I call this edging. I'll do this for hours and will only climax once every hour. I can do it three times in three hours.

Alan: What does it feel like while you're doing this?

Drew: It's just something I have to do. I can't say it feels good. I always feel depressed afterward. Often I'm not even watching porn. I will spend hours looking at personal ads on dating websites, comparing the women, trying to find the perfect one. It's like I'm OCD. All the women that I look at are really earthy and sweet-looking, and I want them to have big breasts. I feel like the looking and trying to meet them is the important part, and once I meet them the sex is less important. I've convinced prostitutes to come to my apartment and spend time with me for no money. I feel like pushing things to the extreme point of danger, but just before the actual act of having sex is what's exciting for me. Though if I do meet them, I want them to hold me in their arms, against their breasts, for hours on end. This is the only thing that relaxes me.

Alan: You just want to be held?

Drew: Yeah. But I also want them to tease me and hurt me. I ask them to insult me and to punch me in the groin every once in a while. I almost never read, but just the other night, I was with a woman I met on OkCupid doing this, and it relaxed me so much I was able to read a book.

I wondered if Drew, through a warped prism, was recreating his childhood sexual dynamic with his father: pushing sexual titillation and intimacy as close to the edge as possible without actually having intercourse—however, this time, with Drew in control.

Empathy

Hearing about his childhood, I felt called upon to be the person for Drew who makes what Donna Orange (2009), a prominent psychoanalyst specializing in Kohutian self-psychology, calls "the empathic stretch" (p. 239), a stance where I communicate that no matter how alien or pathologized the *other*—Drew— might be, that at some juncture in our shared humanity, there is the ability to understand this other. This empathic stretch, however, is particularly fraught with a patient like Drew. Some psychotherapists, such as Michael Rosenbaum (2009), believe the therapist's words "should allow the patient to feel and recognize that the therapist not only knows what he or she is talking about but has also lived it" (p. xv). I think this goal is too far-reaching. I hoped to convey to Drew that I understood and could relate to his experience of having compulsive behaviors without actually communicating that I had "lived them." Drew said that his sex addiction often aroused sexualized feelings in others, and I did not want to think about this happening to me. I was not concerned about engaging in behaviors like Drew's, but I recoiled at the idea of having Drew's voice in my head when I was working with other patients.

Soon after meeting Drew, I asked a member of my supervision group, Justin, how to work with Drew. Justin worked at a private midtown Manhattan sex addiction clinic and suggested keeping count, with Drew, of how many days he'd been sober and to make this our primary focus; without complete sobriety, Justin said, any other work would be impossible. I wondered if in some ways this was a kind of safety net that the clinic employed: by creating an almost unachievable goal that was solely the patient's responsibility, if the therapy failed, then all the fault could be laid at the feet of the patient and would never be due to a lack of empathy or support on the part of the therapist or clinic. I considered this authoritative approach, but I sensed that Drew wasn't looking for this kind of external control any more. Before coming to see me, Drew had been in a 12-step group, Sex Addicts Anonymous (SAA) for the previous 5 years, and I sensed that by seeing me, he was looking for a different experience from what his 12-step meetings offered him. I sensed that after years of 12-step meetings, where he'd been yelled at by his sponsor and felt violated in various ways by other members, Drew was looking to be heard, to be seen, and to feel accepted—not shamed or surveilled.

About a month after we began working together, Drew started dating a 35-year-old woman named Debbie. Over the course of the following few weeks, it became clear that Debbie was turning into a girlfriend. With Debbie spending more time at his place, Drew talked about how nice it felt to be making changes to his apartment and to make the space more reflective of him. Yet, Drew still struggled between a budding intimacy with Debbie and a pervasive dissatisfaction with their sex life.

Drew: This relationship with Debbie is ridiculous. What am I doing? I get the opportunity once a week to have sex, I'm a sex addict, like I desire sex every minute of the day. I get once a week where I can have it and the woman I'm with doesn't like it [*he laughs at this*]. I'm like, what the hell? It just doesn't add up. And her response is "we are having sex." We're just lying around and hugging and kissing. I'm like you don't understand what I'm looking for. I'm looking for pain and suffering. I'm looking to hurt you a little bit and me to be hurt a little bit. That's what is calming to me.

Alan: How would you hurt each other?

Drew: Just fucking the shit out of each other. Not violent, but I want rough sex. That's what calms me. It stays with me. Now I feel like I'm losing my ability to work. I'm like ugghhh and depressed. I'm becoming so depressed, like low. I don't have the sex fueling me up. All of this I'm just saying out loud. I'm not doing anything. I keep in touch with Debbie every day. I text with her three to four times a day and talk on the phone with her for an hour each night. I see her, and I take care of her when I can. You know, she takes care of me, and I'm honest with her, so in essence, I have a relationship [*he laughs*], and I'm enjoying that.

I felt confused by Drew's desire for rough sex and obsession with pornography, yet his commitment to Debbie and desire to be honest and loyal to her. He was cheating on her, in a sense, as he continually watched porn; however, he made it very clear that he never met with other women, and he never physically cheated on her. It's as if the porn was a cut-off, secret part of himself that filled him with a certain kind of intimacy of which he could never have enough; yet, by not meeting with other women, he was not fully transgressing and could keep his deepest feelings of guilt at bay. While Drew was single, he was able to dissociate for hours into a porn dream world, but the presence of Debbie, a subjective other, seemed to act as a mirror that woke Drew from his dream and confronted him with a certain awareness of his emptiness that in some ways the porn helped to hide. Also, by keeping most of his hidden porn life separate from his relationship with Debbie, he was, in a psychoanalytic sense, using the primitive defense of splitting wherein he kept sex and intimacy separate. When children are treated as narcissistic extensions of a parent rather than as independent subjective entities, then these children, according to Vaknin, "develop to become adults who are not sure that they do exist (lack a sense of self-continuity) or that they are worth anything (lack of stable sense of self-worth, or self-esteem)" (2003, p. 309). It's as if Drew felt that at any moment he would fall off a cliff—this was the metaphor he used to describe the feeling he had when he desperately yearned for sex—and that the thought of sex was the harness that could brace him, keeping him from free-falling and disintegrating into nothingness.

Over the next few months, Drew and I worked on helping him confront, accept, and sit with his painful affective states—to do what is now commonly referred to as mentalization, which is one's ability to "understand the thoughts, feelings, and behaviors of oneself and others" (Berry & Berry, 2014, p. 246). Hopefully, our alliance would allow Drew to mentalize the overwhelming affect he experienced when Debbie felt too close. Over time, Drew did begin to become aware of and mentalize these typically unreflexive, unformulated, and unconscious feelings and patterns. At a later session, Drew was able to reflect on his habitual emotional patterns.

Drew: I had this fantasy about asking Debbie to go to the Grand Canyon. I think that's escapy behavior on my part.
Alan: How is it escapy?
Drew: I think it's to avoid being with Debbie in the here and now. I can't relax and enjoy my time with Debbie now.
Alan: That wouldn't surprise me considering everything you went through as a kid. It can take a long time to change old patterns.

If Drew can manage to stay with Debbie and feel the anger and frustration that a real other brings, hopefully he'll slowly learn to tolerate closeness with another person without feeling an overwhelming impingement and imminent annihilation. If he can allow himself to be touched by Debbie's authentic feelings for him, he may even begin to sprout some empathy for himself. If Debbie is a fantasy stand-in for the nurturing, loving mother that Drew always wanted, she can't possibly play this role successfully, and Drew frequently ends up furious with Debbie. With his own mother, this anger—for not doing enough to protecting him—crystallized, and he never moved past it. I hoped that, with Debbie's help, Drew could catalyze a new script where he realizes that Debbie is not the one that is causing him so much pain and frustration (this comes from his developmental needs that were never met), and he can have some guilt (the healthy kind) for taking his anger out on Debbie. This guilt (or empathy) will not only allow him to connect and have a relationship with Debbie, but might be a model for how he can learn to feel empathy toward himself and quiet his tormenting inner voice.

When Drew watches porn for hours with what he describes as his "porn family," he is in some ways independent and in control. From a Kohutian perspective, it seems the safety and control Drew feels when watching porn is superficial and destined to leave him empty; only real, messy, and challenging relationships with three-dimensional people can give him a deeper sense of connection and safety. Heinz Kohut, the creator of the self-psychology school of psychoanalysis wrote,

Values of independence are phony, really. There is no such thing. There can be no pride in living without oxygen. We're not made that way. It is nonsense to try and give up symbiosis and become an independent self. An independent self is one that is clever enough to find a good selfobject support system and to stay in tune with its needs and the changing of generations. To that system one must be willing to give a great deal.

(1985, p. 262)

Drew was living an airless life enveloped in a fog of porn and sexualized thoughts, obsessions that kept him from disintegrating, yet also kept him from the interpersonal connections he deeply yearned for.

At Drew's next session, I met him in the waiting area a couple minutes after our scheduled start time. I gestured for him to follow me, and we walked silently, me in front and Drew behind, down the 20-foot-long hallway that led to my office. I imagined Drew staring at the back of my head, and that gaze felt like a stick pressing into me. I was reminded of a guard and an inmate walking down death row to the execution chamber. Eventually, we reached my office, and I sat in my customary spot, furthest from the door, while Drew took the other chair. I looked at Drew and sensed frenetic activity behind the impassive expression on his face.

Alan: What's going on?

Drew: Oh just my normal thoughts [*said nonchalantly*].

Alan: What normal thoughts?

Drew: [*Grins sheepishly*] That you don't care about me and that I'm not important.

Alan: What makes you feel that way?

Drew: [*Knits brows and looks vexed as to whether it's safe to share*] When you start the sessions late.

Alan: What's that like for you?

Drew: It makes me angry. Like you're just leaving me there and don't care or think about me. It's kind of like when I was a kid with my mother. When my dad was away on business, my mom was like a friend or even treated me like a little boyfriend, but as soon as my father came home she was really neglectful and would forget about me. My father was the opposite. He paid a lot of attention, but it was lots of negative attention. [*Drew's body recedes into the chair and his head lifts up. It feels as if he is simultaneously moving toward and away from me.*] Like when I was a kid, I bit my nails, and this became a thing with my father. My father would have me come into his room, and he would look at my nails. If they were bit, which they always were, he would ask me if I thought I deserved to be punished. If I said no, he would let me go, but then would give me the silent treatment for a couple of weeks and be really mad at me and eventually punish me anyways. So, I'd say yes, and then I would have to go pick the belt from his closet that he would use to give me three lashings. I would hand it to him and then pull my pants and underwear down and lay over his lap. He would then give me the lashings. There was a bin of *Playboys* next to his bed that I would stare at while he hit me. If I cried, he would keep hitting me, and if I didn't cry, he'd stop just after the first three. Sometimes, he and Mom would leave the house after, and I'd be alone. I'd lie down on the sofa and cry into the cushion. I can clearly remember the smell of that wet cushion on my face like it's in front of me right now. Then I'd get the bin of *Playboys* from my parents' room and take them to the living room and lay them out in a grid. I'd put Post-Its on them, so I could remember in what order to put them back. Then I'd dream about and compare the different women in the pictures. I'd try to decide which ones had which flaws, and which ones were the most perfect. There was one centerfold that I was the most obsessed with. She was softer and curvier than most of the others. Maybe that's why I'm so attracted to large-breasted women. This is when I really started masturbating. At around 12 years old, I started doing this like four times a day and really learned to get instant sexual gratification all the time. I never learned any impulse control around sex.

I'm devastated hearing this story. By making Drew answer whether he deserved his punishment, Drew's dad was drafting Drew as a co-conspirator against Drew and creating a voice in Drew's head that his natural instincts and physical desires, such as biting his nails, were to be avoided and punished, or at the very least hidden and kept out of sight. Looking back at his childhood, it's not much of a surprise that Drew spends his days thinking he's not good enough and regularly dissociates into a private, dream world of porn and online fantasy objects.

Psychoanalysis

Visualizing Drew's intrapsychic structure through the lens of his early beatings, Drew may have imagined he was being beaten for his overly close and intimate relationship with his mother, while simultaneously fantasizing about joining forces with his dad, and being part of the team that beats himself—with all the sexual energy that accompanies those beatings. He also escaped into a *Playboy*-fueled dream world of sex with inanimate images, but in his internalized mental schema, he was never allowed to consummate these sexual relations with an actual woman because if it wasn't secret and hidden (as with the *Playboys* or internet porn) it was too risky; his father might find out and then beat or even castrate him. Despite Drew's occasional descriptions of aggressive sexual fantasies, he was generally terrified of sex and of disappointing his partner. This often caused Drew to ejaculate prematurely, which caused him great shame. He combated this shame by cuddling and masturbating with women and generally avoiding intercourse. These feelings of shame began to lessen with Debbie, however, and Drew proudly reported the event whenever they had "good, normal sex."

In *A Child Is Being Beaten*, Freud (1919) describes children who fantasized about beatings. For Freud, the male fantasy of being beaten by a woman represents, for the boy, "I am loved by my father" (p. 390), and it has been transformed into "I am being beaten by my mother," which is passive and "derived from a feminine attitude towards his father." In his theory, Freud strongly believes that even though the object in the fantasy was a woman, if there was a beating involved, then the cathexis must be a positive homoerotic valence toward the father. For the male patient, "the beating-phantasy has its origin in an incestuous attachment to the father," and what Freud later called the "inverted attitude, in which the father is taken as the object of love" (p. 390). Drew may have formed a sexualized bond with his father (whom he both feared and idolized), but due to internalized injunctions against homosexuality (per Freud's theory) transformed his fantasy object into an earthy, large-breasted woman, who occasionally punched him in the groin. This sadomasochistic fantasy may have been further fueled by guilt over attraction to his mother, who sexualized him whenever his very intimidating father was not home—an attraction for which he likely felt guilty, and for which he deserved punishment.

A few months later, another pattern emerged: after particularly intense sessions, Drew would leave hurriedly without making eye contact. I decided to ask him about it at the beginning of a subsequent session:

Alan: I was wondering if what we were talking about at the end of our last session made you uncomfortable. I felt as if you left quickly.

Drew: No. I was very interested, but I don't know how to leave or how to do transitions, so I quickly ran away. If it were up to me, I would have stayed for hours, and I know I'm not allowed to do that, so I quickly ran away.

Alan: You've mentioned you have a hard time transitioning before.

Drew: Yeah. That's why I'll stay in my apartment looking at porn for hours and not go to work; the transition seems overwhelming. Sometimes, I'll play porn on my phone and watch the video as I leave my apartment, so that I can make the transition to outside. It reminds me of when I was a kid. I had a large stash of ice cream bowls and spoons hidden under my bed because it seemed too hard to take them back downstairs.

I have a sense of the ice cream bowls and spoons as a metaphor for Drew's sex addiction. Besides the obvious phallic and yonic symbols that a spoon and bowl might point to, one can think of the ice cream (sweet mother's milk) as a sense of returning to a very early state of fusion with his mother, arguably the best possible feeling Drew could have. If Drew's life was a permanent self-torture, at the hands of his internalized father imago, then taking a "hit" of ice cream would be an escape from his chronic mental pain, albeit a short one. But wary of his father's watchful gaze, any evidence of this escape must remain hidden, and in the case of the bowls and spoons, hidden under his bed. One can imagine sex working the same way as the ice cream, but the "hit" can last much longer. In Drew's case, he can "edge" for hours at a time. Ruth Cohn (2014), a therapist who specializes in working with couples dealing with intimacy issues, equates this kind of sexual escape into pornography, which Drew does for hours on end, to a way of managing the almost ever-present overwhelming affective states that are a residue of early attachment trauma:

> In the sexually compulsive partner, I usually find a desperate attempt to self-regulate or manage intense affects and body states. Beneath that, however, is nearly always some expression of trauma. It may be attachment trauma owing, for example, to a parent who was physically intrusive and emotionally neglectful, a parent whose rage was overwhelming, or a parent who was seductively over-stimulating or sexually abusive.
>
> *(p. 79)*

According to Cohn's blueprint, Drew would have suffered a double dose of traumatic antecedents: a physically intrusive father and an emotionally neglectful mother.

Later in the same session there was at point at which neither of us spoke. I looked a Drew, and he was nervously smiling, almost giggling. The silence was awkward.

Alan: What is it like when there's a silence between us?
Drew: It's terrible. I feel scared of you.
Alan: Does it remind you of anything?
Drew: I think in general I'm uncomfortable around men, and I've felt that way my entire life. I think that may be partly why I'm a sex addict, and why I'm obsessed with women.

It was a recurring pattern that Drew became uncomfortable if we sat together without talking. I sensed that I became too much of an other, of a real person, when we sat silently, and this was intolerable to him because *real* other people, according to his "internal working model of social relationships" (Bowlby, 1969), were likely to annihilate him. Drew's constant talking acted almost as a cloak, or even a blanket, to protect him from my presence overwhelming him. I felt that if Drew could learn to tolerate more silence between us, it might help him with affect regulation in his other relationships. I didn't want to torture him though, and I didn't think he was ready for long silences, just yet. We shared another stretch of quiet, which I decided to interrupt.

Alan: Where are you?

Drew: I went to an SAA meeting the other night. I hadn't been in a couple of
months, and it was helpful.

The 12 Steps

Whenever Drew mentioned SAA (Sex Addicts Anonymous), I felt conflicted. He
often described SAA as having a shaming quality, which made me question its
helpfulness. But, when I questioned Drew about some of the shaming messages
he'd received from SAA, he quickly backtracked and ascribed this negativity to
just a few bad apples in the group, which, he said, he could choose to ignore. I
had a sense of SAA replacing his father as the feared authoritarian voice in his
head, and although he wanted me to commiserate and console him about the
shame SAA sometimes made him feel, when I agreed with his angry feelings
about SAA, the rebellion became too real, which was just too dangerous: in
much the same way that standing up to his dad felt too dangerous. Drew told me
more about the SAA meeting he'd been to:

Drew: The first 45 minutes were crazy. It was an older man who was obnoxious
to me, and I thought to myself I'm not going back, and then someone
shared in a way that touched me, and it made it all worth it. People
always say that's what SAA is like.

Alan: What touched you?

Drew: The man who shared said he wanted his obsession with sex to go away,
and I understood how he felt.

Alan: What would you replace it with if it went away?

Drew: Well, when I stopped sex completely 5 years ago, when I first started
SAA and tried to be abstinent, I became obsessed with cars and with
counting and organizing things and also with work and jobs and having
as many as possible.

Drew seems to shift between different views of SAA. The more positive story is
that he was at a low point in his life when he first went to SAA, and it gave him
a place to be honest about himself and feel accepted. If Drew's addiction comes
out of a need to assert a cut-off, hidden part of himself, then being able to coax
that part out into the open through safe interpersonal relationships would be a
good first step toward recovery. Having a place with structure and support could
help Drew with his lack of self-cohesion and overdependence on his father's
subjectivity, which he has internalized. Lance Dodes, a professor of psychiatry
at Harvard University, believes that group structure and support are the keys to
the success of 12-step groups such as AA and SAA. He writes that the principal
benefit of any 12-step group "is its social function. AA is a place where, with
some notable exceptions, people feel accepted. Early in the process of quitting

drinking this can be valuable for those who can make use of it" (Dodes & Dodes, 2014, p. 122). When Drew first joined SAA, it provided a feeling of acceptance and community he had desperately been searching for.

However, despite the many benefits of programs such as SAA, there are some dark undertones. The cornerstones of 12-step programs are the actual 12 steps and the literature associated with them, such as the Big Book of AA written by Bill Wilson (2013). This literature communicates to its members that they have a disease. Framing one's problem as a disease can help remove external judgments about the addict's behaviors because the addict's actions are, based on this view, the product of a genetic, biologically determined disease and not a conscious choice. However, despite the 12-step insistence on the disease model of addiction, currently, there exists no convincing research backing it up, there exists no legitimate scientific test, clear genetic marker, or pathogenesis to this *disease*. And by strictly adhering to this model, wherein the addict has not only a disease but a defect, they are communicating to the addict that they are congenitally and permanently damaged, with no hope of recovery, only the possibility of eternal maintenance of their disorder. This can lead not only to hopelessness, but the word "defect" has a shaming quality reminiscent of the language that the addict may have heard as a child—a language that would have led feelings of helplessness and shame, possibly the root causes of their compulsive, addictive behavior.

Interestingly, in the 12-step diseased (neuroessentialized) view of addiction, the diagnostic criteria for whether someone has the disease is not tied to the quantity, symptoms, or effects of the compulsion but seems to rest solely with the subject's decision (or requirement by an outside force) to attend a 12-step meeting and interact with the leaders and members of the 12-step group, who tend to have no scientific training. From my anecdotal experience of working with many patients who have attended 12-step groups, I've never heard of someone attending their first 12-step meeting, sharing their story, and then being told by a leader or other members of the group that they are not an alcoholic, sex addict, food addict, and so forth. Because the labels we and others give ourselves inevitably define us and delimit the ways in which we can inhabit our lives, one might think twice about attending a 12-step group, where one is almost guaranteed to be categorized with a very harsh label.

Despite these questions about the validity of the science behind the disease model of the 12 steps, some believe this model should be embraced because it contributes to positive self-worth on the part of the addict. If the addict was born with a disease, then he can argue that he is not morally to blame for his actions. This has both positive and negative consequences. In studies conducted on the general public's perception of people with mental illness, Buchman, Illes, and Reiner (2011) find that "investigations examining public views of people with mental illness found that moral responsibility was mitigated when individuals were described as having a mental illness based on biological rather than psychosocial factors" (p. 74). This seems to show that *neuroessentializing* a person's problem lessens the moral judgments that the average person will make about them, but there is a serious consequence to this benefit; the average person, when presented with the disease model, then thought it "less likely that a person could be successfully treated" (Buchman et al., p. 74). Stigma against the person with the "brain disease" also increased, and this stigma is so strong that it leaks into anyone who is seen as being genetically related to the diseased entity. In their study, Buchman, Illes, and Reiner (2011) find that when subjects of the study were presented with a brother or sister of the person with a purported brain disease, "levels of social distance from the sibling of the affected person were found to increase, particularly as it related to the intimacy of dating, marriage, and having children" (p. 74). Sadly, for the addict, the moral release inherent in a disease model is a steep price to pay; less moral judgment, but increased alienation.

For SAA, its members are always in recovery. "Ultimately this leads to dependency," Dodes and Dodes (2014) argue, "on the group rather than on a healthy self-reliance. I believe that there is a method to this madness. It keeps the revolving door constantly revolving and the money keeps rolling in" (p. 114). Dodes and Dodes see sinister motives at work in the continued success of AA and other 12-step groups, despite what they claim are their incredibly low success rates. They believe, based on a meta-analysis of multiple studies, that the AA 12-step groups only succeed for "5–10%" (p. 1) of the people who join them. They believe an industry of extremely profitable rehab clinics based on the 12 steps is invested in funding research and lobbying that perpetuates the ubiquity of 12-step programs despite their failures and weaknesses.

Turning yourself over to a higher power—God—is another tenet of the 12 steps. For Drew, I imagine, the group itself represented God. Thus, when the group would let Drew down, it was particularly painful for him, as he hadn't yet developed the inner resources to withstand this abandonment. Drew told me that his first sponsor would often verbally abuse him with yelling and insults; Drew then blamed himself for being attracted to and choosing an abusive sponsor. Later, Drew decided to try therapy with a man who was a psychotherapist and leader in his SAA group. This man deeply betrayed his trust by inappropriately sexualizing the relationship. It took Drew 2 years to give therapy another chance, and he vowed never to see a "sex addiction specialist" again, which is how he ended up in my office, because I had no particular training in sex addictions.

Erving Goffman, a sociologist who specialized in group structure, social relationships, and the creation of self through interactions with social structures, spoke of our need to both belong to groups, yet at the same time, to assert our individual identity by resisting the group. Being part of a group can give us a sense of safety and acceptance, while our resistance to that very same group can give us a feeling of selfhood and individuality. "Without something to belong to," Goffman writes (1964),

> we have no stable self, and yet total commitment and attachment to any social unit implies a kind of selflessness. Our sense of being a person can come from being drawn into a wider social unit; our sense of selfhood

can arise through the little ways in which we resist the pull. Our status is backed by the solid buildings of the world, while our sense of personal identity often resides in the cracks.

(p. 320)

Maybe a group experience, such as a 12-step group, can help Drew feel belonging and structure, while a less structured and more open psychodynamic psychotherapy, with someone like me, can allow his personal, subjective identity to blossom.

Narrative Identity

Illness narratives, like those espoused by SAA, can also contribute to "the experience of symptoms" (Phillips, 2003, p. 321). If one is told that he is a defective sex addict with an incurable disease, then it is quite easy to take on that identity and lose the ability to occupy other self-positions, including ones that might offer a healthier alternative. An illness narrative (in Drew's case an addiction narrative) does not capture the quality of an expansive "narrative quest" (Macintyre, 1984, p. 219) that has "a meaningful and intelligible narrative structure" (Phillips, 2003, p. 315). I've found that as Drew and I work together, engaging in the complicated and never-ending process of reauthoring his narrative into something more agentic and heroic, Drew often finds himself unraveling into a series of disconnected self-recriminations.

I want Drew to be able to shift between various gradations of narrative self-positions, but he tends to be limited to only the extreme poles, splitting himself into a binary of good and evil, without any strata in between. Drew is either grandiose, the puppet master, God (while he is masturbating to online porn or lecturing and pontificating to his girlfriend), or he is filled with an annihilating self-loathing. These black-and-white narrative poles eliminate any substories in shades of gray. According to Lysaker, Lancaster, and Lysaker (2003), trauma like that experienced by Drew leads to the "collapse of the ability to converse with oneself" and the inability "to construct meaning in an ongoing manner about oneself" (p. 214). When the shades of gray are too scary to access (in Drew's case it would include questioning his parents' motivations), then sticking to "singular monological self-positions" (Lysaker et al., p. 213) can be a way for Drew to make sense of his life. The problem is that such a rigid story resists narrative evolution and his different self-positions end up shutting down any communication with each other. Lysaker, Lancaster, and Lysaker (2003) believe that when self-positions become monologic, we "may see authoritarian attempts to reconstruct or rebuild a person" (p. 214), which is what seems to be happening to Drew when he's at SAA.

I believe that if I can accept Drew's different self-positions, even the seemingly self-defeating ones, it can help allow Drew to have "more than one perspective at a time, and deliberations between these perspectives can be a useful way to adapt to the realities of one's situation" (Roe & Davidson, 2005, p. 92). This is important, because "rather than simply being a byproduct of recovery, these processes of re-authoring one's life story are actually integral components of the recovery process itself" (Roe & Davidson, 2005, p. 89). If Drew could learn to move freely between new and subtle self-positions, he can "construct a sense of self independent of his illness" (Roe & Davidson, 2005, p. 92) and experience "the novelty and richness of life experience" (Lysaker, Lancaster, & Lysaker, 2003, p. 214) that would in many ways transcend his addiction narrative.

In fact, I think many of Drew's thoughts are coming from an internalized selfobject representation of his father. Because Drew was not allowed to develop his own sense of self, he became dependent on what Kohut calls "borrowed cohesion" (Kohut, Goldberg, & Stepansky, 1984, p. 167), where "the child develops no sense of inner referents" (Jones, 2009, p. 217). Drew becomes dependent on what he thinks his Dad would think and because this isn't in his best interest, he becomes agitated, which leads to compulsive thoughts and behaviors in order to quiet the turmoil. "The child implicitly feels that something is wrong," Jones (2009) explains, "but does not have the ability to know what the problem is or how to set it right" (p. 217). Drew vacillates between wanting me just to listen to him on the one hand, and wanting me to tell him exactly what to do on the other hand. But if I tell him what to do, I become a replacement for his father and SAA. And if I don't tell him exactly what to do, because he never learned to trust his own instincts, he says he feels lost at sea. A more traditional "one-person psychology" psychoanalytic approach might try to puzzle out the emotional antecedents to Drew's problematic, sexual acting-out behaviors; however, I am trying to nurture a growing self-cohesion in Drew by providing what Jones (2009) calls a "responsive selfobject milieu" (p. 224), rather than focusing on traditional psychoanalytic interpretations. Even though I've seen a psychodynamic approach offer valuable support to people struggling with compulsive behaviors, there is a danger, with long-term psychoanalytic psychotherapy, that the patient can become too dependent on one person—the therapist. Individual therapy also has other drawbacks: it can be difficult to schedule, costly, and hit-or-miss in terms of patient–therapist fit. This is why it could be helpful for someone like Drew to be able to find an empathic support group that helps *addicts* by offering a fellowship or brotherhood similar to current 12-step programs, but with a less shaming and authoritarian set of tenets.

The authoritarian discourse of an SAA meeting subsumes Drew in a "power relationship" and "ritual of discourse" (Foucault, 1990, p. 61) that in some ways reduces Drew's power to self-author his own story. It also changes Drew. Foucault (1990) says just the act of confessing "produces modifications in the person who articulates it" (p. 62). If Drew is induced to parrot the dominant discourse of SRA, that he has a defect and a disease that will never be cured, might this not be a performative act that creates and reifies a more abject identity for Drew, while also working as a hypnotic suggestion? A suggestion that he must achieve total abstinence, notwithstanding normophilic sex with a long-term partner, or he will be destined to a life of misery. For some, this could easily lead to feeling powerless and giving up, which could lead to even more use of the substance or compulsive behavior.

Foucault (1990) contrasts the subjugated Western man who has become a "confessing animal" (p. 59) with those who advocate for themselves through "testimony" where there is a witness who is affected by the testimony and feels compelled to take action. I endeavor to be that witness for Drew, and one could say that by writing this chapter I have been impelled to act as a result of Drew's testimony. Foucault might describe Drew's testimony to me as a "performative discourse," a political act of resistance against SAA, as well as his internalized selfobject representation of his father, and a political stand to stop pathologizing himself.

If Drew can see himself in a richer narrative than the simple defect/disease model of SAA, he will be taking part in a political act whereby he posits an alternate to the hegemonic discourse of SAA. He will depathologize himself and be able to use SAA for its social network and strengths while not ingesting its harmful dominant discourse. He will see himself as someone who masturbates for the sake of self-preservation, battling his internalized demons rather than solely as an "addict."

A fellowship can help create meaningful relationships by providing a space for sharing stories. When Drew speaks at an SAA meeting, he is sharing his story in a place where "experiences are shared, commonalities discovered, and relationships built" (Woods, 2013, p. 47). This is what a fellowship or peer-support group can offer that I can't offer in my psychotherapy office. A member-run collective—without the shaming, authoritarian tone of the 12 steps—modeled after the survivor movements of the schizophrenia or self-harm communities would allow Drew and other survivors of compulsive behaviors to depathologize themselves and author new self-narratives.

The tenets of this collective could take inspiration from a growing movement in the Asperger's and autism spectrum disorder (ASD) communities called *neurodiversity*, whereby the members of these *categories* argue that autism is not a disease requiring treatment and that its members should be considered *neuroequals* with the rest of the *normal* population. This group argues that ASD is just a different way of being, and that the ASD citizen's "brain is wired in an atypical—but not pathological—fashion" (Buchman, Illes, & Reiner, 2011, p. 70).

Dissociation

My work with Drew seems to spiral in fits and starts toward shared meaning, with every insight or connection eventually followed by a need for distance and emotional space. For example, after about a year of working together, I began to notice more and more moments where there was a charged energy in the emotional space between Drew and me. Yet he also seemed very far away in what felt to me to be a dissociative process. I'm not sure if the dissociation was in Drew, myself, or in the therapeutic dyad. One session in particular stayed with me:

Drew: Tomorrow's my dad's birthday. I sent him something on Amazon, so I feel like I didn't fuck that up entirely [*he nervously laughs*].

Alan: What do you mean?

Drew: [*Interrupting*] Well, when I don't send a gift, or I send it late and I don't really get it done, I suffer even worse. I suffer the day coming up even worse than I'm going to suffer anyways. Like, I hate the fact that tomorrow I have to call him, but if I didn't send a gift I would feel even crazier.

Alan: What would be crazier about not getting him a gift?

Drew: Just I feel I'd be pushing his buttons [*his voice slows and his eyelids lower a smidge*], just basically rubbing it in his face that he's not loved. I always had to be the good boy, the golden boy in the family. It was like I was trained to be sexually abused. I'm the type. If there are types I'm probably the type because it happened again and again [*his voice slows even more*]. So I have to get him a gift or I'd be telling him that I don't care about him.

Alan: What's wrong with that?

Drew: It just goes against my fear of him or my traditional . . . [*Drew loses his thread, then continues*] I was sitting on the steps in Union Square Park before coming here, and I thought to myself, I have no proof that I got incested. Like, I just don't think I did. Like when I sit in a social environment like that I still think [*speaking as if to himself*] "oh you're just making all this up. You're just an awkward person. You're just a fuckup. You don't have anyone to blame. You're just a fuckup." So, I think, sometimes with my dad I feel bad that behind his back I'm telling people that he's this monster and I question that, and yet [*Drew laughs*] I suppose or know that he is. I can't put the two together really. It's so confusing.

Alan: I don't think you're making it up.

Drew: Yeah, well, yeah.

Alan: But it's normal that you would think that you're making it up.

Drew: Yeah, like right now, I can barely see. It's really weird. Like everything in the room looks like a cubist painting as I talk about this, I see aftershadows on every single thing in the room. It's weird. Literally, right now it's like I can see every light source in front of your face. I'm having trouble focusing.

Alan: Does it seem scary that I might know something against your dad?

Drew: I'm worried that I'll get paranoid that you're lying to me, you know. That you're just doing it for the money. Once you agree what happened to me and say it's definitely sure, then I'm like, oh this is a conspiracy,

I have to get back to my dad, we've got to get together, like everyone's against us. I have to get back there, like, my safest place is in that bathroom with him. Twice this week I followed Debbie into the bathroom, and I was sitting talking to her, and then I looked at her, and I said, "can you fucking believe this is happening," and she was just laughing [*Drew begins to smile*] and I was like, "I'm sitting on the goddamned toilet watching you get ready, can you believe I followed you in here? Can you see how fucked up this is?" She was like "yeah it's weird." I was like "yeah I know; I hadn't realized that I walked in here." Like I didn't know, and now I'm sitting here, and I didn't realize it.

Alan: And she knows you used to do that with your dad?

Drew: Yeah, I've told her about it, and every time I do it I tell her. I'm like look at me—this is crazy. Every time she gets ready for work, I sit on the toilet and watch her just like when I was a little boy with my father. I'm feeling strange right now. I feel like in the end you'll say I'm fine and think I'm cute and funny, and I'll have wasted all this time and money. I have this feeling that I should just go back to my dad. That feels comfortable and right. [*Drew pauses. His eyes roll up a bit, and his facial muscles go limp, flattening his face, not unlike a heroin addict after a hit.*]

Alan: Where'd you go?

Drew: The lights are really going crazy. I can see every light in the room swirling right in front of me, and it makes it hard to see your face.

I imagine, for Drew, talking about his dad feels dangerous—when he was a boy it would have been—and he loses connection to the present. The trigger to this kind of dissociation seems to be whenever we become too close, and in particular, when I communicate a belief that I think he's a good person, a person who deserved love and happiness. It seems this story and these feelings contradict what his parents told him, and to defy them is terrifying. Even now, to defy them risks breaking an imaginary bond, a bond that at one time his life depended on.

Martha Stout (2002) describes how for people like Drew, when they were young, dissociation was a survival strategy necessary to separate his parents' abuse of him from his love for them. As time wore on, and Drew continued to escape into these altered states at the slightest provocation, he was actually, through repetition, strengthening this habit. Even though the present has drifted further away from the original trauma, Drew's dissociative triggers and dysfunctional responses have reified and become even harder to change.

Building on the work of Pat Ogden, one of the pioneers of sensorimotor psychotherapy for the treatment of trauma, Giuseppe (2014) observes that the faulty mechanism in "a sexually addicted individual is his/her inability to recognize emotions as signals" (p. 48) whose etiopathogenic origin is typically early trauma. Giuseppe posits a recursive emotional dialectic between states of hypo- and hyperarousal in the trauma survivor. When traumatic emotions come up, they lead to physical symptoms of higher or lower affect in the form of altered heart rate, blood flow, and tension, which then flood the brain with the message that danger is actually present. Dan Siegel (1999), the founder of interpersonal neurobiology, posits that over time there is a loss of range within which "various intensity[ies] of emotional arousal may be processed without disrupting the functioning of the system" (p. 263). This narrowing window of normal affective function, and the activation of overwhelming biological processes in response to difficult and intrusive emotions, "hamper more complex cortical functions which foster metacognitive processes of self-reflection and impulse control, as well as causing a progressive fragmentation of the sense of self that generates disorientation" (Giuseppe, 2014, p. 48). This fragmentation of the self that Giuseppe refers to aligns with Drew's dissociative symptoms of feeling almost not himself and that he's losing the ability to see the world in a way where things fit together in a clear picture.

The challenge in helping someone like Drew is that the original trauma is ever-present. Any allusion to these original memory traces can be terrifying for him. If we don't integrate these memories into a story that is satisfying and meaningful, then these fragments can stay mired in the foreground of his emotional brain. Drew's constant flashbacks and dissociations have been like picking at a scab. Because of this constant picking, the memory traces of the original trauma have never healed and integrated into a confidently felt and cohesive personal narrative. Hopefully, my acceptance of Drew's unfolding story will act as a bandage to give his traumatic memories the space and time necessary to self-author a restorative personal narrative.

During a session a few weeks later, Drew mentioned the progress that he had made in his relationship with Debbie.

Drew: The other night I had nice, good sex with Debbie that was just regular missionary position, and I felt like I'd never done that before. On Valentine's Day, I got her flowers, and we went to Central Park and walked through the zoo, and it was like we were a nice normal couple. I felt like I was Neo in *The Matrix* and not following my script. Normally, I would want to run so fast from something like that, but I was able to stay in it, yet I felt almost out of body watching myself do it. I thought you'd think I was crazy.

Alan: Why?

Drew: I guess just because I'm like two different people. I'm the bad sex addict, and then suddenly I'm being the nice normal boyfriend.

I'm gratified that Drew is trying to have a more stable relationship with Debbie; yet, he thinks I'll think he's doing something wrong for being "normal." This reminds me of the double-bind that his parents put him in by sexualizing and belittling him, and then as he put on a "false self" (Winnicott, 1960) of being the nice, smiley little boy, they shamed him for this as well. Drew says his parents made fun of him for being a goody-goody when he was growing up. He couldn't win then, and he can't win now—at least not according to his internal working model of social relationships bequeathed to him by his parents. It doesn't surprise me that he would feel stuck, either in my office or at home, masturbating to porn and feeling incapable of transitioning to the next part of his day. If his internal objects (parental voices) are constantly criticizing him for any choice he makes, it's easy to imagine him giving up and just lying in the fetal position sucking his thumb or the adult equivalent—sitting for hours looking at porn on his computer screen. I feel the goal in our work together is to help Drew change his story from one where he is shameful and bad to one where he is loved and accepted, thus widening his window of tolerable affect, allowing easier access to a richer array of self-states, which will not only help him to move through life alone, but can help him attach to other people.

Conclusion

As the population of sex addicts has grown, various groups have sprung up to tackle the problem of the sex addict. There are the high-priced rehab clinics run by licensed medical professionals and the ostensibly bottom-up self-help societies (SAA) modeled after the 12-step groups originated by Alcoholics Anonymous. These two groups—the clinics blanketed with an overlay of medical prestige, and the member-run, religious, 12-step groups—which might at first glance appear at opposite ends of the spectrum, are actually constantly in dialogue and creating meaning around addiction in a mutually constitutive recursive loop. The disease model of addiction embraced by the psychiatric establishment, as well as the 12-step literature, seeks to decontextualize the *subject* by using the *addict* label to dissociate individuals from their social context and place all the pathology in the *addict's* brain. This model, which indelibly etches the abject label of *sex addict* onto Drew's self-identity, can lead to hopelessness and continued compulsive behavior. But in a looping effect between a subject who lives in a discourse and a discourse created by its subjects, people like Drew are providing testimony that will eventually alter the label of "addict" through papers such as this one, altering the way a future *sex addict* views himself, and so on ad infinitum.

By engaging Drew as a three-dimensional person rather than as a category, I hoped to allow Drew, as well as myself, to open up parts of ourselves that we had cut off, parts necessary for us to embody narratives that were both open and fluid. By holding his story and his various self-states between us, in a non-shaming, non-blaming space, Drew could hopefully, eventually, experience himself as the author and hero of his journey rather than a static, shameful, and abject label.

Close Reading Questions

1. The writer foregrounded the client's personal life narrative in the treatment. Did this seem appropriate and/or helpful? Use specific passages in the text to support your answer.
2. Did the author's clinical interventions seem helpful or harmful? Did you agree with the authors assessments of why his interventions were having the effect they did? Were there other variables or mechanisms at work in the treatment outcome that the author seemed blind to?
3. How would you relate Drew's experience of shame to the way you generally define shame?

Prompts for Writing

1. Would you describe Drew's issues and what he needed help with? Redescribe Drew through the lens of an explanatory model (psychoanalytic, neurobiological, cognitive behavioral, etc.) other than the one used by the author. Then write how your intervention with Drew might have unfolded using a treatment modality commonly associated with the explanatory model you chose (i.e., if you chose neurobiological, what diagnosis and medications might you have prescribed). How would you have intervened or worked with Drew?
2. Read Martha Stout's short essay, "When I Woke Up Tuesday, It Was Friday." How does her description of dissociation jibe with what Drew experiences here?
3. How does Oxman's description of Drew's online behavior relate to that of Busfield's description of Olivia's online behavior?

References

Benjamin, J. (2004). Beyond doer and done to: An intersubjective view of thirdness. *Psychoanalytic Quarterly, 73*(1), 5–46.

Berry, M. D., & Berry, P. D. (2014). Mentalization-based therapy for sexual addiction: Foundations for a clinical model. *Sexual and Relationship Therapy, 29*(2), 245–260.

Bowlby, J. (1969). *Attachment: Attachment and loss, vol. 1: loss.* New York: Basic Books.

Buchman, D. Z., Illes, J., & Reiner, P. B. (2011). The paradox of addiction neuroscience. *Neuroethics, 4*(2), 65–77.

Cohn, R. (2014). Calming the tempest, bridging the gorge: Healing in couples ruptured by "sex addiction." *Sexual and Relationship Therapy, 29*(1), 76–86.

Dodes, L. M., & Dodes, Z. (2014). *The sober truth: Debunking the bad science behind 12-step programs and the rehab industry.* Boston: Beacon Press.

Fisher, T. D., Moore, Z. T., & Pittenger, M. J. (2012). Sex on the brain? An examination of frequency of sexual cognitions as a function of gender, erotophilia, and social desirability. *Journal of Sex Research, 49*(1), 69–77.

Foucault, M. (1990). *The history of sexuality: An introduction.* (R. Hurley Trans.). London: Penguin.

Freud, S. (1919). A child is being beaten: A contribution to the study of the origin of sexual perversions. *International Journal of Psycho-Analysis, 1,* 371–395.

Giuseppe, C. (2014). The dissociative nature of sexual addiction the role of traumatic emotions. *Procedia-Social and Behavioral Sciences, 114,* 45–51.

Goffmann, E. (1964). *Asylums: Essays on the social situation of mental patients and other inmates.* Oxford: Doubleday.

Jones, B. (2009). Addiction and pathological accommodation: An intersubjective look at impediments to the utilization of alcoholics anonymous. *International Journal of Self Psychology, 4*(2), 212–234.

Kohut, H. (1985). *Self psychology and the humanities: Reflections on a new psychoanalytic approach.* New York: W. W. Norton.

Kohut, H., Goldberg, A., & Stepansky, P. E. (1984). *How does analysis cure?* Chicago: University of Chicago Press.

Lysaker, P. H., Lancaster, R. S., & Lysaker, J. T. (2003). Narrative transformation as an outcome in the psychotherapy of schizophrenia. *Psychology and Psychotherapy: Theory, Research and Practice, 76*(3), 285–299.

MacIntyre, A. (1984). *After virtue.* Notre Dame, IN: University of Notre Dame Press.

Orange, D. M. (2009). Kohut memorial lecture: Attitudes, values and intersubjective vulnerability. *International Journal of Psychoanalytic Self Psychology, 4*(2), 235–253.

Phillips, J. (2003). Psychopathology and the narrative self. *Philosophy, Psychiatry, & Psychology, 10*(4), 313–328.

Reay, B., Attwood, N., & Gooder, C. (2013). Inventing sex: The short history of sex addiction. *Sexuality & Culture, 17*(1), 1–19.

Roe, D., & Davidson, L. (2005). Self and narrative in schizophrenia: Time to author a new story. *Medical Humanities, 31*(2), 89–94.

Rosenbaum, M. (2009). *Dare to be human: A contemporary psychoanalytic journey.* New York: Routledge.

Siegel, D. J. (1999). *The developing mind* (Vol. 296). New York: Guilford Press.

Stout, M. (2002). *The myth of sanity: Divided consciousness and the promise of awareness.* New York: Penguin.

Vaknin, S. (2003). *Self love: Narcissism revisited.* Prague: Narcissus.

Wilson, B. (2013). *Alcoholics anonymous: Big book.* Retrieved from eBookIt.com

Winnicott, D. W. (1960). Ego distortion in terms of true and false self. *The Maturational Processes and the Facilitating Environment, 1965,* 140–152.

Woods, A. (2013). Rethinking patient testimony in the medical humanities: Schizophrenia bulletin's first person accounts. *Journal of Literature and Science, 6*(1), 38–54.

INDEX